THE FAME GAME

THE
FAME
GAME

AN INSIDER'S PLAYBOOK FOR
EARNING YOUR 15 MINUTES

RAMON HERVEY II

AMISTAD

An Imprint of HarperCollins*Publishers*

This book is memoir. It reflects the author's present recollections of experiences over time.

HarperCollins books may be purchased for educational, business, or sales promotional use. For information, please email the Special Markets Department at SPsales@harpercollins.com.

FIRST EDITION

Designed by Leah Carlson-Stanisic

Library of Congress Cataloging-in-Publication Data has been applied for.

ISBN 978-0-06-304803-4
ISBN 978-0-06-327585-0 (ANZ)

22 23 24 25 26   LSC   10 9 8 7 6 5 4 3 2 1

I DEDICATE THIS BOOK TO MY CHILDREN,

Melanie, Jillian, and Devin, who have enriched and brought more love, joy, and happiness into my life than I could have ever dreamed or fathomed.

CONTENTS

INTRODUCTION

Over the past four decades, I've passionately invested my professional career and livelihood in playing "the fame game." As a seasoned proliferator of fame, I find it impossible to ignore our fascination, insatiable desire for, and obsession with fame, branding, celebrity cachet, and social media influencer stardom. Its allure, pomp, pretense, and enviable rewards are more coveted now than at any other time in modern history.

However, there is no failsafe expert playbook, foolproof recipe, magic potion, serum, diet, spiritual path, holistic herbs, manager, Svengali, mentor, coach, agent, performance school, or university that can guarantee stardom and fame. The challenges and strategies are not universally the same for everyone. There's no spin bible that offers the secrets on how to craft an effective strategy to counter and create a positive spin on a major crisis or canceling that arises. If there were, someone would be selling it.

I've never had a desire to be famous, but the perception of fame and its link to success has always intrigued me. Andy Warhol popularized the iconic pop culture phrase "In the future, everyone will be world-famous for fifteen minutes." It surfaced in a program for a Swedish exhibit at the Moderna Musset in Stockholm in 1968. But photographer Nick Finkelstein claimed credit for the phrase which was said in a conversation with Warhol while doing a photo shoot of him. As a crowd gathered to get a peek of Warhol, Warhol remarked, "Everyone wants to be famous," and Finkelstein replied, "Yeah, for about fifteen minutes, Andy." Regardless, once I heard the expression, I latched on to it and made it my mantra—adding my own twist to it. I don't think it's possible for everyone to get fifteen minutes of fame. But, in the entertainment business, if you're lucky enough to get fifteen minutes, used wisely, you can milk it and sustain a lengthy career.

If you only get ten minutes, you'll reach a lower plateau of fame, but can still experience a moderate level of sustainable success. From five to ten minutes, you can be popular and quasi-famous, but you're not in the upper echelon. Anything under five minutes and you can hang on to your anonymity and walk freely wherever you go. There is an internal industry system that assesses a talent's commercial success and fame. Major film studios, broadcast networks, and record labels set their own rating prerequisites. In turn, they pay the most famous the highest fees, rewards, access, and benefits. People who earn fame have the right to exploit and use it however they see fit. There is no right way, only the way that works best for the person. They reap the benefits or deal with the adverse consequences of their choices.

I chose the title *The Fame Game* because it captures and personifies the inherent spirit of the unpredictability of fame. While not a frivolous game, it requires that the players possess the comparable level of talent and skills to compete and play any professional game at its highest level. Add to that, all the games that we love and are most fascinated by don't have a pre-determined outcome. In most instances, the behind-the-scenes powerbrokers in the entertainment industry who play, and fuel, fame are guessing; the talent is guessing—and I've guessed hundreds of times myself. It's not rocket science or based on scientific methodology. It's a crapshoot. It's bias. There are inherent risks. Developing a successful and famous star takes a collective and concerted team effort. There is no *I* in team or fame.

I'm not posturing to be a wunderkind, nor is this a tell-all exposé filled with mudslinging and innuendo, a vanity project, or a how-to guide. It was premature for me to write a memoir because I'm an eternal optimist and believe my best years are looming in my future. Hence, I framed this work as a career retrospective and my "promoir." My inspiration for authoring my book is to share my unique story and put you in the passenger's seat to experience my roller-coaster ride representing a cavalcade of prominent Black and white entertainers in contemporary pop culture in the twentieth and twenty-first centuries. It's an insider's glimpse of their career journeys; my perspective, philosophy, and path; influential historical context; and the invaluable lessons I learned from guiding and collaborating with them on their trek to fame.

My first personal interactions with famous people happened while I was living in London, England, working as a flight attendant on Pan Am Airways as one of the first Black males hired as a steward in the early seventies. I served stars like Miles Davis, Richie Havens, Peter Jennings, Shirley MacLaine, and Keith Moon from the Who, among others. After an eighteen-month stint I landed a job as writer/publicist at a talent agency, Starlite Artists, owned by Peter Walsh, who represented the Bay City Rollers, the UK's biggest pop band, Marmalade as well as Clem Curtis & The Foundations, and Mac and Katie Kissoon, among others.

After moving back to the States, I worked in the same capacity for Motown Records, when Berry Gordy's label roster of famous superstars included Stevie Wonder, Diana Ross, Marvin Gaye, the Jackson 5, the Temptations, and Smokey Robinson, among others. Later, I earned my stripes working at one of the premier entertainment public relations companies in the industry—Rogers & Cowan—and represented the top talents in the world. I embarked on my own as an entrepreneur in the mid-'80s, which is the path where I've logged the most miles in my forty-year career.

The geneses of my link to fame are the consequences of coincidence, resiliency, luck, and invaluable tutelage that prepared me to serve in a myriad of entrepreneurial roles, launching public relations and management companies and serving as an entertainment publicist, personal manager, management consultant, brand consultant, music supervisor, and a live event, film, and TV producer.

I've been blessed and lucky to be in the trenches and experience hundreds of iterations and variables of fame firsthand while representing

Richard Pryor, Bette Midler, Paul McCartney, Little Richard, the Bee Gees, Quincy Jones (*The Wiz* soundtrack), Harry Belafonte (and his artist-driven non-profit Sankofa.org), Herb Alpert, Peter Frampton, the Carpenters, James Caan, Nick Nolte, Rick James, Anita Baker, Natalie Cole, George Benson, Vanessa Williams, Kenny "Babyface" Edmonds, Luther Vandross, Andraé Crouch, the Jacksons with Michael Jackson, Daphne Rubin-Vega, the Commodores with Lionel Richie, Motown Records, Don Cornelius, Soul Train, Philippe Saisse, Sweet Honey in the Rock, the Soul Train Music Awards, Hall of Famer St. Louis Cardinal star Lou Brock, Chic, Alabama, Muhammad Ali, Caitlyn Jenner, and NBC-TV's long-running music series *The Midnight Special*, to name just a few.

I've built my own brand identity based on the relationships and bonds I forged with them. They shaped my brand persona as much as I helped shape theirs during our engagement. I believe there's an art to creating and building larger-than-life personas, a skill set and an intuitive sense which are not unique to me but that I covet and share with my peers—many of whom have been successful as publicists or managers.

Fame can produce huge egos, inordinate stress, anxiety, self-doubt, or it can strengthen and empower. Every rise to fame has a different story, heartbeat, ebb and flow, set of unforeseen challenges; different celebratory high notes, rejections, failures, and faux pas. In each chapter, I highlight a myriad of transparent and uncensored behind-the-scenes sagas I learned managing all phases of fame; creating, conceptualizing, manifesting, shaping, molding, sustaining, preserving, fixing, mopping up after a crisis occurs and things go awry, and launching comebacks to resurrect damaged and famous reputations that were tottering and on the brink of disaster, or by today's standards, canceled. I chronicle the clients that most influenced, peppered, and spiced up my career, their roots, big breaks, greatest successes, inflection points, and downfalls. And I portray my own triumphs and failures, and how both affected me emotionally and psychologically and impacted my career trajectory.

One of the most valuable lessons I've learned about collaborating with famous celebrities is that fame isn't a destination; it's an arbitrary reward and outcome that emanates from achieving success—but it's not promised. It's one of the thirteen "Tenets of Fame" I've listed, which have helped me to stay balanced, even-keeled, and realistic about how to approach, treat, and embrace fame.

It's a rare distinction to be famous, and only a minuscule number of people in the world have achieved that distinction. Noted American mathematician Samuel Arbesman, a scientist and author (*Overcomplicated: Technology at the Limits of Comprehension*, 2017), estimated that just a fraction, 0.000086 percent, of living people are famous. He came up with a clever shortcut for calculating that number in 2013 by using Wikipedia's "Living People" category (604,174 people in its ranks), and estimated the fraction of living people who have Wikipedia pages (Wikipedia requires a certain threshold of notability for someone to get a Wikipedia page). He then divided Wikipedia's 604,174 by total global population, 7,059,837,187, which equated to 0.000086. Of the estimated 160,000 members in SAG (Screen Actors Guild), 95 percent of all the work goes to just 5 percent of the members. In the contemporary music industry, only about 0.000002 percent of musicians become "successful." In a *Rolling Stone* article (September 9, 2020), data showed that 90 percent of all digital streams go to the top 1 percent of artist (from 1.6 million artist releases, just 16,000 account for 90 percent of streams).

The sparsity of famous people who have emerged over the past decade of nouveau "social media fame" is minuscule as well. As of July 2021 (per Data Reportal), the estimated number of global social media users is 4.48 billion, which equates to 57 percent of the world population. Instagram averages over one billion monthly active users and has five hundred thousand influencers, but only 0.5 percent are mega influencers (have one million followers). YouTube averages two billion monthly active users; fewer than 1 percent are influencers. There are thirty-one million channels on YouTube. To qualify as a YouTube partner, you must have a minimum of one thousand subscribers and have accumulated four thousand hours of watch time. Only 0.25 percent of all channels make money. Facebook averages 2.89 billion active users every month, but they only contribute to 45 percent of the influencers market. And upstart TikTok influencers with one million or more followers represent just 0.26 percent of its influencers. Influencers on TikTok need a minimum of ten thousand subscribers and over 270 million views a year just to generate $100,000.

The data aptly demonstrate that the odds for acquiring success and fame in the entertainment business do not favor bona fide artistic talent. However, social media has opened the doors, giving young people the freedom to express themselves as entrepreneurs and commercially exploit their own brand personas, if they're able to use marketing tools backed up by a comprehensive business strategy.

The one reality it hasn't changed is that regardless of your innate talent, brand concept, or the expertise and track record of your support team, the public at large and the media subjectively arbitrate who becomes "famous." They determine when someone becomes famous and when they're no longer relevant. Parlaying and creating fame is easier said than done because there's no guarantee that your vision or strategy is going to be effective. There are marketing and public relations strategies which are brilliant that work magically and others that completely miss the mark.

In a deeper context, this is also my personal story and plight as a Black man. I illuminate and share historical and contextual accounts of my professional challenges and the adversities that I endured to compete and rise to the comparable level of my esteemed white counterparts. These experiences shaped my psyche and philosophy, and impacted my ability to navigate success in a game where the rules for famous Black superstars, executives, and peers heavily favored our counterparts.

We're all dealt a different hand in life as human beings—and how we choose to play it differs as well. I've always viewed being Black as my reality—but not as a handicap. I've felt fortunate, empowered, and a personal responsibility to mentor and pass on the knowledge I've gained to the next generation. Millennials need torches and encouragement and to be aware that people of color like me, and many before me, exist and have played an integral role in shaping the global evolution of the entertainment industry. I hope millennials who read my book will learn something from my story that they can apply to make their own life journeys and paths to achieve success less cumbersome. I've always encouraged my children not only to chase their dreams, but also to concentrate and focus on being the best at whatever they want to be. Regardless of the dream, an elixir of dedication, discipline, arduous work, resiliency, self-confidence, and self-belief will give realizing it an incredible and sustainable boost.

Fame is chameleon-like and influenced by factors that are impossible to predict and control. It can also become addictive and a liability if you allow it to manipulate and control you, rather than the other way around. If one can successfully monetize and strike the right balance between art and commerce, fame can become currency and an extremely beneficial tool. However, if achieving fame is your only objective, then you've already lost the game. Albert Einstein once said, "Strive not to be a success, but rather to be of value." That is a truth that aligns with my perception of success. If you fuel your pursuit of success and fame with integrity and a sense of purpose, attaining them will be more meaningful.

Authoring this book has been the most solitary and ominous challenge in my life. I've gained so much respect for writers and authors who have dedicated their lives to this art form. It has been a painstaking and enlightening process that has taken more than three years to complete, from drafting the initial book proposal to soliciting agents and publishers, receiving rejections, finding an agent, and securing a publisher.

I embarked on authoring the book at the onset of the pandemic in March 2020 and wrote the contents over the next eighteen months. I wrote the lion's share at night, usually starting around 7 or 8 p.m. after my regular business day ended. Most often I finished writing around 2 to 3 a.m., and sometimes not until 5 a.m. I set a handful of personal records becoming a first-time author. I spent more hours and time sitting on my ass in front of my computer than ever before. I reflected, reminisced, dissected my past, used *I*, and talked about myself more than I ever deemed possible. I far surpassed my threshold and tolerance for self-absorption—which previously was not more than an hour at any given time.

Fortunately, I survived a contemptuous love-hate relationship with my computer. I love the technical and functional purpose it served to help me give life to my thoughts and store them. But there were countless days I hated waiting for it to turn on, knowing it would control me for hours. I resented having to deal with its erratic, rogue, and abusive behavior: clicking off without warning, freezing, deleting text I didn't ask it to delete—just a litany of unwanted torturous impediments and breaches that thwarted and stymied my creative process and nearly brought me to tears on more than one occasion. We managed to finish it together, so I'm thankful for that.

A PATH OF SELF-DESTRUCTION
CAN SABOTAGE FAME

In most cases, a star's success illuminates his or her level of fame, but sometimes people obsess even more when they endure failures. The mercurial nature of fame and infamy, and the fine line between them, evoke intrigue and fascination, especially when the celebrity engages in a pattern of self-destruction and becomes a victim of fame. It can happen when stars are ascending or have reached their pinnacle. Due to a variety of contributing factors, there's a meltdown, and things start spiraling out of control.

During the late 1970s until the mid-'80s, I represented a talent many irrefutably revere as a genius and the greatest comedian of all time, Richard Franklin Lennox Thomas Pryor, who struggled with fame—and sabotaging it—throughout his career.

Richard was paradoxical and brilliant, with an acute lens for break-your-face storytelling humor imbued with arresting and biting social commentary about racism, sex, drugs, marriage, nature, politics, and sports. He also created a plethora of colorful characterizations of amalgamated people he vividly animated and portrayed.

On his dark side, he had an unpredictable and combustible personality. He openly admitted to being addicted to alcohol and drugs. He self-victimized and was desperately searching to find an equitable balance between his fame, his personal life, and his shortcomings. Richard wasn't a publicity hound, but he was cognizant of the role it played in bringing attention to projects he opted to promote. And he understood the inner workings of the entertainment business and the inherent power of his celebrity and fame, even though he never felt deserving or comfortable with it.

Other than talking about his marriages, he kept the rest of his personal life private, particularly his children. One of his liabilities was his tendency to cancel commitments at the last minute. Over time, it became clear that my principal role was to handle damage control, protect his fame, and reduce the risk of collateral damage and public embarrassment when he made missteps, being careful to keep the media at bay.

Fame is currency, but it only belongs to the person who earned it. It's not yours to exploit or like having a shared bank account. Regardless of how much you contribute to elevating it, extending it, or protecting it, ultimately the possessor arbitrates what it means: whether they want to abuse it and suffer the consequences, or honor it.

Interestingly, Richard always understood when he messed up and would try to offer retribution to lessen the tarnish on his reputation for being professionally irresponsible or a flake. He made me his cancellation consigliere and tasked me to extend an olive branch or make a payment on his behalf on multiple occasions. In that respect, I was complicit and did my best to shield him from potential negative media attention when necessary.

A NO-SHOW

Sometimes his calls came in the wee hours of the morning. One time I received a 3 o'clock Saturday morning call from Richard and his wife, Jennifer. He spoke first and said he wasn't feeling good, then put Jennifer on the phone to explain. Still half-asleep, I could hear them unsuccessfully trying to whisper to each other in the background. Richard was coaching her on what to say. Jennifer explained that he was suffering from gastro-enteritis, as diagnosed by his doctor.

I wasn't familiar with the term, so I jumped out of bed to look it up in the dictionary and found out it's a medical term for a stomachache or flu. Richard was set to headline an annual benefit concert for the Brotherhood Crusade that night. He requested I send out a press release to announce he was canceling his appearance because of his "doctor's prognosis." He subsequently insisted I go to the event and arrange for the organization to read a prepared statement (which I would write). It would include an apology and a $10,000 donation to the organization.

It was obvious they were both high, so I proposed we wait until around 10 a.m. to see how he felt in the morning. I reminded him that showtime wasn't until 9:30–10:00 p.m., which gave him at least eighteen hours to feel better. And I explained as a professional courtesy that it was impera-tive I contact Danny Bakewell, the CEO of the Brotherhood Crusade, before making a public announcement about canceling.

Although I had not met Danny, we had spoken on the phone several times. He was excited about Richard's performance. His participation had lifted their ticket sales and fundraising efforts considerably. The only way to reach local papers and local news on the same day as the event was to use the AP and UPI wire services. However, I didn't feel that sending out a press release using gastroenteritis as the reason for canceling was the optimum strategy.

The Brotherhood Crusade was founded in 1968, and it became one of most prominent Black community organizations in Los Angeles. Bakewell took over as CEO in 1973. Its mission was to help individuals overcome the barriers to their pursuit of success in life and promote improved health and wellness; facilitate academic success and personal, social, and eco-nomic growth; encourage artistic excellence, cultural awareness, and financial literacy; and build community agencies and institutions.

When I connected with Danny, we agreed not to alert media in advance about Richard canceling. We planned to break the news after people got seated for the concert. I advised him I'd have an official statement from Richard apologizing for his illness and announcing his $10,000 donation. Richard approved the plan. Our strategy reduced the collateral damage considerably and limited potential media exposure to the beat writers attending the concert.

That night I went to the event. Upon my arrival, I immediately sought Danny to give him the statement. Meeting him under the circumstances was awkward. We were both uneasy but congenial. I handed the statement to him, and without looking at it, he said very matter-of-factly that he would not read it. He told me, "You're here, he's your client, so you can go out there and tell the audience he's not coming." This possible glitch in my strategy had never even crossed my mind. I tried to talk my way out of it, but Danny wouldn't budge.

I was not thrilled about announcing to a large, predominantly Black audience that their most revered comedian (whom they had paid good money to see) was a no-show. In fact, it petrified me. I received a brief introduction. Before I got to Richard's apology, most of the theater was booing loudly and repeatedly in unison. I waited a few moments for the booing to die down, so I could announce the $10,000 donation. It received some minuscule clapping, and then the booing resumed as I walked off the stage. Danny knew exactly what he was doing and how the audience was going to respond. I got played, but we shared a laugh afterward and remained friends for many years. His event went well, and in the aftermath, Richard didn't suffer any media fallout. I had a premonition that similar scenarios would occur in the future.

Miraculously, Richard rarely got admonished by his fans or the public for his misbehavior. They always forgave him. People continued to rally behind him, much the same way fans of famous controversial megastars with similar drug problems, such as Elvis Presley, Michael Jackson, Prince, Robin Williams, Marilyn Monroe, Eminem, Whitney Houston, and Amy Winehouse, rallied around them. It's the exception and not the rule. Within the industry, they never blackballed or ostracized him completely, but his erratic behavior and drug use cost him potential starring roles in major films because studios wouldn't insure him.

PEORIA

I knew about Richard and was an avid fan several years before I started working with him. When I lived in London, I listened to his early comedy records on Laff Records, *That Nigger's Crazy* (1974), . . . *Is It Something I Said?* (1975), and *Bicentennial Nigger* (1976). Whenever I felt lonely and needed a laugh, I would play one of his records. He wasn't well known in the UK, but by the early seventies Richard was wrapping up the first decade of his career. He had a tumultuous childhood growing up in Peoria, Illinois, where he was born and raised. His mother, Gertrude Thomas, was an alcoholic and a prostitute. His father, Leroy "Buck Carter" Pryor, was a former boxer and hustler.

His mother worked at a brothel owned by his grandmother Marie Carter. When he was ten, his mother abandoned him, and his grandmother raised him for the rest of his childhood. His grandmother also beat him consistently. At seven, he endured sexual abuse. He got kicked out of school when he was fourteen and stopped going to school completely after ninth grade.

In 1963, when he was twenty-three, Richard moved to New York and started booking stand-up gigs as an opening act for some big names, including Bob Dylan, Woody Allen, and Nina Simone. He launched his stand-up career as a straitlaced comedian. Bill Cosby inspired him, and he fashioned his stand-up routine to reflect the less controversial middle-of-the-road tone that made Cosby famous.

That style of comedy propelled regular bookings on the premier television talk and variety shows, including the *Ed Sullivan Show*, the *Merv Griffin Show*, and the *Tonight Show Starring Johnny Carson*. In just three years after moving to New York, his popularity and fame were on the rise. He started securing gigs in Las Vegas when the city earned the title of being the "Entertainment Capital of the World." The premier strip hotels featured headlining superstars such as Frank Sinatra, Dean Martin, Sammy Davis Jr., Joey Bishop (the Rat Pack), Elvis Presley, Wayne Newton, Milton Berle, Tony Bennett, Flip Wilson, Lola Falana, Liberace, Andy Williams, and Paul Anka, among others.

Amid his increasing popularity, he suddenly changed course. During a live sold-out performance at the Aladdin Hotel in September 1967, he looked straight at the audience and abruptly asked, "What the fuck am I doing here?" Then he exited the stage. In his autobiography (*Pryor Convictions*, 1995), he referred to the moment as an epiphany. In this same period both his parents died, his mother in 1967 and his father in 1968.

A TRANSFORMATION

Although he continued to perform in Vegas, that epiphany ushered in the second phase of Richard's rise to fame, with a fresh brand of comedy that was more controversial and in-your-face, laced with a healthy dose of profanity and frequent use of the racially controversial slang word *nigger*. He showcased his new, edgier stand-up routine on his debut album, *Richard Pryor*, released in 1968 on Dove/Reprise Records. In 1969, he moved to Berkeley, California, where he developed friendships with Black Panthers cofounder and political activist Huey P. Newton and the celebrated poet, author, and essayist Ishmael Reed, and became entrenched in the counterculture and the civil rights movement—which he integrated into his comedy.

Over the next eight years, starting in the early '70s, Richard's level of fame and notoriety mushroomed to superstar status. He became a sought-after comedy writer, recorded several more comedy albums, and started acting in motion pictures. He wrote for *Sanford and Son* and the *Flip Wilson Show*. In 1971, he recorded his second album, *Craps (After Hours)*. That same year his first comedy film was released, featuring his stand-up at the Improvisation Comedy Club in New York.

In 1972, he appeared in the historically significant *Wattstax* documentary. Wattstax was a benefit concert organized by Memphis-based Stax Records to commemorate the seventh anniversary of the 1965 riots in the Black neighborhood of Watts in South Central Los Angeles. It was held at the Los Angeles Memorial Coliseum on August 20, 1972. David L. Wolper Productions produced, and Columbia Pictures released it. Richard was the only comedian on the bill, with several top R&B artists, including Isaac Hayes, Albert King, the Bar-Kays, and the Staple Singers. He also appeared in Motown's Billie Holiday biopic, *Lady Sings the Blues*, which starred Diana Ross in her motion picture debut that same year.

His run from 1973 to 1975 was pivotal. He signed with Stax Records. He contributed as a writer to the CBS-TV special *Lily*, starring Lily Tomlin, which earned him a shared Emmy Award, and he cowrote *Blazing Saddles* with Mel Brooks (1974). Brooks directed, and the film starred Gene Wilder and Cleavon Little. It won the American Writers Guild Award and the American Academy of Humor Award in 1974. Brooks wanted Richard to play the lead role of Bart, but because of his known drug use the studio would not insure him.

He appeared in *The Mack* (1973) and *Uptown Saturday Night* (1974). His third album, *That Nigger's Crazy* (1974), was a breakthrough commercial and critical success. It went gold, selling over five hundred thousand copies, and captured the Grammy Award for Best Comedy Album (1975). In 1975, he was the first Black guest host in the debut season of *Saturday Night Live*.

In 1976, Stax Records closed, and Richard returned to Reprise/Warner Bros. Records, which released . . . *Is It Something I Said?* (1975, certified platinum with one million in sales). The album earned him his second consecutive Grammy Award for Best Comedy Album (1976). Reprise also rereleased *That Nigger's Crazy* and *Bicentennial Nigger*. The latter became his third consecutive gold album and won a Grammy Award for Best Comedy Album. He also starred in a string of films and box office hits, including *Silver Streak* (1976, the first of four buddy films that starred Richard and Gene Wilder), *Car Wash* (1976), *Bingo Long Traveling All-Stars & Motor Kings*

(1976), *Which Way Is Up?* (1977), *Greased Lightning* (1977), *The Wiz* (1978), and Paul Schrader's *Blue Collar* (1978). Richard also cohosted the 47th Annual Academy Awards in 1977.

On May 5, 1977, NBC-TV broadcasted *The Richard Pryor Special*. It was Richard's first television special, and it featured guest appearances by Maya Angelou, John Belushi, LaWanda Page, Shirley Hemphill (*What's Happening!!*), Glynn Turman, and Sandra Bernhard. Burt Sugarman Productions produced it. Sugarman had created *The Midnight Special* for NBC too, and I was working on that account. Richard's special was a ratings and media hit. Its success led to him securing his own comedy series, the *Richard Pryor Show*, which Sugarman also produced for NBC.

During a meeting about *The Midnight Special*, Burt mentioned the possibility of me working on Richard's series if he could get it on the air. From the first episode, which premiered on September 13, 1977, the show's controversial sketches drew red flags from the network censors. ABC programmed it during the prime-time family hour on Tuesday nights opposite *Laverne & Shirley* and *Happy Days*. Richard's cast featured mostly unknown comics: Tim Reid, John Witherspoon, Sandra Bernhard, Vic Dunlop, Edie McClurg, and Marsha Warfield, and writers Robin Williams and Paul Mooney.

I made it a priority to watch the show and thought most of the skits were hilarious. His writing and sense of humor always resonated with me. Even without him saying a word, his arsenal of animated facial expressions, eye movements, and body gestures would make me laugh. The possibility of working on his series immediately sparked excitement, and I was chomping at the bit.

The most celebrated characters on Richard's television series included the first Black president of the United States at his first press conference, a hustling preacher (Reverend James L. White), a white rocker who machine-guns his fans, and a raunchy, legendary New York Friar's Club Roast to Richard. Yet the most controversial bit Richard tried to pull off was him appearing wearing only a body stocking matching his skin tone to open the show. It was a direct provocation aimed at the network censors.

Richard made sure it appeared in the final cut of the episode, but it was deleted before the broadcast. NBC canceled the show after the fourth episode. It had only averaged a 14.5 rating and ranked 86th out of 104 shows in the 1977–78 season. Richard was resolute and would not water down his material to appease the censors. During the last part of 1977, our paths crossed again briefly. While I was representing Quincy Jones, I visited the film set of *The Wiz* a few times. Richard portrayed the Wizard, and Quincy produced the soundtrack. I witnessed him in action, which was a treat.

Richard kicked off the new year by making headlines for a shooting incident at his home in Northridge. Police issued a warrant charging him with assault with a deadly weapon. Two female friends of Richard's wife, Deborah, filed the complaint. They alleged that after they got into Deborah's Mercedes Benz, Richard chased them around the yard in another car as they were trying to leave the residence. He rammed her Benz a half-dozen times, shot at the car, and shot the tires flat. No one suffered injuries. The next day he turned himself in, and they released him on $5,000 bail.

ALI VERSUS RICHARD

In early spring 1978, I started working on one of my most memorable and fun events, one that featured Richard as a participant. It was a boxing exhibition benefit hosted by Muhammad Ali for one of his dearest friends, his longtime personal photographer Howard Bingham. I had met and talked with Ali a few times and was friends with Howard. Howard called to tell me he was running as a Democrat for a seat in Congress representing the 31st District in Los Angeles.

A few months earlier on February 15, along with millions of others, I had watched in shock and dismay as Ali lost his heavyweight championship title to upstart Leon Spinks in a fifteen-round bout in Las Vegas. Howard and I commiserated about the loss, sharing our acute disappointment, but he expressed confidence that Ali would redeem himself in his next fight.

He explained that Ali had volunteered to host a celebrity boxing exhibition match as a fundraiser for his campaign and would use his influence to secure a few celebrities for the match. He asked me to produce the event and said he had received Ali's blessing for me to do it. I felt flattered and accepted his request. Ali had received verbal interest from his superstar friends Sammy Davis Jr., Marvin Gaye, Richard, and actor Burt Young (of *Rocky* fame), but no one had contacted them yet. He wanted to hand everything over to me. I didn't have any experience as a live event producer, but I had helped organize and oversee similar entertainment events for my clients.

I welcomed the opportunity and enlisted my longtime friend Hamilton Cloud to coproduce with me. He was a seasoned producer and one of the few Black executives to work at NBC or any other major network.

We decided I'd handle booking and be the principal contact for the celebrities, and Hamilton would oversee the production elements and schedule for the day of the show. Fortunately, they didn't have to worry about getting knocked out: Ali had great comedic timing, and we just wanted to make it a fun and entertaining event.

To add a hint of authenticity, we booked the event at the legendary Grand Olympic Auditorium for Monday, May 8, 1978. It was in south downtown Los Angeles and had hosted many top boxing, wrestling, and roller derby championships and events from the 1920s through the '70s. Walking through it was like time-traveling back in history. The dressing rooms were dingy and had the stench of thousands of fighters' sweat and blood ingrained in the wood. It was all a little too authentic for our celebrity boxers, so we rented several film trailer dressing rooms and parked them outside the back entrance. We sequenced the exhibition with Sammy Davis Jr. starting off. (His longtime manager, Mrs. Shirley Rhodes, demanded we call him Mr. Davis and open the show.) Mr. Davis had starred as a prizefighter in the Tony-nominated musical *Golden Boy*. Ali dwarfed him. During their bout Ali used his long reach to palm the top of Sammy's head and hold him stationary. Sammy was flailing with wild air punches. They clowned around to the crowd's delight.

Marvin Gaye was next. He was coming off his smash album *Got to Give It Up*. Marvin exuded coolness, wearing a T-shirt and one of his classic beanies, and showed off his natural athletic ability. He was closer to Ali's height and did enough not to embarrass himself.

Richard stole the show. When he entered the ring, he started talking trash, sneering at Ali, shadowboxing, imitating Ali's flashy footwork, and insinuating he was going to whip Ali's ass. Ali was smiling and sneering back and had his corner team pretend they were holding him back from going after Richard. When the bell rang for the first round, Richard jumped off his chair, stood up, and then acted like his feet were glued to the mat and couldn't move. The auditorium erupted with thunderous laughter. They were hilarious together.

The last bout featured Burt Young, who had received an Academy Award nomination for Best Supporting Actor for his role as Paulie Pennino, Rocky Balboa's brother-in-law, in the first *Rocky*. He was the most game fighter. He pressed and tried swarming Ali, determined to land a couple of punches, but Ali easily thwarted his efforts.

We succeeded in making it entertaining, and I gained even more respect for the friendship Howard and Ali cultivated and shared. Ali even penned a poem we used in the flyer, "Bingham is smart. Bingham is wise. Elect Howard Bingham. Cut our problems down to size." We had a decent media turnout, and all the participants posed and took photos with Ali. It didn't sell out, and Howard lost the election, but it was memorable experience to add to my résumé. And there was a happy epilogue for Ali. On August 15 at the New Orleans Superdome, he became the first fighter to win the heavyweight championship title three times by defeating and avenging his earlier loss to Spinks in their fifteen-round bout.

*   *   *

In early 1979, David Franklin, one of Atlanta's top Black attorneys and a burgeoning entertainment manager, reached out to me. I had not formally met him but had seen him a few times. He was a political power broker in Atlanta and a partner with Maynard Jackson in one of Atlanta's most influential law firms. They credited him with galvanizing the clout it took to get Jackson elected as the city's first Black mayor in 1973.

He had built an impressive roster as an attorney and entertainment manager, working with Richard, Miles Davis, Cicely Tyson, Roberta Flack, Donny Hathaway, Peabo Bryson, Andrew Young, and Julian Bond. He had managed Richard for four years. When we spoke, he was direct, speaking deliberately and fast. He briefly noted that he had heard a lot of good things about me, and he thought Richard could use someone like me on his team. He asked me about Rogers & Cowan's monthly retainer fee and requested that I set up a meeting with my boss.

David insisted that I be the account executive for Richard. He barely took a breath and only stopped talking long enough to give me a few seconds to answer his questions. I was fishing for an appropriate response while still trying to process the broad implications of what he had proposed. It felt fortuitous that after being in Richard's orbit several times over a period of months, I was suddenly on the cusp of representing him—which had never crossed my mind. I expressed my appreciation and profuse thanks to David for the opportunity he was giving me.

His gesture to mandate that I serve as Richard's exclusive account executive in the contract exceeded the norm. He wanted to make sure I received full credit for signing Richard. It wasn't a common practice, but he understood the prevailing racial inequities that existed in the industry, and he felt that taking these precautionary measures made sense.

I didn't have to do a song and dance, court, write up a publicity campaign, or audition for Richard—nothing. All I had to do was schedule the meeting. It stupefied me. Despite his checkered history, he was a megastar as a comedian, writer, and actor. He would become one of my most famous clients and my biggest Black client, and the same for Rogers & Cowan.

While I appreciated what David was proposing on my behalf, I explained that it was equally important to keep the upper-echelon executives (especially my boss) strategically involved and supportive of Richard. I assured him I would assume responsibility for Richard's account and make sure he received the full extent of the company's network and resources.

Richard had a new album coming out and a small tour of live dates. He was coming off his failed comedy series, although they perceived it mostly as a minor bump in the road and a show that was ahead of its time. Shortly after I started representing Richard, I received a cold call from noted producer Bill Sargent. Sargent had received major media attention for announcing that he had offered $50 million to film a Beatles reunion concert. He knew about Richard's forthcoming album and tour and wanted to film one of his live concert performances for theatrical release.

I told him the tour was already booked and it was too late to add a broadcast component to any of his engagements, but he was persistent and committed to covering the costs of filming at a venue in Los Angeles. In addition, he even offered me a production credit if I could help secure Richard. It was a generous offer, but I told him I'd have to run it by David. If he was interested, I'd hook him up directly.

I also let him know I didn't need a credit. Even though it would have been a nice feather in my cap, I didn't want to create the perception that I was hustling to get my name attached or trying to make side money on deals I brought to Richard (or anyone else) as his publicist. It was an ethical liability I wasn't willing to risk.

I contacted David, who was interested and asked me to push Bill to submit an offer in writing. I shared David's request with Bill and added that I thought anything less than six figures wouldn't pique their interest. Within days he made a six-digit offer. I submitted it to David, and they worked out a deal for Richard to headline concerts at the Terrace Theatre in Long Beach, California. I was ecstatic about the deal closing. On paper, it was a win-win scenario for all parties. It was also in Los Angeles, which meant major media coverage, and I'd be able to cover it.

In the fall, Richard embarked on his first stand-up mini–concert tour in two years. It featured three dates, the John F. Kennedy Center in Washington, DC, on September 3; City Center of Music and Drama in New York on September 19; and the Auditorium Theatre in Chicago on September 28. Richard agreed to have all three concerts recorded for inclusion on his first double album, *Wanted: Richard Pryor—Live in Concert*. It was Richard's twelfth album. He produced it with Biff Dawes, and Warner Bros. Records released it on November 17, 1978.

The album opened with "New Year's Eve," where Richard illuminated his version of the night he shot at his wife's car. He thanked the audience for coming out and then started his account: "Shit wasn't that bad; all I did was kill a car. . . . My wife was going to leave me, and I said, 'Not in this motherfucker, you ain't!'" Richard's candidness and his ability to turn his personal upheavals into comedic fodder endeared him to his fans. The album also included a story about being in the ring with Ali during the benefit I produced, as well as stories about Jim Brown, Leon Spinks, animals, nature, and his classic "Heart Attacks," when he gives life and voice to a Black heart attack bullying him.

The public and media response to his shows and the album was phenomenal. He rolled into Los Angeles on a wave of momentum for a sold-out engagement in Long Beach on December 10–11. Since the performances weren't on the album, the title was shortened to *Richard Pryor Live in Concert*. The Terrace Theatre had a capacity of 3,051 and a spacious proscenium stage. Patti LaBelle opened the concert. It was a predominantly white audience, which wasn't always the case, but there was also a noticeable mix of ethnicities sprinkled throughout audience.

Richard was in exceptional form and delivered a captivating performance. He enthralled the audience from beginning to end. The night was running smooth as butter, with no hiccups. I roved around throughout the concert. During the second half of the show, one of the production staff had noticed a suspicious character lurking around the backstage area. We determined he was a process server trying to serve papers from Richard's estranged wife.

We had invited celebrities backstage after the show but didn't want to risk this guy getting to Richard, so we canceled all backstage access after the show and arranged for security guards to meet Richard at the stage and usher him straight to his limousine. They parked it six feet from the backstage exit. We didn't advise Richard until the show was over, so it wouldn't affect his performance. It added a touch of drama to an otherwise spectacular night.

Although I wasn't expecting to play the role of secret service agent at the concert, seeing my clients perform resonated and inspired me. It's what fueled my passion and kept me motivated. Artists feel the most freedom when they're able to share their gifts and express their passion for their chosen art form. The stage is their safe haven, and their performances can often be transformative. Richard had an uncanny ability to take you on an emotional roller coaster. He could make you teary-eyed, or make you laugh so hard you might slobber, get snotty-nosed, suffer knots and pains in your stomach, lose your balance, flail your legs or arms, scream, holla, or shake. Witnessing the monstrous laughter he drew from audiences was a separate show that never failed to be entertaining. And for those seventy-eight minutes, you could tell Richard felt free and safe—not knowing that a few minutes later he would abruptly return to the reality of being rushed to a limousine to avoid getting served.

While Richard continued to enjoy success and fame, his pattern of self-destructive behavior was tampering with his professional reputation as a reliable talent. He was also generating adverse media coverage that I couldn't counter meaningfully. I thought I would have the power to generate media coverage—instead of constantly reacting to it.

However, he gave me the latitude to find a few opportunities that would heighten his fame and present his image in a positive light. We intended to accomplish that by making him more visible and proactive in the Black community. Richard could be very warm and genuine, but at other times he was totally unpredictable, not only to the people he worked with but to himself. I didn't feel he could predict his own actions. So every idea had an inherent risk factor—and could backfire. Like headlining the Brotherhood Crusade gala.

THE ALI INCIDENT

In 1979, Muhammad Ali invited Richard to take part in a Celebrity Sixty-Yard Dash for the Second Annual Muhammad Ali Invitational Track Meet, held in Long Beach. He was hosting it with Dick Enberg for broadcast on NBC. Ali launched it to bring attention to track and field stars in the US, many of them Black.

Stars attending the meet included the highly touted hundred-yard dash champion Houston McTear, the legendary Wilma Rudolph, and high-jumper Dwight Stones. With Ali branding it, the meet instantly became a major sporting event. He naturally added his inimitable charisma and humor to the event, and while promoting it he commented, "I'm so fast that last night I turned off the light switch in my hotel room and I was in bed before the room was dark."

I was looking forward to attending the event, hanging out with Richard, and seeing Ali. It was also good timing for the release of *Richard Pryor Live in Concert*, which was coming out at the end of the month. The itinerary I arranged for the day was to meet Richard at his home so we could travel together to the track meet. It was about an hour's drive. I allocated a little extra time to make sure we arrived before the call time for talent competing in the race.

When I arrived at his house, he was upstairs in his den, chilling with his close friends David Banks and Paul Mooney, both hilarious characters. Paul was a talented comedy writer and stand-up comedian in his own right. He was Richard's most influential and consistent collaborator. David was a writer and actor who had contributed to several of his projects in both capacities. I could tell they had been getting high, but wasn't sure for how long.

Richard invited me to sit down. They were full of funny stories and constantly traded quips. After about fifteen or twenty minutes I reminded Richard about our time constraints and the need to get going. He said he needed to take a quick shower before we left. David and Paul left, so I was sitting in the den alone waiting for Richard. After about ten minutes, the phone rang. I heard it ringing downstairs and presumed Richard was in the shower, so I picked it up.

I answered, "Hello, Pryor residence." It was Richard calling me from downstairs. He said he didn't feel he was in the right condition to go to the meet. I reminded him that they had used his name in promotional ads and Ali was expecting him. But if he didn't feel up to it, it was his call. He opted not to go. Instead, he wanted me to apologize to Ali in person on his behalf and proposed that his longtime bodyguard Rashon accompany me. I was exasperated but didn't feel I could refuse, so I agreed to honor his request.

Rashon and I jumped in the limo and headed down to Long Beach. Rashon was Black, average size, not imposing, but muscular and well cut, with a shaved head, and he usually wore a suit. He was low-key and talked minimally. He usually had an intense look on his face, but occasionally I would see him break his tough guy veneer and crack a smile. In our limited strands of conversation, he discussed a training regimen he had developed for Richard and said that he was consulting on his diet. He was an expert in the martial arts, a man of few words who could be intimidating at times. When we arrived at the track meet, one of the staff members from the talent check-in area helped connect us with Ali.

I didn't have a lengthy statement or a foolproof excuse to give Ali to justify Richard's absence. Richard and I had agreed I'd sincerely apologize, saying he felt weak this morning and his condition had worsened. When we finally reached Ali, he acknowledged me and was welcoming. I delivered my spiel, and he asked me to give Richard his best wishes for a speedy recovery. I thanked him for his understanding and suggested we try again next year. Our exchange lasted for five or six minutes, and then we headed back to Richard's.

It was a low point for me. It felt terrible lying right to Ali's face, and I couldn't deflect or blame Richard. I accepted full culpability for my actions. Lying to Ali compromised my integrity, but I wasn't willing to risk suffering repercussions from Richard if I stood my ground. As I matured professionally, I eventually gained the self-confidence I needed to say no to client requests that I felt compromised my integrity.

Sargent's company, Special Events Entertainment, released *Richard Pryor Live in Concert* nationally on January 26, 1979. The production budget was $750,000, and it grossed $15 million at the box office. In addition, the box office gross for the concerts generated another $300,000. Many ranked it as the most important live comedy film in the modern era by any comedian, Black or white. Only Lenny Bruce's live comedy film, *Lenny* (1965), received comparable ratings from a few critics. Janet Maslin, the noted *New York Times* film critic, stated, "It's not Mr. Pryor's individual lines that make his show so wickedly funny, nor are the comic conceits that launch his various routines automatically uproarious. Mr. Pryor is a superb mime and a fabulous mimic, and he can use almost any topic, intrinsically funny or not, to introduce the brand of physical comedy that is especially his own."

Pauline Kael, top film critic for the *New Yorker*, proclaimed, "Probably the greatest of all recorded-performance films." The film set the standard for the genre's next generation of Black comics. Eddie Murphy, then a burgeoning star in his early twenties, praised it as "the single greatest stand-up performance ever captured on film."

Richard's album was an immense success as well and received a nomination for the 1980 Grammy Award for Best Comedy Album. In 2017, the National Recording Registry by the Library of Congress selected it for preservation as being "culturally, historically, or artistically significant." The momentum from his album and film success continued for months. On May 3, I scored my second cover story for *Rolling Stone*, penned by

David Felton. It featured a head shot of Richard beaming under the banner "Richard Pryor Live in Concert."

A ROUTINE FOR RICHARD

I began feeling more comfortable with my business relationship with Richard, although our interactions remained unpredictable. Sometimes he'd call in the morning to say hello and ask me if I had seen the box office numbers on the film. We didn't hang out socially. Occasionally, he would do unannounced impromptu sets to try out new material at the legendary Comedy Store on Sunset Boulevard and tell me to drop by. After watching his set, I usually hung out with him for a bit backstage. Robin Williams was a big fan, and I talked with him more than once. I thought Robin was brilliant. He was one of my favorite comedians.

On other days, I received crazy calls from Richard or from weird fans. Richard had a habit of getting high and staying up late at night watching fundraising telethons. He would get emotional and call the 800 number on the TV screen to donate. On one occasion, I got a call from an organization that said he had donated $100,000 and given them my name and number to call to facilitate receiving the funds. I advised the caller that Mr. Pryor had not notified me about making the donation, but I'd check with him. When I called Richard, he had no recollection whatsoever and swore he didn't call to donate.

Richard also attracted a wide range of strange characters and fan requests for cash loans, donations, and appearances at weddings, anniversaries, or surprise parties. The most outlandish calls I received was from a man who claimed he was from "planet Zircon." I said, "Excuse me, you're from where?" He reconfirmed he was from Zircon. He said he needed to deliver an important message to Richard personally. I responded succinctly, "That can't happen, but if you want to send a letter, I'll include it in his fan mail and send it to him." I thought that was a better option than rudely hanging up, but he called incessantly for a while.

BUSTIN' LOOSE

In October, Richard started filming the comedy-drama *Bustin' Loose*, directed by Oz Scott, who was a friend I met through our mutual network. He had directed the off-Broadway play *For Colored Girls Who Have Considered Suicide / When the Rainbow Is Enuf*, which earned him a Drama Desk Award in 1977, and *Bustin' Loose* was his first feature film. He was one of just a few Blacks hired to direct a major studio film, so I was pulling for him and the project to be successful. Cicely Tyson starred in the film with Richard, who also served as a producer with Michael Glick.

Richard invited me to drop by the set a few times, and I found out his relationship with Oz had been deteriorating. One day around 9 a.m. I stopped by before going to the office. He was in his trailer relaxing, doing a couple lines of blow and drinking straight vodka. He offered me both. I smiled and said it was early and I was cool nursing my cup of coffee.

They were running behind on the first scene, and he resented the lag time after being asked to report so early. Once they started shooting, there were a series of technical glitches and they had to reshoot the same scene numerous times. Finally, Richard was so disgusted he stormed off the set and, while departing, told Oz he'd come back when Oz got his shit together. I followed him to the trailer. He was livid and felt as a comedian it was impossible to make the same lines funny sixteen times in a row, with several *motherfuckers* added for emphasis. Oz irritated him because he felt he was indecisive and didn't know when to lock a scene and move on. Not too long after that incident, they suspended production, and I found out Oz was no longer involved with the project. Several months later filming resumed after another notable Black director, Michael Schultz, was hired.

My memory is hazy and I don't remember the specific circumstances, but I stopped representing Richard later that year or the beginning of the following year. In late winter of 1980, Richard started filming the hit comedy film *Stir Crazy* with Gene Wilder, directed by Sidney Poitier.

A few months later, while watching the news, I found out Richard was in the ICU in critical condition at the Grossman Burn Center in Sherman

Oaks. They said he was a victim of a self-inflicted explosion in his home. He was thirty-nine and had suffered severe third-degree burns to most of his upper torso. It was a disheartening revelation. Even though Richard perpetuated a pattern of habitual self-destruction, I didn't think it would get this dire.

Flames had engulfed his body, and police reports claimed he had jumped out of the window of his house in Northridge, California, and ran down Parthenia Street, staggering around until two police officers could help him. I had been to his house several times and knew the area, and understood that he had gone a considerable distance before running into the police officers. Neighbors and the two officers recounted that they heard him pleading, "Lord, give me another chance. There's a lot of good left in me. Haven't I brought any happiness to anyone in this world?"

I reached out to his assistant to see if the news was accurate and find out how serious his condition was. She said it was too early to tell. I was getting calls from my family and friends, who knew I had represented him.

Richard had apparently set himself on fire while freebasing cocaine and drinking 151-proof rum. They gave him a one-in-three chance of living. Eventually, he and his wife, Jennifer, admitted that he had attempted suicide in several articles and television interviews. He spent six weeks recuperating in the burn center. I felt relieved when I heard they released him from the hospital.

In his first major television appearance after the accident, on the *Tonight Show Starring Johnny Carson*, he shared a story about turning on the television while lying in his hospital bed one afternoon. A newscast popped up announcing he had died. He joked that he started touching himself to make sure he was still alive.

Around the same time, I learned that Richard had a falling out with his lawyer/manager David Franklin and fired him. Early the following year, February 18, 1981, he filed a $1 million lawsuit alleging that David had illegally mingled hundreds of thousands of dollars of his money with other people's money. Richard won the case, and the California State Labor

Commission ordered David to pay Richard $3.1 million in damages. It was disappointing to find out that David had embezzled this exorbitant amount of money from Richard. It seemed out of character, but I had misjudged him.

Columbia Pictures released *Stir Crazy* in December 1980, and although the reviews were mixed, it grossed $101,300,000. It was the third-highest-grossing film of the year, Columbia's third film to gross over $100 million, and the third-highest-grossing film of all time, after *Close Encounters of the Third Kind* and *Kramer vs. Kramer*. The box office total marked the first time a film directed by an African American earned more than $100 million.

Bustin' Loose premiered on May 22, 1981. It opened number one at the box office in 828 theaters and grossed $31,261,269. Vincent Canby of the *New York Times* wrote in his review, "Only the incomparable Richard Pryor could make a comedy as determinedly, aggressively sentimental as *Bustin' Loose*, which is about eight needy orphans and a $15,000 mortgage that's due, and still get an R rating." Richard returned to doing stand-up in 1982. He followed up *Richard Pryor Live in Concert* with his second live comedy film, *Richard Pryor: Live on the Sunset Strip*, filmed at the Hollywood Palladium on March 12, 1982. He produced and cowrote it with Paul Mooney. Joe Layton directed, and Columbia Pictures released it. The film grossed $36.3 million, which was the highest-grossing concert film of all time. Five years later, *Eddie Murphy Raw* eclipsed it, grossing $50 million. He also recorded a companion album with the same title, which won the Grammy Award for Best Comedy Album (1982). It was his seventeenth album release.

One of most poignant and funny parts of the film came when he shared his personal account of how he caught on fire. He told the audience it happened while he was dunking a cookie into a glass of low-fat pasteurized milk, which caused an explosion, and that scientists were still trying to figure it out. At the end of his performance, he extended thanks to the many people who sent caring and loving messages to him. And he jokingly chastised those he knew were telling nasty-ass jokes about him. He said, "Like this one." He lit a long match, held it in his hand, then moved it from one side to the other. He paused and asked, "What's that?" And then delivered the punchline: "Richard Pryor running down the street." The audience burst into laughter, and he walked off stage.

In early 1983, Richard called to express interest in working with me again. He was developing a script for a biopic that would mark his debut as a director and planned to do another live comedy film and album. Most significantly, he was negotiating a history-making deal with Columbia Pictures, which included establishing his own film production company. He was set to cohost the 55th Academy Awards on April 11, his second time hosting, and had a couple of other films coming out.

It was an opportune time for Richard to land a deal of this magnitude. Blacks were barely visible in motion pictures and television. In fact, in 1981, at the seventy-third national convention of the National Association for the Advancement of Colored People (NAACP) in Boston, a special Hollywood film task force reported to delegates that jobs for Blacks in the entertainment industry were direly needed. The unemployment rate among Black actors was nearly 90 percent, compared to 60 percent among white actors.

Curtis Rogers, NAACP assistant general counsel in charge of the task force, said their goals were to encourage Hollywood to use Black actors on the screen in "real-life roles" beyond maids, servants, or clowns and to have studios hire Black directors, producers, technicians, cameramen, and others. He also noted, "Of the 240 movies made for Hollywood studios in 1981, only twelve featured starring roles for Black men, and only one starred a Black woman." Paul Brock, another member of the task force, stated, "Blacks are almost being filmed out of existence." The national office of the NAACP was pressing for inclusion and change, as was the Beverly Hills chapter of the NAACP, headed by Willis Edwards. Some felt he was a spirited and effective antagonist, while others viewed him as a self-serving opportunist who exploited the NAACP platform to elevate himself. I was friendly with Willis and felt he was a fusion of both. Even in the fight for social justice and racial equality, having some level of fame can be an asset—when you know how to use it to advance your efforts. He helped convince NBC-TV president Brandon Tartikoff to broadcast the NAACP Image Awards for the first time in 1983, which was a significant accomplishment.

Guy McElwaine, who became president of Columbia Pictures in 1981 and later its chairman and CEO, brokered the deal. He was formerly Richard's agent and had been one of his longtime friends and champions. During his tenure at Columbia, McElwaine supervised production and distribution for over sixty films, including *Ghostbusters*, *The Karate Kid*, *A Passage to India*, and the Oscar-winning Best Film *Gandhi*. He had been a powerful agent and founding partner at International Creative Management (ICM), where he helped package talent for many top films, including *E.T. The Extra-Terrestrial*, *Close Encounters of the Third Kind*, the Alien trilogy, and *The Towering Inferno*.

I worked with Guy directly on the bullet points for the media release to announce his new film deal with Columbia. He felt it was important to reinforce that the deal was a partnership and felt it should be a joint release made by Columbia and Richard. It would position Columbia Pictures as the first major studio to initiate tangible action in response to the NAACP's plea to eradicate the existing racial inequality in the industry. Columbia's PR department would handle the announcement. The release would also include a couple of quotes from Richard, which he agreed to provide. On May 20, 1983, Columbia Pictures and Richard announced that they had signed a five-year contract worth $40 million, which included Columbia financing Richard's own film production company, Indigo Productions. Richard's financial package was the highest ever paid to a premier Black talent by a major Hollywood movie studio.

The partnership called for Richard to produce four moderately budgeted films via Indigo Productions, which he could star in or not. Columbia also committed to signing him to star in a minimum of three motion pictures for the studio over the next five years. Richard would have artistic control over all his Indigo films, and the right to star in or produce projects at other major film studios.

Richard had surprised many people by hiring Jim Brown, the Hall of Famer and former Cleveland Browns star turned actor, as president of Indigo. They had been friends for fifteen years. Throughout Richard's stay in the hospital, Brown spent time daily at his bedside and helped keep his personal and business lives running while he was recuperating. I had worked as Jim's publicist for a short period during my early days at Rogers & Cowan. My boss, Paul, represented him while he was developing his acting career. We became friendly, and I attended some of the popular house parties he hosted regularly. He lived up in the West Hollywood Hills at the top of Sunset Plaza Drive.

He invited me to play in three-on-three basketball games on Saturday mornings on his driveway court with a mix of sports execs and athletes. He had a deadly corner bank shot he could hit nonstop—probably with his eyes closed too. The games were fiercely competitive and fun. I played with former Laker Hot Rod Huntley and former NFL wide receiver Lance Rentzel (veteran of the Vikings, Cowboys, and Rams) on several weekends. Jim was one of my favorite NFL players, and I could only imagine what an intimidating figure he was on a football field. I felt much safer and had a blast playing basketball with him. I was looking forward to working with him again.

The Columbia announcement on May 20, 1983, generated considerable media coverage, all positive. It was good public relations for Columbia, and it refreshed and added some luster to Richard's stardom and level of fame. He was mounting a reasonable comeback from being on the brink of death. About a month later on June 17, Columbia released *Superman III*, which grossed $100 million. Richard received $4 million for his role in the film, the highest fee ever paid to a Black actor.

On December 16, Richard ignited another firestorm when he fired Jim Brown as president and three other Black employees. It caused an earthquake of dissonance and sent shock waves throughout the Black community. Willis Edwards, who had aligned himself closely with Brown, hoping to develop Indigo as an outlet for Black projects, actors, and jobs, incited and fueled the backlash against Richard. Willis and the NAACP's visceral reaction was to rally behind Brown and vehemently accuse Richard of being unfair and racially insensitive.

Edwards called Brown's firing a "slap in the face" and levied attacks on Columbia Pictures and Coca-Cola, its parent company, for allegedly pressuring Richard to fire Brown. His accusations intimated they were using Richard as a scapegoat and puppet. He claimed the Brown firing happened because he was developing too many Black-oriented projects. Neither was true. Richard and Jim had a personal falling out that carried over into their business relationship. In the press release announcing the firing, Richard cited their parting was "due to creative differences."

To extricate itself from the fracas, Columbia issued subsequent press releases to reinforce that Richard had full autonomy and control of his company and the exclusive right to hire and fire its employees—without their input. Richard stood by his statement and refused to elaborate further.

Columbia's $40 million pact spread out its financing such that Richard could make only low-budget Black-oriented films, spending $5–6 million per film. And if Richard starred in them, he would essentially need to waive the acting fee he could earn starring in other films to get films produced by his company Indigo Productions. Columbia agreed to pay him $5 million on any other Columbia film he starred in, which was a slight bump up from the record-setting $4 million fee he had just received for *Superman III*.

At the same time, it became evident that Richard was an extraordinarily gifted comedian and actor, and that's what he did best. But he didn't have the personality, discipline, or passion to become a spokesperson, activist, humanitarian, or film production mogul. That realization shifted how I approached working on his behalf. I focused on honoring who he was— and not what I thought he could become.

In October 1983 Columbia released *Richard Pryor: Here and Now*, his third live comedy film. It was filmed earlier on August 9 at the Saenger Theatre in New Orleans. Richard directed and wrote the film, which was part stand-up and part documentary. It also featured comedian Paul

Mooney. Andy Friendly, Bob Parkinson, and Jeff Scheftel produced it. Jimmy Jam and Terry Lewis did the music. Warner Bros. Records released an album of the same title on November 12.

Development of Richard's biopic, *Jo Jo Dancer, Your Life Is Calling*, continued. Richard hired a talented young Black producer, George Jackson, to replace Brown and serve as executive vice president of Indigo Productions. George and I had been casual friends for a couple of years. Along with his producing partner, Doug McHenry, also a friend, they became hot and filled the void left by the post-'70s blaxploitation film era. They scored commercial successes with the urban and hip-hop lifestyle films *New Jack City* and *Krush Groove*.

George was very likable and could talk passionately for days about Black culture and Hollywood's ingrained stigmas and inequities regarding Blacks. I thought he could be an asset in helping Richard develop Indigo into a viable player and content producer of Black films that could be competitive and commercially successful in the marketplace, if that was Richard's mission.

In early 1985 filming started on *Jo Jo Dancer, Your Life Is Calling* in Peoria, Illinois, where Richard was born and raised. Peoria is about 160 miles southwest of Chicago along the Illinois River. During Prohibition it was popular for its speakeasies and as a haunt for bootleggers and known Mafia leaders like Al Capone who hid large qualities of liquor there and then trucked them into Chicago. Shooting was scheduled for three weeks.

Richard emptied his soul into the film as the star, director, producer, and cowriter with Rocco Urbisci and Paul Mooney. It was his directorial debut and the first Indigo Productions film under his pact with Columbia. The cast included Carmen McRae, Debbie Allen, Art Evans, Fay Hauser, Barbara Williams, Paula Kelly, Diahnne Abbott, Scoey Mitchell, Billy Eckstine, and E'Lon Cox as Little Jo Jo. Herbie Hancock did the music. In the prepromotion of the film, Richard insisted it wasn't autobiographical, so we followed his directive.

It was an enlightening, surreal experience to see where Richard grew up, to walk on the same street and see the brothel his grandmother ran, where she raised him as a child. It was once a thriving red-light district and the only area of the city that wasn't segregated and allowed interracial interaction. The house had three levels, a big front porch, a high pointed roof, and dark wood floors. Richard admitted that the days we filmed there were eerie for him. During breaks, he was discernibly more reflective than usual.

I spent most of my time hanging with Paul Mooney on shooting days at various locations. He provided an endless stream of hilarious stories, jokes, and social commentary. His favorite retort was "break face," a slang inference for inciting robust laughter. He asked repetitively, "Did I break face?" Each time I responded, laughing, "Yeah man, you broke face." Paul was a cerebral comic and storyteller. His take and Black perspective as a comic were unique, which is why I think he and Richard collaborated so well.

After three weeks in that small Midwest city and experiencing similar views, I felt that a moderate and unapologetic segregation and racism still permeated the city. I could only imagine what Richard might have experienced growing up there when Black people had no access to any of the areas, restaurants, and bars we visited.

Soon after *Jo Jo* wrapped, Universal released *Brewster's Millions*, a comedy film that teamed Richard with John Candy. Walter Hill directed it, and Lawrence Gordon, Gene Levy, and Joel Silver produced. Richard played Montgomery Brewster, a minor league baseball pitcher, and Candy, Spike his catcher. He discovers that a distant uncle left him a $300 million inheritance, but in the will, his uncle posed three challenges he must choose from to retrieve it. The film grossed $45,833,132 at the box office.

The last project I worked on with Richard was overseeing the *Jo Jo Dancer* premiere. It was an organizational disaster. Over the years, I've been moderately successful erasing the horrid details from my memory—but not all of them. We set up the premiere to be a fundraiser for a Los Angeles–based Black community organization. My larger mission was to restore Richard's image in the Black community and silence the uproar Willis Edwards had stirred up with his rhetoric after Jim Brown was fired.

I recommended hiring Pat Tobin, a Black twenty-five-year veteran publicist and entrepreneur, to work on the premiere and help identify a worthy beneficiary. She had heavily pursued me and had deep roots with the prominent Black business, political, and social strata in the city. She also had ties to some major white corporations that invested financially in the community. Richard approved retaining her services.

We worked out a final itinerary for the event, expecting to have a full house and a great premiere. The only glitch was that Richard had decided not to attend. It would have been optimal but he gave us enough warning to work around it. The premiere was on May 2. Some of Pat's team had arrived, but I found out she had many of the tickets. A crowd was gathering waiting for the theater doors to open, and she was more than fashionably late. I was infuriated and thought it was rude and unprofessional.

She finally showed up in a limousine, fully glammed up in a fancy gown, grandstanding like she was a star in the movie. She had a photographer taking pictures of her getting out of the limo. It infuriated me. When I confronted her, she shrugged off her lateness like it was no big deal.

We discovered that she had sold more tickets than the theater could accommodate, so we had an overflow crisis and missed our start time. Fortunately, the theater manager was able to arrange seats for some people to view the film in an adjacent screening room.

Once the film started, Pat and I got into a volatile argument in the lobby area. I had put my ass on the line to get her involved, and she had let me down. I berated her and didn't mince words. Minutes after our confrontation, I regretted losing my cool. It was an organizational failure that happened on my watch, and I had to accept culpability for it. I was glad Richard didn't attend. We met a few days later so I could give him a recap on the premiere, and I apologized for my role in what transpired. I also apologized to Pat but never worked with her again.

The film budget was over $14 million, and it only grossed $18,034,150.

The media reaction and reviews were mostly unflattering, although certain critics felt Richard's effort was courageous. In a few interviews, he came clean and admitted his freebasing explosion had been a suicide attempt. I arranged for noted *Chicago Tribune* critic Gene Siskel to interview Richard: "The triumph of 'Jo Jo Dancer' is that Pryor does not spare himself—neither his talent nor his mistakes—filling his life story with hilarious episodes from his strip club beginnings to his pathetic scratching for cocaine crystals on the living room carpet of his California mansion." He quoted Richard: "Here I was, as the film shows, a snotty little kid from Peoria, who was allowed to rise to the top, who became a very big star—as big as anyone could want—and I couldn`t handle it. I became a drug addict." "I did try to kill myself," Pryor admits freely. "I have only fragments of memory about exactly what happened that night, but I know I tried to kill myself. The pain . . . it had come to that."

A month or two later, I stopped representing Richard, and we didn't stay in touch. I read that he had multiple sclerosis and in 1991 underwent quadruple bypass surgery. Due to his weak heart and MS symptoms, he was forced to use an electric scooter to get around for the final years of his life.

Before his death in 2005, he became the first recipient of Mark Twain Prize for American Humor from the John F. Kennedy Center for the Performing Arts in 1998. In 2004, Comedy Central voted him number one on its Top 100 Greatest Stand-ups of All Time. The National Academy of Recording Arts and Sciences (NARAS) posthumously awarded him the Grammy Lifetime Achievement Award in 2006.

From my retrospective view, Richard was a transcendent talent who achieved an unprecedented and herculean level of fame. His influence on the genre was not just as a megastar of stand-up, motion pictures, and television, but also as a seminal and prolific writer, producer, and director. And he did it despite his drug addiction, a reputation as an erratic malcontent, and a string of humiliating self-destructive acts.

I have often contemplated the path his career might have taken if he could have prevented his infamy from overtaking his fame. In most cases, when celebrities fall from grace due to self-inflicted poor choices, you encourage them to confront it and move on. You urge them to take a personal and mental hiatus. Time heals holistically, so give the public time to forget—or forgive. Avoid talking to the media. Whenever the issue comes up, change the narrative, and emphasize that you've moved on.

Richard did the exact opposite: He wouldn't let you forget it. He owned it. Then he regurgitated and transformed his infamy into hilarious stories that drove the content of his live films and albums. It became a cathartic and ingrained part of his creative process.

Toward the end, I'm not sure which was driving his career more, the infamy or the fame. It doesn't matter; he did it his way! And I think it's safe to say he took the mold with him.

BE AUTHENTIC AND
DON'T LET FAME DEFINE
YOUR SELF-WORTH

There is an unavoidable ebb and flow to being famous, regardless of your inherent wealth of talent. One can become delusional and lost while traversing the lofty peaks and depressing valleys. Navigating and managing those periods requires a defiant and resilient spirit. You can't allow fame, or the lack thereof, to dictate what you can and cannot do.

In my formative years as a publicist, I represented Bette Midler for a half-dozen years and felt she struggled emotionally at both ends of the spectrum but never let either define her. She is fortunate to possess an abundance of diverse talents, which enabled her to pivot seamlessly across all the prevailing entertainment mediums: recordings, diverse music genres, live performances, film, television, theater, and the literary world. Which is an exception—not the rule.

It's impossible to manage fame without interacting with people who have achieved it. As in any other profession, there is an inherent learning curve and a dues-paying component to get game-ready. After you've learned the ropes, quantifiable fame can be a powerful commodity in leveraging, influencing, and negotiating favorable advantages for its possessor.

Bette's level of fame gave me access to the top editors in media and major talent bookers and producers in electronic media (radio and television). Sometimes, it gave me the power to dictate the time frame when an article would be published, the writer assigned for the interview, the theme of the article, boundaries on issues that were off-limits, photographer and image approvals, and whether an interview was for a regular feature or cover story.

Most A-level media editors abhor giving "superstars" (or more directly, their publicists) the ability to manipulate or control how they're presented in a publication or featured on a broadcast. I preferred a balanced approach that allowed for some give-and-take. I also strived to be strategic and avoided wasting major media coverage on vanity PR, which might help a publication sell more copies but is ill-timed and doesn't serve the interest of artists or their brand.

The fact that she was already a superstar sped up my professional growth exponentially. Just as important, she and her manager, Aaron Russo, embraced me from the onset. They trusted me and gave me access. The more you know your clients, the better you can serve them. Most relevant is to have a firm grasp of how they view their fame, and how they feel they should leverage it. If they have an inflated sense of its value, and the level they have achieved doesn't match their self-perception, it can be detrimental. It's also instructive to know their personal nuances, pet peeves, what time of day they're most responsive, red flags or prior tiffs with journalists or publications, their attention span, their media awareness, and the length of their decision-making process. In Bette's case, I learned her nuances and preferences quickly.

Bette was usually amenable to speaking in the midmorning hours. She hated doing interviews and would decline most that required more than an hour. It was more effective to send her media requests in writing. Unlike other clients, she was an avid reader and familiar with most prominent media outlets and journalists. Most important, she understood the importance of strategic timing and wasn't interested in seeking publicity unless it served a purpose.

Bette was also the first female superstar I represented. All my initial clients at Rogers & Cowan were men, and I noticed that there are distinct differences. There were more media outlets focused on women than men, especially with beauty-, fashion-, and lifestyle-themed formats. It's also a misogynistic and sexist industry. Numerous times I witnessed women being unfairly judged for their physical attributes in a way that men were not.

The timing for becoming a point person with Bette was serendipitous. She had logged a dozen years in developing her career, but her rise to becoming a superstar occurred in a six-year run from 1971 to 1977. During that period, she won a Grammy and a Tony, released three commercially successful albums, headlined a couple of sold-out national concert tours, and became a media darling. She created a one-of-a-kind persona, and media compared her to megastars like Barbra Streisand, Liza Minnelli, and Judy Garland. Her level of fame contributed to the invaluable knowledge and lessons I learned representing her.

FIRST STEPS

When I started working with Bette, we were both living in Los Angeles. She was thirty-two, and I was twenty-seven. Paul Bloch, my boss at Rogers & Cowan, asked me to join him for a meeting with her manager, Aaron Russo, to discuss Rogers & Cowan representing her. Paul advised me that he had communicated with Aaron and felt confident we'd sign her. The meeting was more of a formality than a pitch meeting. He also wanted Aaron to meet me.

When we walked into Aaron's office, his assistant's desk was next to the entryway. I didn't look closely at her until we sat down. When I looked up, she had a look of surprise on her face, as did I. We had met the night before at a film premiere afterparty and had briefly flirted and talked—but not long enough to exchange numbers or find out what we did professionally.

Before the meeting I discovered her full name, Bonnie Bruckheimer. After our meeting, we shared a laugh and relief that our flirtatious encounter had not led to anything else.

Aaron was short and stocky, and carried excess weight in his bulging stomach. He had been born and raised in Brooklyn, had a heavy New York accent and thick, curly black hair he wore shoulder length. His typical wardrobe included weathered, lived-in blue jeans, a cut-off short-sleeve gray sweatshirt, and sneakers. Aaron could be gruff and combative if triggered, but he also had a robust laugh and a jovial spirit. He fused a sharp business mind with street savvy. At his core, he was a rock 'n' roll manager; he didn't fit the traditional slick Hollywood prototype for managers. In 1968, at twenty-five, he opened a popular rock nightclub in Chicago called Kinetic Playground. He booked some of rock's premier artists, including the Grateful Dead, Iron Butterfly, Jefferson Airplane, Janis Joplin, Led Zeppelin, King Crimson, Vanilla Fudge, and the Who. He was also managing the Manhattan Transfer along with Bette.

The meeting went well. Days later, Aaron officially retained R & C to represent Bette. I knew very little about Bette before I started representing her, but I did a lot of research to familiarize myself with her music and career history. Aaron made sure I received her most recent releases and media materials.

Bette was born and raised in Honolulu, Hawaii, and started her career at nineteen, hustling to get work like most young singers and actors. She landed her first paid gig as an extra playing a passenger beset with seasickness in the film *Hawaii*. In 1965, she used the money she had earned to move to New York and pursue a career in theater. Upon arrival, she studied with Uta Hagen at HB Studio and landed roles in off-off-Broadway plays, including Tom Eyen's *Miss Nefertiti Regrets*, her first professional gig. A year later she secured the role of Tzeitel in *Fiddler on the Roof* on Broadway and then became an original cast member in *Salvation*.

Every artist has a career-breaking hit or project. In the summer of 1970, five years after pounding the streets, Bette landed her game-changing gig, performing an avant-garde cabaret show at the Continental Baths, a gay bathhouse in the basement of the Ansonia Hotel. The Ansonia, built in 1904, was a lavish and massive French Renaissance luxury residence hotel that became a historic landmark.

During a down period for the hotel, the Australian opera singer Steve Ostrow and his wife, Joanne, leased the basement swimming pool and Turkish baths and created a design approach that reimagined "the glory of ancient Rome." He named it the Continental Baths. It ushered in the era of gay liberation and revolutionized gay bathhouses in New York. Twenty-four hours a day, the baths served a capacity of one thousand men, who wore only bath towels while on the premises.

Bette's tour de force stage presence, her comedic proficiency, and her habit of often performing in just a bath towel earned her the affectionate moniker Bathhouse Betty. During her residency there, she also birthed her Divine Miss M character and created a musical collaboration with a young songwriter and singer named Barry Manilow, who accompanied her on piano. Manilow helped Bette develop her trio of backup singers, the Harlettes. She enlisted the services of choreographer Toni Basil, who added another interesting dynamic to her live performances. Bette was getting her first taste of fame and had become a must-see darling for the in-crowd movers and shakers who fueled the New York underground club scene.

During the height of Continental Baths, the venue attracted top entertainers, including the Manhattan Transfer, John Davidson, Melba Moore, Peter Allen, Lesley Gore, Patti LaBelle, Gladys Knight & the Pips, Dick Gregory, Minnie Riperton, and Gloria Gaynor. It also birthed the electronic disc-jockey movement with top DJs Frankie Knuckles and Larry Levan, among others.

Her bond with and allegiance to the gay community lifted her to diva status and led music mogul Ahmet Ertegun, head of Atlantic Records, to give her a record deal after seeing her perform for the first time. Her popularity also led to a starring role in the first theatrical production of

Tommy, the Who's groundbreaking rock opera, in 1971 and her debut appearance on the *Tonight Show Starring Johnny Carson*, which introduced her to a national television audience.

Two years later, in the summer of 1972, she met Aaron Russo. They dated briefly, and he took the reins as her manager. Atlantic Records released Bette's debut album, *The Divine Miss M*, on November 7, 1972. Arif Mardin and Barry Manilow produced the album, which featured three hit singles, "Do You Wanna Dance?," "Friends," and "Boogie Woogie Bugle Boy." "Bugle Boy" was originally a classic swing "jump blues" hit for the Andrews Sisters in 1941. It reached #6 on the *Billboard* Hot 100 Singles chart and became her first #1 on the Adult Contemporary chart. The album reached *Billboard*'s Top 10 and sold a million copies. She also won her first Grammy Award in 1973 as Best New Artist. I remember hearing "Boogie Woogie Bugle Boy" when I was in college.

That was an auspicious debut, but what accelerated Bette's level of fame was her conceptual live performances and her frenetic pace of releasing records and touring. In the next four years, she launched the Divine Miss M character with her first national concert tour, opening for Barry Manilow in thirty cities, and followed that up with her second album, *Bette Midler*, which reached #6 on *Billboard*'s Top Album chart and nearly went platinum. The entire tour sold out and wrapped up in New York with a nineteen-day engagement at the Palace Theatre on December 3–23.

On April 14, 1975, the original production of *Clams on the Half Shell Revue* premiered at Broadway's Minskoff Theatre, which earned her a special Tony Award for "adding luster to the Broadway season." She followed it with her third album, *Songs for the New Depression*, which marked Bette's first outing as composer, producer (along with Mardin), and engineer. She penned two of the album's tracks. Kanye West sampled lyrics from "Mr. Rockefeller" on the song "Last Call" from his debut album, *The College Dropout*. She followed that up with the "New Depression Tour" and then released her fourth album and first live album (a double-album package), *Live at Last*, in June 1977. The album is culled from her performance on the "New Depression Tour" at the Cleveland Music Hall in Cleveland. Her performance was also filmed and became a television special titled "The Bette Midler Show." *Live at Last* reached #49 on *Billboard*'s Albums chart in the fall of 1977.

When we signed Bette, *Live at Last* had just been released. Paul advised me that Aaron wanted to meet with me at his office. I hoped it was to meet Bette, but he had beckoned me to go through about five hundred color slides of Bette's *Clams on the Half Shell Revue*. He wanted me to pick twenty-five or thirty of whatever I felt were the best shots so he could run them by Bette for approval.

It was an inauspicious first assignment that didn't thrill me. He set me up in a room at a table with a carousel slide projector that used a rotary tray capable of storing about eighty slides. There was a pull-down ceiling projector screen so I could view the slides. They needed to be taken in and out one at a time. He advised me to let him know when I had finished, then showed me how to turn down the lights and left. It was a tedious process. Bette was rarely ever still for more than a second, and often the angles weren't flattering.

After about forty-five minutes, I had picked some thirty images. When I showed them to him, he said Bette wouldn't approve them and told me to find better ones. He gave me one hint: to pick images where the left side of her face was more prominent. It's the side she preferred. I reviewed the slides again and found enough images to satisfy his request. It was a menial endeavor, but learning that she preferred the right side of her face paid dividends down the line.

When I finally met Bette, she was warm and friendly, not standoffish or effusive but pleasantly talkative. When she committed to talking, she was engaged and focused, and always established strong eye contact. On first impression, she seemed down-to-earth and had a profound sense of humor. Her core character traits stayed consistent and never changed dramatically.

A STAR-SPANGLED NIGHT FOR RIGHTS: A CELEBRATION OF HUMAN RIGHTS

My first extensive project with Bette and Aaron was a historic benefit concert at the Hollywood Bowl. The singer and anti–gay rights activist Anita Bryant was the face and spokesperson for Save Our Children, a coalition formed to spearhead a campaign to repeal a local ordinance in Dade County, Florida, passed in January 1977, which prohibited discrimination based on sexual orientation. She was also a brand ambassador for the Florida Citrus Commission (1969–80), which promoted the orange industry, crops, and orange juice made from frozen concentrate and initially supported her position.

Gay rights activists condemned her involvement with Save Our Children, the first organized opposition to the gay rights movement, which dated back to the historic Stonewall riots in New York in 1969. On June 7, 1977, Dade County repealed the antidiscrimination ordinance, a major setback to the gay rights movement, and it resulted in gay rights marches and gay pride parades across the country.

Aaron wanted to produce a major concert event and fundraiser headlining Bette to support the gay rights movement. He sensed there was angst brewing in her gay constituency, which felt she should be a more active voice and advocate for their cause, and he wanted to quell it before it escalated. Bette was a fervent supporter of gay rights but was reticent about using the event to promote her stance.

She committed to headline the event, and Aaron assembled a production team to put the event together. Besides booking the artists, we had to create an interesting title and select the beneficiary. One faction had trepidations about inserting *gay rights* in the title. They felt it might make it more difficult to attract headline artists and a mainstream audience. I felt if the title didn't include gay rights, it would dilute the messaging and purpose of the event.

Finding a reputable beneficiary was more challenging. We needed to identify an organization the gay community recognized as a legitimate and worthy supporter of their cause, and Aaron felt we should meet with potential beneficiaries in person. I was tasked with researching and creating the list of candidates. We identified twenty-five or thirty candidates, most based in San Francisco, and met with three or four organizations every day for a week at Aaron's house.

The meetings were enlightening, sometimes emotional, funny, and frustrating. The range of organizations covered the gamut. Representatives came wearing suits and ties, others wore leather outfits, and others were straight-up impostors who had created fake organizations thinking they were going to meet Bette. Aaron and I were out of our milieu, but the meetings educated me about the underpinnings of the gay movement. Aaron opted to make the Save Our Human Rights Foundation the beneficiary for the event. The foundation was the best-funded pro-gay rights organization in the country, was aggressively fighting against Bryant's Christian anti-gay crusade, and agreed to invest in promoting the event.

The event's final credits read, "Aaron Russo Presents: A Star-Spangled Night for Rights: A Celebration of Human Rights," to be held at the Hollywood Bowl, September 18, 1977. The featured performers included Christopher Lee, Lily Tomlin, the Lockers, David Steinberg, Aalon, War, Tom Waits, Baked Potato, Helen Reddy, Tanya Tucker, Richard Pryor, and Bette. Ticket sales and press interest were robust, and the event was heavily promoted and advertised.

It was a warm and lovely summer night. The audience comprised seventeen thousand predominantly gay men. The atmosphere was festive and celebratory, with a charged-up audience anxiously ready to party. Celebrities were sprinkled throughout the crowd, including Paul Newman, Olivia Newton-John, Valerie Harper, Robert Blake, and noted Hollywood columnist Rona Barrett. It had all the trappings and buzz of a hugely successful event. I had arrived early to cover sound check and get VIP guest tickets, media, and photo passes to the will-call window for pickup.

THE RICHARD PRYOR INCIDENT

The audience response to the first few performers, which included the street dance group the Lockers, was lukewarm. The biggest names were performing toward the end of the show. Besides Bette, I really wanted to see Richard Pryor. He was performing right before her. I had never met him or seen him perform live at this point, but I was diehard and loved his early comedy albums *That Nigger's Crazy*, . . . *Is It Something I Said?*, and *Bicentennial Nigger*.

I stood in the wings, stage left. Right before Pryor went on, he was standing about six feet from me. He briefly acknowledged me with a smile and a head nod but looked tense and hyped up. I opted not to introduce myself. When he stepped on stage, he historically altered the night.

He strutted to the middle of the stage and perused the audience with a snarling stare. They welcomed him with a thunderous applause. He hesitated momentarily and then opened his set by saying, "I came here for human rights, and I found out what it was really about was not getting caught with a dick in your mouth." The audience responded with sheer laughter. "You don't want the police to kick your ass if you're sucking the dick, and that's fair," Pryor continued. "You've got the right to suck anything you want!"

Then he shifted gears and started a rant of vitriolic attacks on gay people, even including an attack on women's rights. The crowd had stopped laughing and was booing and yelling expletives at him. He didn't relent. "When the niggers were burning down Watts, you motherfuckers were doing what you wanted on Hollywood Boulevard and didn't give a shit about it. Fuck you and everything you stand for." Then he lifted the back of his suit jacket, turned to point his backside at the audience, and said, "You can kiss my happy, rich Black ass!"

He immediately exited the stage, passing right by me, got in his limo, and drove off. I never witnessed a rant by a performer that came remotely close. The crowd was shocked and incensed. In a matter of minutes, it had ripped the heart out of the event.

Bette was backstage and didn't see it happen. After Aaron explained what transpired, she was pissed off. Like everybody else, she didn't understand what had triggered Pryor. While the crowd waited for Bette to come on, Aaron and the director came on stage to apologize. The audience greeted Bette with infectious joy and a sense of relief. She opened her set by asking, "Does anyone want to kiss my rich white ass?" With that one line, she resuscitated the show, and the crowd went wild. She delivered an inspired performance, and all the performers joined her on stage for a finale to close the show.

The postmortem on the event included many disparaging views of the incident that lingered in media coverage in Los Angeles and San Francisco for two weeks. Pryor's tirade grabbed the headlines and overshadowed the purpose of the event.

Bette felt embarrassed at having her name dragged through the mud, and Aaron took a hit as the producer. There wasn't a practical way to spin what had occurred. It was an anomaly. Aaron's intent hadn't been misguided. The concert was not a failure, but the outcome was shrouded by controversy. Its historical significance is remembered annually by the media in retrospective articles. Pryor wasn't canceled by today's standards, but he did suffer a few minor repercussions from the industry and incendiary rebukes from the gay community.

The event helped fuel the movement and ignite a national boycott of orange juice produced in Florida. In turn, the boycott forced the Florida Citrus Coalition to dump Bryant as its spokesperson. It was the country's first successful national gay boycott.

On November 17, 1977, Atlantic released *Broken Blossom*, Bette's fifth album, fourth studio album, and second album of the year. It featured a fusion of cover songs from rock, pop, jazz, blues, and genres, including most notably Edith Piaf's most celebrated tune, "La vie en rose." The album reached #51 on the *Billboard* Albums chart but didn't produce a hit single.

ROLLING STONE'S 10TH ANNIVERSARY SPECIAL

Jann Wenner, the founder and publisher of *Rolling Stone*, retained Rogers & Cowan to represent *Rolling Stone's 10th Anniversary Special*, a two-hour special scheduled for broadcast on CBS on Friday, November 25, 1977. He hired Steve Binder to direct and the produce the show. Binder, also a Rogers & Cowan client, was one of the industry's top music directors and producers, and had produced music specials featuring Elvis Presley as well as the Rolling Stones. I was working with Binder on the *Rolling Stone* special.

Wenner anticipated it being an epic show, but many of the top artists, including Mick Jagger, Paul McCartney, John Lennon, and Paul Simon, had personal issues with him and refused to take part. John Belushi and Dan Aykroyd had agreed to perform, but they pulled out at the last minute. Bette was invited to perform on the show and accepted.

The featured performers also included Keith Moon (legendary drummer for the Who), Steve Martin, Art Garfunkel, Richie Havens, Gladys Knight, Patti LaBelle, Teri Garr, Yvonne Elliman, Donny Osmond, Mike Love, and Ted Neeley. Bette performed "La vie en rose" with the Harlettes—Charlotte Crossley, Ula Hedwig, and Sharon Redd. Television and music critics panned the special, and it also embarrassed several *Rolling Stone* editors. The special was a poor representative of the most iconic music and pop culture publication in the 1970s, and it was the first project I worked on that totally tanked.

Bette maintained a torrid schedule and had little time to lament about miscues or failed projects. She embarked on her first club tour in five years, "An Intimate Evening with Bette Midler," which featured shows from late November through New Year's Eve in Vancouver, San Francisco, Chicago, and Los Angeles.

She also taped her first network special for NBC-TV, *Ol' Red Hair Is Back*, in Los Angeles on December 7. Frank Sinatra's *Ol' Blue Eyes Is Back* inspired the title. Her friend Dustin Hoffman and Emmett Kelly guest-starred on the special, which was highlighted by her duet with Dustin, who played the piano on a song they cowrote, "Shoot the Breeze." Dwight Hemion, director and producer for specials featuring Frank Sinatra, Elvis Presley, Bing Crosby, and Barbra Streisand, directed and produced it. It earned her an Emmy Award for Outstanding Special—Comedy-Variety or Music.

A WILD NIGHT AT THE ROXY

Bette closed out the year with a ten-day sold-out engagement on December 21–24 and 26–31 at the legendary Roxy Theatre on Sunset Boulevard. It was one of the longest engagements at the Roxy, the most prestigious live performance club in LA during the 1970s. The theater was intimate, with a capacity of five hundred people.

On the day of the show, I would log eight or nine hours just at the venue. Starting around 3:30 p.m. and continuing almost nonstop until showtime, I handled TV crews, tickets, photo passes, VIPs, getting a song list to reviewers, and arrivals. Before the show I advised Bette on whether photographers were shooting—which was usually for a maximum of three songs.

Bette had agreed to host a meet and greet for about twenty journalists in the upstairs backstage area after the show. She'd talk for a few minutes with each person and take a picture with them. I gathered everyone together, asked them to get in a single line, and escorted them up the stairs. I walked a little ahead to take a peek and make sure the coast was clear. I peered down the hall and saw that Bette and Aaron were arguing.

Bette was yelling expletives, pushing, flailing, and trying to punch Aaron, who was yelling back and doing his best to deflect Bette's punches. Fortunately, the line of journalists was far enough back that they couldn't hear or see what was going on. I rushed to stop them, apologized, and told them Bette needed a little more time.

As soon as I had resettled them downstairs, I ran back up to make sure they had stopped fighting and find out if Bette still wanted to meet the journalists. Bette agreed to do it. When I brought them up, she had flipped her mood. She was warm-spirited and generous, allowing ample time to chat with each journalist. In heated moments like that, I felt my role was to mitigate. I avoided playing the role of a therapist and never took a side. I found out later that Bette was infuriated about the sound quality—and blamed Aaron for not fixing it.

The pop music editor at the *Los Angeles Times*, Robert Hilburn, one of the most influential music critics in the country, whom I knew and had pitched several times for other clients, reviewed the show. He respected Bette and showered her with plaudits: "Bette Midler's spectacular Roxy opening was easily the pop concert of the year in Los Angeles. Despite strong bids by Rod Stewart and Linda Ronstadt, Midler's show was in a class by itself. . . . She may well be the most arresting American female performer since Judy Garland." His review was a redemptive high that helped minimize the havoc of opening night. The rest of the run went without a glitch.

THE ROSE

There was a lot of excitement about Bette doing *The Rose*. She was my first music client to star in a major motion picture. She had received other film offers, but none they felt were right. This one fit like a glass slipper—and seemed destined to make her a movie star. Making Bette a movie star had been Aaron and Bette's dream from the beginning. It was her debut, and she was getting paid a half-million dollars. It put her on the same pay scale as prominent actors such as Barbra Streisand, Faye Dunaway, Jane Fonda, Diane Keaton, and Jill Clayburgh.

The Rose was an inspired by a story set in the late 1960s that chronicled the life of a self-destructive rock star who struggles with the perils of success and coping with her intimidating and ruthless business manager. Veteran film producer Marvin Worth had the rights to the script, which was intended as a biopic of Janis Joplin. He had been trying to develop it for five years. The original title was "Pearl," Joplin's middle name, but her family refused to sell the rights to her life story. Worth saw Bette perform at the Troubadour, pursued her to star in the film, and agreed to coproduce it with Aaron.

Worth had managed jazz greats Billie Holiday and Charlie Parker, and produced the Oscar-nominated documentary *Malcolm X* (starring Denzel Washington) and the Oscar-nominated film of Lenny Bruce's Broadway hit, *Lenny*.

Marvin agreed to make the adjustments in the *Rose* script that Bette and Aaron requested, and they signed Mark Rydell to direct. The cast included Alan Bates, Frederic Forrest, Harry Dean Stanton, Barry Primus, and David Keith. They shot the film on the 20th Century Fox lot and various locations throughout the city in June and July 1978. Highlights of the filming were two live concerts Bette performed, one on June 23, at the Wiltern Theatre, Los Angeles, and one at Veterans Memorial Stadium, Long Beach, on July 14.

Aaron and Marvin Worth couldn't be more different—they were worlds apart. Aaron dressed the same every day. Marvin was a lean and diminutive man whose wardrobe comprised high-priced clothing from swanky Beverly Hills men's boutiques like Mr. Guy and Bijan. He sported a long flip hairdo that skimmed his shoulders, and not a single strand moved. He always looked like he had just stepped out of a beauty salon chair. Aaron was an outlier, making his motion picture debut as a producer. It was a partnership made in hell. The toxicity between them was palpable. On some days when I was on set, the off-camera drama overshadowed what was being filmed. They infuriated each other and argued incessantly—but needed each other. Marvin had industry clout, and Aaron had Bette. Aside from that, Bette experienced stoked levels of nervous anxiety. She knew there was a lot riding on the film, and the added pressure heightened her insecurities.

Two months after filming ended on *The Rose*, Bette launched a world tour that included dates throughout the US, her first European tour, and a major tour in Australia. She hit all the major markets—the UK, France, Germany, and Holland—and was well received. In Australia, she performed in Sydney, Melbourne, Perth, Adelaide, and Brisbane.

While the film was being edited, Bette worked on music for the soundtrack, completed her fifth studio album, *Thighs and Whispers*, and ended the West Coast run of her US tour. I joined the tour for her dates at the Gammage Auditorium in Tempe, Arizona; the Concord Pavilion in Concord, California; the Greek Theatre in LA; and Pine Knob Music Theatre in Detroit.

In early December she premiered her first live production with Aaron, *Divine Madness*, at Broadway's Majestic Theatre in New York. The title credit read, "Ron Delsener Presents 'Bette! Divine Madness!'" She collaborated with director Jerry Blatt, who directed all her live shows, and Ron Delsener, one of New York's most celebrated promoters, presented it. It opened on December 5, 1979, and ran through January 6, 1980.

She continued her tour with a date at the Concord Pavilion—the most memorable on the tour for me. We stayed at the Four Seasons Hotel in San Francisco, and it was about a thirty-minute drive to the venue. I had planned to accompany Bette in the limo to the venue for sound check, but I had a meeting that ran behind. I let her know I was running late and to leave without me.

When I arrived in the hotel lobby, the only person waiting was one of her backup singers, Luther Vandross. I had not met him before. I grabbed one of the rental car drivers and suggested Luther come with me. We both sat in the backseat. He weighed over 350 pounds, which left me pinned against the car door. It was over 100 degrees. He was sweating profusely and experiencing increasing bouts of quick breaths and gasping for air. I thought his health might be at risk, so I asked if he wanted to stop and get some water. He deferred and said his symptoms were normal because of his weight—the same thing happened when he walked up a single flight of stairs.

Luther had built a solid reputation backing up such top recording stars as David Bowie, Roberta Flack, and Donny Hathaway, and he was a featured vocalist on national commercials for several top product brands, including NBC, Mountain Dew, Kentucky Fried Chicken, Burger King, and Juicy Fruit. His backup singing role for Bette was out of the norm—at least for me. Every night he sat behind a curtained area on stage and sang all the high notes for Bette and the Harlettes on a handful of songs. They set up a small table with a full plate of food on it, so he could munch when he wasn't singing. He was gifted with one of the best voices I had ever heard.

*   *   *

Being on the road with Bette was eye-opening. Her shows were elaborate productions that took between thirty and sixty people to pull off. In the limo after every show, the director, Jerry Blatt—one of her dearest friends and a very skilled and likable man—her assistant Bonnie, and I would sit and listen to Bette critique every aspect of the show. She noticed when a lighting cue had been missed, a musician played the wrong note or chord, one of the Harlettes sang out of tune—or when any miscue occurred. Even though she typically received several standing ovations during the show, it never overshadowed her concerns about how the shows fell short. It's impossible to attain perfection in live music presentations, but I respected Bette's passion and desire to try. Sometimes I wished she took greater joy from the performances she and her cast gave audiences night after night.

In October, shortly after the tour ended, Atlantic released *Thighs and Whispers*. It leaned heavily on disco/dance tracks and was produced by Arif Mardin. A few tracks made some noise on the dance charts, but the album only reached #65 on *Billboard*'s Top 200 Pop Albums chart, which fell short of expectations.

THE ROSE OPENS

Bette's motion picture debut, *The Rose*, opened at the Ziegfeld Theater in New York on Wednesday, November 7, 1979. The reviews were mixed.

Most cited flaws in the script but applauded Bette's performance. Janet Maslin from the *New York Times* wrote in her film review, "There are so many finely drawn episodes, so much brittle, raunchy humor, and such an unexpectedly alluring performance from Bette Midler in the title role that the movie maintains its momentum even after it's gone off the track." It grossed $793,063 in its opening weekend on forty-four screens nationwide, making it the second-highest-grossing opening weekend for under fifty screens, behind *Star Wars*. The film eventually grossed $29.2 million in the United States and Canada.

Bette was getting prominent media coverage across the board, but I was most thrilled about securing my first *Rolling Stone* cover story. Iconic veteran *Rolling Stone* photographer Annie Leibovitz was set to shoot the cover, and Timothy White was assigned to do the interview.

Normally, I would confer with photographers or their reps in advance to go over the objectives and flow for the shoot. Bette liked being prepped with details and a plausible direction—for example, the number of setups, whether there would be props, any styling directions, the approach to hair and makeup, and the length of the shoot. All I could get from Annie was that she wanted Bette to look natural and to not overdo her hair or makeup. I shared the little direction I had gathered with Bette, and she seemed willing to roll with it.

The photo shoot took place at a moderate-size studio in Hollywood. Annie is tall and thin, and at the time had long black hair. She was also a fast talker, and her spontaneous approach wasn't putting Bette at ease. The setups weren't working, and the frustration was escalating. We were also exceeding the allocated time set for the session, and Bette was secretly raising her eyebrows and giving me her "I'm ready to throw in the towel" look.

Annie had two big buckets of long-stemmed red roses, four or five dozen, sitting on a table, but she hadn't used them yet. After three hours of shooting, as a last-ditch effort, she asked Bette to lie on the floor. Along with her assistant, she started gingerly arranging roses around Bette to give the appearance that she was lying on a bed of roses. Bette was wearing a black bustier body suit that left her shoulders and arms uncovered. She clutched her hands behind her head, with her elbows extended. They covered the rest of her body in roses and left her barefoot with her legs exposed up to the top of her thighs. For the final touch, Annie asked Bette to cradle a single long-stemmed rose in her mouth. It took less than thirty minutes to shoot. It was an amazing setup and instantly felt like a killer cover image. Annie was exuberant, and Bette felt relieved. On December 13, *Rolling Stone* featured the image as their cover story.

Just shy of a month later, Atlantic released the soundtrack for *The Rose*. The album's second single, "The Rose," written by Amanda McBroom, peaked at #3 on the *Billboard* Hot 100 Singles chart. It also went to #1 and stayed at the top of the Adult Contemporary Singles chart for five consecutive weeks. In the spring of 1980, the album hit #12 on the *Billboard*'s Album charts. It was certified double platinum in the United States alone. "The Rose" became her first gold single, and the album was her most successful in seven years.

The latter part of the year ended on a somber note. Besides separating from Aaron, Bette's mother died. Her breakup with Aaron didn't surprise me. They both confided in me, and I was around them often enough to witness their unraveling firsthand. We never discussed her mother's passing or the breakup.

THE AWARDS SEASON

The first major awards show of the year was the Golden Globes, which was broadcast in January from the Beverly Hilton Hotel. *The Rose* received five nominations. Bette earned nominations for Best Actress in a Motion Picture—Musical and Comedy and New Star of the Year in a Motion Picture, Female. Her fellow nominees for Best Actress included Julie Andrews in *10*, Jill Clayburgh in *Starting Over*, Marsha Mason in *Chapter Two*, and Shirley MacLaine in *Being There* (which is one of my all-time favorite films).

I remember getting to the hotel early. Bette had gathered some team members to give input on an acceptance speech in case she won. She was crafting it with Bruce Vilanch, her longtime friend and comedy writing collaborator. Bette and Bruce would throw out lines to us to get everyone's input. They kept the lines that won everybody over, scratched the misses, and wrote the speech spontaneously based on everyone's feedback. Bonnie and her agent, Arnold Stiefel, also contributed to the process.

They came up with a hilarious acceptance speech, which she gave after winning Best Actress. The most memorable quip was, "I'm reminded of when Joan Crawford actually won her Golden Globe, and she said, 'I'll show you a pair of Golden Globes,'" while cupping her breasts. The crowd loved it.

BARBARA WALTERS

About two weeks later, Barbara Walters asked about featuring Bette as a guest on the *Barbara Walters Special*. ABC had made Walters the highest-paid TV journalist the year before. Initially Bette was reticent about doing the interview. She knew Walters was a mega media star but deplored her reputation for baiting guests with surprise questions about intensely sensitive personal issues. She didn't want to become one of the victims who broke down in tears. I advocated in favor of Bette doing the interview. I thought she could deflect any darts Walters threw. I also encouraged her to request a break if she began feeling vulnerable so that she could gather herself. After a little coaxing, she committed to do it.

We set up the interview at the house Bette was renting in Los Angeles. Walters had a large camera and technical crew. Wires were strewn everywhere, along with lighting stands and several cameras. The living room felt like a soundstage. They seated Bette in a comfy oversize armchair. Barbara sat near her on a chaise longue, leaning in for the interview.

Within the first couple of minutes, Barbara went straight for the jugular and brought up Bette's mom dying and her parting company with Aaron, pointedly framing what a difficult year it must have been for her. Bette was silent. She leered slightly at Barbara, and I knew she was seething inside. I had expected Barbara would strike at some point, but she bypassed any warmup or foreplay. After an extended pause, Bette calmly responded. She affirmed that it had been a challenging year, that she was still reeling and trying to plot her course for the future.

Bette requested a break a few minutes later and came into the kitchen infuriated. She couldn't believe that Barbara had ambushed her to start the interview. She wasn't sure she could get through it and was defiantly proud that she had not cried. Having gathered herself, she walked back to the staging area. She looked at Barbara and jokingly said, "Get out of my house." It was a payback zinger that caught everyone off guard. Bette made it clear that she was just teasing, and everyone laughed. She sailed through the rest of the interview seamlessly. ABC broadcast it during prime time on April 1—which was excellent positioning for the Oscars. Barbara asked guests to rate themselves on a scale from 1 to 10. Bette responded, "Oh, I think I'm about a 55. I don't know. I'm a happening girl." It was the most prominent media coverage she received during the awards season.

Next up was the 23rd Annual Grammy Awards. For the first time, it was moved to the famed Radio City Music Hall in New York. Paul Simon hosted, and it was televised on CBS-TV on February 25,1981. Bette won Best Female Pop Vocal Performance for *The Rose*.

In the middle of award season, Bette made her debut as an author with the release of her memoir, *A View from a Broad*, published by Simon and Schuster. It chronicled her massive 1978 world tour and retraced her family roots and early ascension to stardom. Her range of talents and mediums were assets in building her multifaceted brand identity. Each medium mandated pitching different media editors, which was a plus. But it was challenging to maintain optimum media coverage when projects from different mediums overlapped. Mostly, it made it tough on Bette and stretched her too thin.

The last hurrah of the award season was the Academy Awards. Bette happily received a nomination for Best Actress in a Leading Role. *The Rose* also received three other nominations: Best Actor in a Supporting Role (Frederic Forrest), Best Film Editing, and Best Sound. The other nominees in Bette's category were Sally Field in *Norma Rae*, Jill Clayburgh in *Starting Over*, Jane Fonda in *The China Syndrome*, and Marsha Mason in *Chapter Two*—tough competition, but it was a feather in Bette's cap to receive the nomination in her film debut.

The Academy Awards ceremony was held in April at the Dorothy Chandler Pavilion in Los Angeles. Johnny Carson, one of Bette's biggest fans, hosted it. Bette presented an award but lost in the Best Actress category. *The Rose* was, however, a triumphant debut and validated her as a film star capable of carrying a movie and delivering at the box office. It completed the circle of fame she had aspired to attain in all the major entertainment mediums.

After Aaron left, I dealt with Bette and Bonnie to schedule her media activities. Bette and Bonnie had periodic bouts of not speaking to each other. During those times, I'd call Bonnie and she'd tell me to call Bette directly, or if urgent to fly out to meet with her in person. I never asked Bette for more than an hour, and our meetings were most productive if I prepared an agenda listing all outstanding items, gave her a copy, and ran through them one by one.

Bette's *Divine Madness* concert film hit theaters on September 26, 1980. The Ladd Company produced the ninety-four-minute film, and Warner Bros. distributed it. It featured sixteen live performances of her most popular songs and some of her comedic characters. The response at the box office was tepid. Bette had implanted her handprint in every creative element of the filmmaking, and it was her follow-up film to *The Rose*, which made it particularly disappointing.

Bette had contributed immensely to my professional growth and success at Rogers & Cowan, and based on the success I had achieved with my client roster, I felt I deserved a raise. They agreed to only a nominal pay bump but offered a promotion to vice president as a trade-off—so I settled. After serving as a VP for two years, I began to seriously contemplate branching out on my own. I received an offer to become a partner in a small boutique public relations firm, the Gibson Group, founded by the highly respected rock 'n' roll music publicist Bob Gibson. It was an offer I couldn't refuse, so I resigned. I was apprehensive about my future, but I was also excited and ready to embrace whatever happened next. Representing Bette was the one thing I knew I'd miss. When I told her I was leaving, she was empathetic and gave me her blessing. Shortly after joining Bob, we changed the name of the company to The Group.

JINXED

I checked in with Bette from time to time to see what she was up to, but we didn't stay in touch on a regular basis. I heard she was recording another album. In 1981, about a year after I resigned, Bette received a second opportunity to star in a film, *Jinxed*, which turned out to be a prophetic title on every level. The film derived from the 1980 novel *The Edge* by Frank D. Gilroy. He sold the film rights to the Ladd Company at Warner Bros. (producers of *The Rose*), hoping to direct. Ladd sold the project to United Artists. Bette agreed to star and asked Don Siegel to direct. She rewrote the script with Jerry Blatt, Carol Rydall, and Siegel. She also handpicked the young up-and-coming actor Ken Wahl to costar as her love interest.

Filming started on May 5. The film was shot in numerous locations, including Lake Tahoe and Las Vegas. Bette and Wahl's relationship got off to a contentious start, then continued to deteriorate throughout the production. Siegel suffered a heart attack; it would be his last film. Siegel had been a mentor of the then-struggling director Sam Peckinpah and hired him for the final twelve days of shooting.

After the film was released I read a scathing *Los Angeles Times* article about *Jinxed* failing miserably at the box office. It featured interviews with Wahl, Bette's costar, and director Don Siegel, both unabashedly excoriating Bette.

Wahl recounted, "Whenever I had to kiss her, I thought about my dog," and added that he dreaded doing their romantic scenes. Siegel asserted, "I'd let my wife, children, and animals starve before I'd subject myself to something like that again." Siegel's characterization of Bette as temperamental and unruly lingered, damaging her reputation for years. Bette withdrew into a prolonged depression. I didn't realize the severity of it until she shared it with me personally.

Bonnie called one day to tell me Bette wanted to talk about us working together again. I was surprised and thrilled. Bette could pick any major PR company in the industry, and she was picking mine. Signing Bette to my fledgling company would feel like a coup!

Because of the systemic racism that permeated the entertainment industry, it would be barrier-breaking. When Black superstars signed with white managers, agents, publicists, and lawyers, no one blinked, because it was the norm. But I wasn't aware of a white superstar comparable to Bette who had signed with a Black publicist or management company. Bob and I became partners because we wanted to build an integrated and diverse artist roster. I felt that signing Bette might help change the racial paradigm and open the door for someone else of my color to follow me.

Race was a nonissue in my business relationship with Bette. We shared a mutual respect as human beings and openly engaged in spirited discourse about the prevailing social, political, and economic challenges of the racial injustice plaguing our industry and society. I was immensely grateful that she trusted my professional acumen enough to sign with me based on merit. That's all you can ask for. It was an enormous boost to my self-confidence and helped elevate the stature of our company.

Bette had several projects lined up that she wanted to publicize: a new studio album, a lengthy national concert tour, and her second book, *The Saga of Baby Divine*, which was being released by Crown Publishers. Nothing was happening in the film area, and she was still reeling from the fallout from *Jinxed*.

"De Tour" was Bette's first national concert tour without Aaron. It started on December 8, 1982, and had two segments, a winter leg from December to March, and summer leg from June to September. It included major theaters and amphitheaters in the summer. In many markets, engagements were booked for multiple dates. The summer leg allowed time to support her new studio album, *No Frills*, which had an August 1 release date. She capped the tour with a seven-day sold-out engagement at Radio City Music Hall in New York, which was her first major engagement in New York since the Majestic Theater.

"De Tour" also included two sets of Harlettes. The first set featured Ula Hedwig, Linda Hart, and Katey Sagal (who became a major television star with *Married with Children*). The Harlettes for the summer leg comprised Joanne Harris, Siobhan O'Carroll, and Jenifer Lewis (who became a prominent film, television, and Broadway star, actor, singer, comedian, and activist). They were all talented and fun. Jenifer kept me and everyone else in stitches. She was a guaranteed daily dosage of wild, crazy, and hilarious.

Bette wanted my presence on the road full-time to manage her media interviews and meet and greets. She was doing four or five performances a week, so we moved constantly, but we managed to break away for some fun and carousing. This usually involved going out for late dinners after the shows, preferably at restaurants that had a piano. Bette would occasionally do impromptu performances, which was her way of winding down.

Simultaneously, I was collaborating with Crown Publishing to figure out the media and marketing campaign for *The Saga of Baby Divine*. Bette penned the book, and Todd Schorr illustrated it. It was a colorful story about Baby Divine, a loud, cute, bossy fairytale princess who wears heels. She experiences adventures with three outrageous dames. Her parents are never sure how to deal with their divine baby daughter.

Crown publicist Susan Eilertsen was my contact. She was warm, congenial, and excited about Bette's book. She really wanted her to do a major book tour. Bette hadn't done a tour for her first book, and I doubted a traditional book tour would appeal to her. My instinct was that if I could figure out a way to transform each in-store appearance into a media event and make it a "book event" tour, Bette might do it. The average time allotted for traditional author in-store appearances was one or two hours. I created the idea of having Bette sign books for an undetermined time—until every person in line got a book signed. It would attract her core fan base and potentially generate thousands of book sales in the major markets. It would be more costly, but everyone would get more bang for their bucks. I had to run it by Bette first. If she approved it, Susan would have more leverage with her bosses.

The idea was only plausible because Bette could pull it off. She was charismatic, comedic, and spontaneous, and she could interact with a crowd and media in close quarters, skills she had honed working at the Continental Baths. I pitched the idea to Bette, and she immediately expressed reservations about signing books for an unfixed length of time. I convinced her it was the media hook to make them events. She also didn't want to incur any expenses to have her dresser and makeup and hair person travel with her. I understood and asked, "If I get everything you want, will you do it?" She gave me one of her patented anguish-laden answers: "Oh, all right, I'll do it."

A great idea is only great if you can implement it. I advised Susan that Bette had committed to do the tour. I developed a marketing strategy to secure financial and marketing support from the bookstores and a basic rider. I recommended they get the top bookstores in each market to bid on securing Bette. The store template and rider included the following items:

1. Bette will sign all books purchased at the store for as long as people stand in line.
2. Place a full-page ad in the major metropolitan newspaper the day before the in-store event. Bette will do an interview with the same newspaper to run before the event.
3. Dedicate the front window display case to Bette's book for one week prior to the event.

4. Provide a secure press area in proximity to the signing table to accommodate TV crews, photographers, and journalists. The table must have two comfortable chairs: one for Bette, and one for a person from the bookstore or our camp. Customers will be asked to have the page open in the book they want Bette to sign. Provide ample gold-colored Sharpies, a wired or cordless microphone, and a PA system.

5. Provide a private room for Bette to take breaks and minimal catering: snacks, coffee, tea, water, and juices.

6. Additional security guards to monitor the lines in and out of the store.

7. Commit to purchase a minimum number of books, depending on the size of the market and the store.

8. Two first-class airfares, two economy airfares, four- to five-star hotel accommodations, a one-bedroom suite for Bette, three single rooms, ground transportation, one town car, an SUV or van for luggage and two passengers, plus salaries and per diem for the dresser and makeup person.

9. Arrange for one dry run/rehearsal prior to the event.

10. Bette will arrive the day before each event to do media interviews to promote the event.

The tour focused on eight markets: New York, Los Angeles, Chicago, DC, Boston, San Francisco, Dallas, and Minneapolis. Crown liked the plan and committed to funding it. Bette agreed to welcome the crowds, take media photos, and allow television crews to tape the first fifteen or twenty minutes of the signing session. She enthusiastically embraced the tour and decided to create different customized themed hats for each appearance. We scheduled the tour to start after Bette finished her concert tour.

Atlantic released *No Frills*, Bette's sixth studio album, in August, her first album since *The Rose*. The album mixed rock and new wave music and was produced by Chuck Plotkin, best known for producing Bruce Springsteen and Bob Dylan. The first single was a rock ballad, "All I Need to Know," written by veteran songwriters Barry Mann, Cynthia Weil, and Tom Snow.

I encouraged Bette to commit to visiting radio stations on the book tour. She had been remiss in maintaining her relationship with radio in the past. I suggested she do the morning drive-time talk shows, so she could press some flesh and hopefully restore her relevancy as an artist. I couldn't guarantee all the radio stations would add the song to their playlist, but we could get it played during her interviews. After some convincing, she agreed to do them.

FOREST HILLS

At the end of August, she had an engagement at the legendary West Side Tennis Club in Forest Hills, Queens. It had hosted the US Open and many superstar music concerts featuring such greats as Frank Sinatra, the Beatles, the Rolling Stones, Jimi Hendrix, Diana Ross, Bob Dylan, and the Who.

We arrived at the venue for sound check in the late afternoon. Bette looked out from the stage at the audience seats and was instantly infuriated. It looked like the aftermath of a hurricane. Most of the white wooden folding chairs looked weathered, dilapidated, and broken. She vowed not to perform unless the venue's management agreed to replace or repair the seats. Her concert tickets weren't cheap, and she couldn't stomach her fans paying to sit in those seats.

After contacting management amid considerable consternation, we got them to fulfill her request to salvage the engagement. Within an hour they had assembled a large crew to paint and fix the chairs. Both parties agreed not to reveal publicly what had transpired. It was a prime example of how the power of fame can meaningfully serve an artist's interests, and I respected Bette for standing up for what she believed in.

We set up the meet and greet for after the show outside Bette's dressing room trailer. Such events weren't elaborate and were usually uneventful, but one surprise guest showed up to meet Bette: Gene Simmons, the lead singer of Kiss. They didn't know each other, but she agreed to meet him. After chatting with him for a few minutes, she spontaneously asked, "I've heard tales that your tongue is quite infamous—is it true what they say?" Simmons smirked and flicked his tongue nastily, suggesting she decide for herself. Bette let out an OMG gasp of awe upon seeing it. It lived up to its billing of being extraordinarily long, and Bette found it laughably disgusting. It was a welcome dose of comic relief after what had been a stressful day in Queens.

We ended the "De Tour" in Minneapolis and had three weeks to recalibrate and get ready for the book tour. I was serving as the publicist, manager, road manager, and valet for all the ladies.

The *Saga of Baby Divine* book tour was a phenomenal success and surpassed Crown's expectations. Bette signed for a minimum of five or six hours in every market, generating considerable TV, radio, and print media coverage. Most notably, the book remained on the *New York Times* fiction list for fourteen consecutive weeks, peaking at #5 the week of December 18.

The highlight of the tour was the San Francisco event. We created a red-carpet entry to the store and hired a popular sixty-piece gay orchestra to surprise Bette and play a few songs upon her arrival. People camped overnight on the sidewalk, with the line stretching for several blocks from the store. By morning, the crowd had mushroomed to a couple thousand. Bette was thrilled by the turnout. She signed books for eight hours, and a few times during the day she went outside to talk to fans who were patiently awaiting their turn to meet her.

We only faced one crisis on the tour. In Minneapolis, her in-store event was approaching seven hours, and the line was still long. If we let her finish, we'd miss our evening flight to the next market. There were no commercial flights leaving later, so the only way to avoid canceling the next date was to hire a private jet. Susan wasn't excited about paying for a jet, and Bette hated flying, and was more fearful of flying in small planes. However, Bette didn't want to let her fans down, so she agreed to take the private jet. Luckily, Susan found one. The stars aligned in our favor; we kept on track and finished the tour on a high note.

Unfortunately, *No Frills* was failing to gain traction. And although Bette despised doing the early morning radio interviews, she plodded through. They didn't generate any short-term leverage for the record, but she ingratiated herself with the Atlantic promo team, who felt she'd reap residual benefits down the line. The only bright spot for *No Frills* was her third single, "Beast of Burden." It became a Top 10 hit throughout Europe, and the video, which included a cameo by Mick Jagger, earned three MTV Video Award nominations.

THE *ART OR BUST* HBO SPECIAL

Bette turned her attention to editing her *Bette Midler: Art or Bust* special for HBO. Simultaneously, I was collaborating with HBO on a premiere event to launch the special. We decided to make it a viewing party rather than a traditional screening. I found a hip new club downtown, 20/20, which had wall-to-wall video screens. The venue was packed and buzzing, but Bette was running fashionably late (over twenty minutes), much to the chagrin of Michael Fuchs, the president of HBO. He felt it was rude for her to show up late for her own premiere. She finally arrived seconds before he was about to go ballistic. The crowd gave her a resounding welcome. She gave him a big hug and kiss on the cheek, and the red on his face suddenly dissipated.

The special integrated visuals of art by Van Gogh, Degas, Picasso, Lichtenstein, Kandinsky, and others that were fused with live concert performances of her most popular songs, famed characters like Delores DeLargo, and her patented bawdy jokes. The *New York Times* review exclaimed, "Bette Midler takes risks that other performers do not. On 'Bette Midler: Art or Bust!' she succeeds more often than she fails; she is, in fact, close to being an absolute winner, and if she were an Olympic gymnast, going for a perfect 10, she would get a 9.9."

BETTE AND DAN AYKROYD HOST THE FIRST MTV AWARDS

MTV invited Bette and Dan Aykroyd to host the first MTV Awards ceremony and broadcast. They accepted and asked us to attend all the major creative meetings throughout the show's development. We met with MTV's founding executive team, including the programming chief and CEO Robert Pittman, Tom Freston (who later replaced him), John Sykes, and Fred Seibert. Carolyn Baker, the only Black executive, was head of Talent Acquisition. We had input on all aspects of the show, even choosing the trophy—a replica of a man wearing a silver spacesuit, which they nicknamed the "Moonman."

The highlight and low point of the show was Madonna singing "Like a Virgin" on top of a cake while dancing erotically in a provocative wedding dress. While slithering down the layers, the tulle from her dress got caught in a stair and caused her to fall on the floor. She cleverly attempted to turn it into a choreographed move. Herbie Hancock topped the night by winning five awards, and Cyndi Lauper had the most nominations with nine.

The MTV Awards was my last project with Bette. I shifted my attention to management, as Bette worked on getting back into the film business. It had been over three years since the infamous *Jinxed* debacle. At the end of the year, Bette married artist Martin von Haselberg.

Bette and Bonnie later partnered to form All Girls Productions as a vehicle to produce film and television projects as starring vehicles for Bette. They signed a deal with Disney/Touchstone Pictures, which started with *Down and Out in Beverly Hills*. The film was produced and directed by Paul Mazursky and starred Bette, Nick Nolte, and Richard Dreyfuss (all former clients). Little Richard, whom I was managing, had a minor role. The film's success sparked comebacks for Bette, Nick, and Richard, and helped me revive Little Richard's career.

I hold an enduring love and fondness for Bette. Her relationship with fame for over sixty years and her resolute inner strength to weather its unpredictable rollercoaster effects taught me valuable lessons that influenced the way I approached dealing with other famous superstars later in my career. After collaborating with her, I felt empowered and equipped to manage anyone at her level of fame.

I'm forever indebted to her for taking a chance on me and letting me play a small role on her prodigious career journey. It's impossible to counsel and manage fame without having a few stars of Bette's caliber in your life. On my trek through the land mines of fame, she rates high—one of the best ever.

3

DON'T SELF-ASSESS—
THE PUBLIC DICTATES FAME

Fame is fleeting. By the time you've learned how to deal with it, it may have already dissipated. An obsession with fame can become a destructive force in one's life. Once you give it up, it's almost impossible to regain.

PASSING OF ICONS

It was Saturday morning, May 9, 2020, and I was just waking up, a little after 10 o'clock. Since the COVID-19 pandemic had started two months previous, I was staying up every night until 2:30 or 3:00 a.m. Prepandemic, every Saturday morning I would bolt out of my apartment by 7:30 to catch the 2/3 train from 125th Street to play pickup basketball at PS 4 on 11th Street in the West Village. Since that was no longer an option, there was no rush to wake up.

I awoke beset with some lingering depression about the sudden passing of a longtime friend and former client, Andre Harrell, who was just fifty-nine years old. Andre had passed away on Thursday night in Los Angeles, and *Variety* was one of the first publications to break the story of his death on Friday afternoon. The *New York Times* published an article on Saturday, along with many other publications. Andre had hired me as a publicist when he secured a $40 million distribution for his Uptown Records label with MCA Records. I worked with him again briefly when he was president of Motown Records. And while I was managing Kenny "Babyface" Edmonds, he was Kenny's business partner in his Nu America record label (distributed by Arista Records). We worked closely on Kenny's album *Face2Face*, released on September 11, 2001, the infamous and tragic day when terrorists attacked the Twin Towers in New York and the Pentagon.

Staying at home and quarantining had disrupted my lifestyle, like with so many others. I stopped rushing to get up not only on Saturdays but as a daily routine. Sporadically, I watched movies in bed, and would leave my computer and cell phone on my bed when I crashed—absurd laziness had become the norm. Both were within arm's reach, along with my glasses. When I woke up, I could start working without moving a muscle or lifting the covers. I'm always intrigued by how the media treats the passing of a famous person, celebrity, or business icon in obituaries. It makes me momentarily ponder how mine will read one day. I felt Andre had received an honorable send-off, with every article recognizing his many contributions as a lightning rod and connector for Black culture, Black excellence, R & B and hip-hop music, fashion, social justice, and as a cultivator of the glamorous life. He hosted his own weekly radio show, *Champagne and Bubbles*, on Sunday nights from six to nine on Emmis's urban adult contemporary station, WRKS (98.7 Kiss FM), in New York since 2011. It celebrated his passion for living life to the fullest.

As I scanned through more posts, I noticed an image of the iconic Little Richard and a headline noting that he had died earlier in the morning. I could not believe that I had lost another former client within twenty-four hours. I honestly never considered Richard to be a friend per se—we only hung out for business meetings and projects. But his passing still overwhelmed me with sadness. He was eighty-seven, had been ailing for years, and rarely made any public appearances in his last years. It had been many years since we had spoken.

After reading the initial article, I started scanning my feed more, and many articles and posts about his passing began to crop up. The paradoxical media outpouring, praise, and reverence that he was receiving amazed me. Some articles chastised and ridiculed him for character traits and tendencies that he had mocked about himself. Little Richard desperately craved the fame associated with being the self-proclaimed "king or architect of rock 'n' roll." Throughout the intermittent dalliances of fame that marked his stormy career, he was rarely recognized as the king, including by the public, major artists, or the music industry at large. On this day, I wondered whether he would be happy with how they assessed his career legacy, level of fame, and contributions.

Richard was an enigma in rock 'n' roll history, and the way several prominent music critics eulogized him aptly epitomized the wide view of how his influence and controversial persona impacted the genre.

New York Times, *written by Tim Weiner*

Little Richard, Flamboyant Wild Man
of Rock 'n' Roll, Dies at 87

Little Richard did not invent rock 'n' roll. . . . He raised the energy level several notches and created something not quite like any music that had been heard before—something new, thrilling, and more than a little dangerous.

The Guardian, *written by Tavia Nyong'o*

Too black, too queer, too holy:
why Little Richard never truly got his dues

How did a turbaned drag queen from the sexual
underground of America's deep south ignite rock 'n' roll?

. . . A world-shaking music still associated, to this day, with white male musical acts like the Beatles and the Rolling Stones?

NPR, written by Elizabeth Blair

Little Richard, the King and Queen of Rock 'n' Roll, Is Dead

Little Richard was an explosive performer who inspired generations of musicians from Otis Redding to The Beatles to David Bowie.

Nbc.com, written by Jeff Slate

He was black, sexually fluid, and playing the devil's music. Little Richard terrified America in the mid-1950s, but he was the real king of rock 'n' roll. Little Richard threatened the cultural status quo—straight, white culture, especially—in a way that none of his contemporaries did. . . . In so many ways, Little Richard invented the role of the rock star before the term existed.

Vulture, written by Dan Reilly

Pioneering, flamboyant, eccentric—Little Richard was all these things, and then some. And just as his anarchic performances suggested, the late legend was just as wild away from the piano, living a life full of sex, drugs, spirituality, generosity, sex, bravado, kindness, and some more sex—he was a trailblazer whose personal styling begat Elvis, the Beatles, The Stones, his former sideman Jimi Hendrix, Elton John, Prince and countless others.

He Used His Own *Rolling Stone* Blurb to Proclaim His Greatness

A lot of people call me the architect of rock & roll. I don't call myself that, but I believe it's true." That's how Richard began his self-penned blurb for Rolling Stone's "100 Greatest Artists of All Time" feature.

All those articles rekindled many memories of the business relationship I developed with Richard after meeting him initially in 1984. At the time I was thirty-four. My venture with Bob Gibson in forming The Group had paid off: in just a few years we had become a highly regarded independent public relations firm with a roster of top contemporary music artists, including Bette Midler; Rick James; Natalie Cole; Crosby, Stills & Nash; and Mick Fleetwood of Fleetwood Mac. I was also managing and handling PR for Andraé Crouch and Vanessa Williams.

A lot was going on in this time frame. Madonna burst onto the music scene with her hit "Like a Virgin." Lionel Richie, Prince, Aretha Franklin, Whitney Houston, Tina Turner, and George Michael also had major chart hits. The historic USA for Africa benefit song "We Are the World," written by Michael Jackson and Lionel Richie and produced by Quincy Jones, featured over twenty superstar artists. *The Cosby Show* made its premiere on NBC-TV. Hip-hop's Russell Simmons launched his Def Jam record label. The top news program was *60 Minutes*. Oprah's talk show became nationally syndicated. *The Color Purple*, *Back to the Future*, and *Rambo* were the biggest motion pictures. The Reverend Jesse Jackson ran for president, and Carl Lewis won four gold medals at the 1984 Olympics.

One day, from out of the blue, I received a call from Susan Eilertsen, the publicist at Crown Publishing whom I had worked with on Bette Midler's bestselling children's book, *The Saga of Baby Divine*.

"LITTLE RICHARD: THE QUASAR OF ROCK"

Susan said they were releasing a biography of rock 'n' roll legend Little Richard, *The Life and Times of Little Richard: The Quasar of Rock*, authored by noted UK radio personality and unknown author Charles White. She was interested in me representing the project and asked if I would read the galley of the book. I had not been a perennial Little Richard fan, but I respected him as a seminal music figure in rock 'n' roll. It flattered me that she had reached out. She promised to send the galley, and I told her I would get back to her as soon as I had finished reading it. Once I picked it up, I could not put it down. I loved it. It was riveting, graphic, filled with depictions of orgies and drugged-out parties backstage, the milestones of his storied career, and an abusive childhood.

Little Richard's proper name was Richard Penniman. He was born in 1932 in Macon, Georgia. His father was a brick mason and a bootlegger. He was one of thirteen children, and one leg was shorter than the other. In an old interview with *Rolling Stone*, he said kids harassed him for the way he walked: "The kids would call me a faggot, sissy, freak. They thought I was trying to twist and walk feminine." As a boy, his parents raised him in the Pentecostal Church, where he sang gospel on Sundays with his family group called the Penniman Singers and another group called the Tiny Tots Quartet. His earliest musical influences included Mahalia Jackson, Sister Rosetta Tharpe, and Brother Joe May, the "Thunderbolt of the Middle West." Even as a child singer, Richard was known for his high range and incredible volume. But, in his father's eyes, his unbearable effeminacy could not be tolerated. So, his father threw him out of the house when he was a teenager. When he first started singing live at local clubs and recording, he was also washing dishes in a Greyhound bus station, just to make a living. In 1955, things changed when Art Rupe of Specialty Records signed him. Rupe set him up with some notable musicians, and later that year, he recorded "Tutti Frutti," an uncensored R-rated song that he had been performing in drag bars. It included lewd verses such as "Tutti Frutti, good booty / If it don't fit, don't force it / You can grease it, make it easy." Rupe also connected him to noted Black producer Robert "Bumps" Blackwell to rework the record. Blackwell brought in a songwriter named Dorothy LaBostrie to collaborate with Richard in censoring the lyrics and making the song more mainstream and pop friendly. They also added what would become Little Richard's most famous lyrical line, the infectious and electric howl, "A wop bop a loo bop a lop bam boom!" The record became his first major hit, among Blacks and whites. It became an even bigger pop hit after Pat Boone recorded a homogenized watered-down version. Over the next couple of years, Little Richard experienced a meteoric rise to rock 'n' roll stardom, just as the genre was becoming the rage for young white teenagers across the country. The book also chronicles his often volatile relationships and friendships with rock 'n' roll royalty like Jerry Lee Lewis, Chuck

Berry, Bo Diddley, Jimi Hendrix, the Beatles, the Rolling Stones, Buddy Holly, and his nemesis James Brown, "the Godfather of Soul," among others. His journey emotionally moved me, especially trying to imagine all the adversity and discrimination he had to endure being a Black artist and a homosexual in the fifties and sixties. He had left rock 'n' roll twice, first in 1957 to convert and become a minister. He returned to regain some of his fame and glory between 1969 and 1977, but then left again to continue his ministry.

I met Little Richard in 1984, when he was fifty-one. He had been living in Riverside, California, and out of the limelight for almost a decade. He was devoting his life to Jesus, as an evangelist and a minister—with little fanfare. He did a few gospel performances and recorded some gospel music. He had lost his relevance as a rock star. I doubted mainstream media outlets, or the public, would clamor to read his memoir. And since he was refusing to perform any rock 'n' roll music, I didn't have the option of using live performances of his classic songs as a conduit to get him booked on major network news and entertainment shows like the *Today Show*, *Good Morning America*, the *Tonight Show*, or *Late Night with David Letterman*. My mission as a publicist was to always make sure I had a firm grasp of what I was selling and a shared vision with the artist. Conceptually, trying to manipulate or convince an artist to follow my vision or strategy never really appealed to me. No artist says yes to every idea you pitch. It takes mutual trust, moderate transparency, and a plausible "we" factor to forge successful publicity campaigns. Viable contingency plans are a must, in case your A-plan fails miserably. And trust me, A-plans fail all the time.

I was also curious about how he viewed the book. Did he view it as a chance for yet another comeback? He already had two, and two is extraordinary. Scoring a trifecta is unprecedented. Was he hoping to rejuvenate himself as an old rock 'n' roll star? Or was he hoping the book would create a new platform for him as a reformed gospel minister? I felt the book was too racy to attract church audiences. Regurgitating his past of embracing the devil's music, flaunting his homosexuality, and succumbing to infamous bouts of drug and alcohol addiction could backfire on him. Did he need money? Did the author and publishing company convince him it would make him a lot of money? I also wasn't aware of how he looked. Mostly, I wanted to understand, why now? What was his motivation? I was not sure if he had enough juice left in the tank to drive a national PR campaign, or if he would be vulnerable enough to expose an uncensored account of a lifestyle he now condemned. Was he willing to commit to investing his time and energy to promote and support the book?

The bottom line was that Little Richard was a living legend, at least in my mind. As a Black man in the music biz, I had a heartfelt desire to help him reap the adulation and respect he sought as one of the founding architects of rock 'n' roll. I felt indebted to him. He was a pioneer, and like so many seminal Black artists of his generation, he paved the way for young artists and professionals like me to have access in the music industry. Mostly, I didn't want him to feel compromised, or risk ruining his ministry for the sake of a check and a three- to six-months book campaign. I was also reluctant to risk jeopardizing my reputation with Crown by orchestrating a misguided strategy that would fail. I decided I would request a meeting with Richard before making an ultimate decision about the project. I also needed to know how much marketing and PR support Crown planned to give the book. I didn't expect it would be a huge budget, but I wanted to find out if they would cover travel and hotel expenses, and if there were any plans for a promotional tour and in-store appearances. I called Susan, raved about the book, and asked her if it would be possible to meet Little Richard in person. I was honest and explained that everything I thought I could deliver would hinge on my assessment of him, on my determination of whether he would be a liability or an asset. She understood, appreciated my position, and was enthusiastic about scheduling a meeting. Bette had been a gem. She had breathed life into her book campaign, made it special, and taken it to another level. Richard was an unknown.

SIGNING LITTLE RICHARD

Susan set up a lunch meeting at the Beverly Hills Hotel's ritzy Polo Lounge, which was a favorite haunt of the glamorous, the rich, the famous, and wannabes, all ogling each other, whispering gossip dish, flaunting attitude, and trading fake put-on smiles, hugs, and kisses. In those days, men had to wear sports coats to have dinner there. One time, I was visiting clients Daryl Hall and John Oates, who were staying in the hotel. They had been doing interviews and wanted to grab a drink and have dinner at the Polo Lounge. When we arrived, the host advised us they had a strict dress code. We could not enter unless we wore sport coats. He was polite and said he could provide us with loaners. We shook our heads in dismay, said no thanks, and walked out. So it was not one of my go-to places to frequent, nor was it heavily supported by Black celebrities. A lot of my clients liked it for a power breakfast or lunch, so I had been there several times, just not for dinner.

When I arrived for our meeting, Susan and her associate were already sitting at the table. We chatted for maybe five or ten minutes, but Little Richard was missing in action. It didn't surprise me. I always felt there was "regular time" and "artist time." Artist time was customarily twenty or thirty minutes late. They were getting antsy and were very apologetic, but I was fine. I emphasized that artists showing up late was a normal occurrence for me. However, in the back of my mind, I wondered if this would happen if I scheduled an important interview for him. As I expected, he finally arrived about thirty minutes late. He was wearing a bright, multicolor polyester jogging suit, which had several ominous dirt stains on it. He looked disheveled, with a messy Afro. He seemed somewhat in a daze—not fully coherent. Not stoned or high, just on edge. He apologized for being late and explained that his car broke down on the way there. It did not feel like an authentic story, but we all chimed in to reinforce that we were happy he was safe and could make it. Once he settled in, he seemed to feel more relaxed and engaged.

Richard was more reserved than I had expected. I viewed that as a positive sign. He was humble, with less braggadocio than the book had portrayed. He cracked a few jokes and laughed at them, one of his trademarks. When he did interviews, if he thought he had said something hilarious, he would crack up before the interviewer laughed. Most of the time that would make the interviewer laugh, so I think it was just a clever shtick that he had refined. He stood by the book. He emphasized that all the stories were true and he wanted the book to be successful. When I asked whether he was prepared to invest his time and hard work in promoting it, he said yes. The tipping point in the meeting for me was when he advised us he had filed a $112 million lawsuit against Specialty Records, owner Art Rupe, his publishing company Venice Music, and ATV Music for not paying royalties to him after he left the label in 1959. Most newsworthy was the fact I later discovered that the Beatles' Paul McCartney (a former client) and his Northern Songs Publishing Company had purchased his iconic catalog. ATV Music had acquired and owned Northern Songs. When Michael Jackson recorded the pop hit "Say, Say, Say" (1983) with McCartney, McCartney allegedly advised Michael that ATV Music was willing to sell the Beatles publishing catalog for $49 million. But he just couldn't bring himself to pay that much for a catalog he felt he should already own. About two years later, on August 14, 1985, Michael Jackson (in partnership with Sony Music Publishing) acquired ATV Music (for $47 million) and took control of all Little Richard's most popular copyrights.

Music industry outlets and mainstream media loved stories about alleged impropriety featuring litigious artists and record labels, particularly when Black artists were the alleged victims and the perpetrators were white. His lawsuit was public record, so its legitimacy didn't concern me. I instinctively felt it was a bonus chip that would bring more media attention to the book. If his case received more media and public attention, it might create some negotiating leverage to secure a substantial settlement without him winning the case outright. I found out later that he was counting on winning the case and not settling.

Our lunch meeting lasted for about two hours, and I felt it had been productive. I had a comfortable feeling about Richard but wasn't sure he could deliver on a time-intensive PR campaign. I had discovered that the lawsuit was a lightning rod that he would talk about ad nauseam—but he needed to use some restraint. His image begged for updating. When Little Richard was at the peak of his stardom, he did a lot of guest appearances on talk shows, but he often came across as a caricature of himself. He was innately zany, wild, and funny, but he was constantly reminding everyone of how he single-handedly created rock 'n' roll and how artists and the industry should be forever indebted to him. In his mind, he was being authentic. What he failed to realize is that self-advocating and trying to arbitrate one's fame never ends well, especially during the 1950s, when racial and sexual discrimination was rampant. A few days after the meeting, following some deliberation, I committed to work on the book. I had taken a liking to Richard, although I didn't feel I could trust him. However, if I could generate major media interest and he could give me 60 percent of what I required, I thought we could be successful.

My strategy was to present a more mature, reflective, and humble version of Little Richard, a man who had found a modicum of inner peace and hoped that the industry would one day respect his many contributions to contemporary music and rock 'n' roll. It was imperative to convince him not to use the book promotion to continue lambasting everybody for not recognizing him as the self-proclaimed "king and founder of rock 'n' roll." Whether the industry had failed in giving him his due was not the issue. The reality was the industry had grown tone-deaf to his approach over thirty years, and I felt he needed to take a more passive approach to changing the way he was perceived: a little repentant, laced with a smidgeon of diplomacy. He offended more people than he won over, and that was hard for him to understand and accept. At the core of the issue was that advocating for one's own fame never sends the right message. You can aspire to garner fame, but the public and media must endorse it. And there are no real kings or queens in the music industry. The titles are pure hyperbole, just a conduit to create a bigger illusion and symbolically elevate the perception of fame.

Once we started working together, I laid out what I was expecting from him, and he committed to the strategy. And although he said he wouldn't perform any of his classic rock 'n' roll hits, he agreed to perform gospel songs. There were two songs that he offered, "Someone Worse Off Than I Am" and "Joy, Joy, Joy," which was a rocking gospel song. Richard was a character, but he was intelligent. He was cognizant of the stark financial differences between Black artists and white artists, which ultimately influenced his decision to give up his gospel roots to become a rock 'n' roll star. In his book, he noted that he aspired to create "joyful music" that would bring the races together.

I found out he was living at the Highland Hotel on Sunset Boulevard, next to the famous Comedy Store, a seminal and career-making venue for many of the best comics in the industry, including Richard Pryor, Robin Williams, and Chris Rock. The Highland Hotel was a B or C hotel and had built a storied reputation as a haunt for rock 'n' roll and heavy metal touring bands and musicians in town for shows. It was a haven for groupies, hangers-on, and suspicious characters that were usually drunk or stoned out of their minds. Richard had cut a residence deal with the hotel, but I wasn't privy to any of the details. I didn't ask or feel it was any of my business.

When I started calling Richard at his hotel, he would answer the phone in a fake voice, pretending to be somebody else. I would announce my name. He would pause briefly. About thirty seconds later the "real" Little Richard would speak. His fake voice was laughable. I thought it was silly, but I played along with him. He did it often enough to convince himself that his impression was working. Finally, I couldn't take it anymore, so I busted him. I confessed that I always knew it was him. He acknowledged it was a habit to avoid talking to people he didn't want to speak to. But he didn't explain why he felt the need to do it with me. He stopped doing it, which I sincerely appreciated.

Little Richard was full of colorful stories, and he was an avid and ani-mated storyteller. Many of his stories were even more revealing and wilder than the ones in his book. He was like a human time machine, and I prodded him to share as many stories as possible. I also learned that he consistently embellished the truth. I'm not sure if he could separate the truth from lies. He lied about trivial things that shouldn't matter, so I learned to take everything he said with a grain of salt. When I confronted him, he would go mute.

Before every interview, I would give him key bullet points and issues that he should focus on in the interviews. He would agree and fully under-stand the strategy. We were off to the races, and he was delivering, showing up on time and following the game plan in interviews.

The public relations campaign was unfolding in a positive vein and was building momentum. Noted music writer Stephen Holden reviewed the book for the *New York Times*, Bryant Gumbel interviewed him for the *Today* show. He appeared on MTV, *David Letterman* (where he performed "Joy, Joy, Joy"), *Joan Rivers*, *Bill Boggs*, and other shows. The book was reviving interest in Little Richard's career. The highlight was getting Ed Bradley to do a piece on CBS-TV's highly rated *60 Minutes*, which was a first for one of my clients. Ed was a fan, and his piece was fair and incorporated all the elements we needed: his legacy as a pioneer of rock 'n' roll, his plight of being flamboyantly gay and Black during a time in history when both were extreme liabilities to achieving mainstream stardom, his natural gravitation toward rock 'n' roll—a predominantly white music genre—his multimillion-dollar lawsuit against ATV Music, his book, and everything that I inherently felt made Little Richard's story and contributions histor-ically relevant. I later read that the executive producer and creator of *60 Minutes* felt Little Richard wasn't worthy of a segment. However, Bradley fought and moved forward with the story. *60 Minutes* was the highest-rated network news program. Ed's segment with Little Richard took the cam-paign to another level. Richard was reveling in the renewed acclaim he was reaping. Crown was also happy. I had passed the halfway mark of my term of engagement, and I was almost certain there were no plans to extend it. It would not make practical sense or be justifiable for either of us. The campaign had unfolded amazingly well. We were on a roll.

TAKING A LEAP OF FAITH

One day, while I was driving Richard to an interview, out of the blue he delivered a touching soliloquy thanking me for all my efforts. He was overwhelmingly generous with his praise. It blew me away. He had thanked me before, but not on this level. I effusively thanked him back and conveyed my appreciation for his kind words. A few minutes later he told me he wanted me to be his manager. It was another wow moment—we had never discussed management at all. I let him know it flattered me, but I needed some time to think it over.

I was managing gospel great Andraé Crouch, and I had just started managing Vanessa Williams. I was also fulfilling my role as a partner in my PR firm. I was looking to transition completely into management and give up my PR company, but my PR clients were generating most of my income. I wasn't sure if Little Richard could generate any substantial revenues and, if so, from what areas. He didn't have a record deal, new music, or any recent credibility as a live performer. And as a gospel artist, I didn't feel he would be a big draw coming off the book promotion. I thought there might be a way to fuse some rock 'n' roll with two gospel songs and maybe get two younger name artists to make special guest appearances. In manager speak, I thought if I could get him to commit to one album cycle, roughly eighteen months to release an album, package an event-style concert tour in maybe twenty to twenty-five markets, and shoot a concert special, we could make enough money to justify working together. However, I wanted him to sign a management agreement so I would be legally and financially protected. I figured if we were running on all cylinders and put together a magnificent show, we could gross maybe $500,000 or $1 million. I deliberated about it for a few more days and called him to say I was interested.

I planned to follow up with an overview of my plan for his review, get him to commit to the vision, and sign a management contract.

When we spoke on the phone, he was very receptive to everything I mentioned—except signing a contract. He had not had a manager in a long time and said he had an aversion to contracts, because most of his past contracts took advantage of him. I respected his reasoning. In the past, I had agreed to represent several artists without a contract and got stiffed each time. Without a contract, artists can cut you out of deals with no warning. Or they will try to negotiate deals directly, so they don't have to pay you a commission. Little Richard swore he desired to be honorable and that he would not try to cheat me. He emphasized that he wanted to work with me. There were a lot of ifs hanging in limbo, but I opted to take the risk. I had no plan to invest in Richard's career. I was committing time and energy to implement my strategy. Worst-case scenario, I would walk away penniless and only lose the time I invested. And if we won, I would make some decent money and get the credit for pulling off a third miraculous comeback for Little Richard. I adopted the adage "No risk, no reward."

Not too long after I agreed to manage him, Stuart Griffen, a junior agent at Creative Artists Agency (CAA), called me. He was a Little Richard fan and wanted to know if he had an agent. I told him no, and he asked if we'd meet with him and some of his associates, including Bryan Lourd, a fast-rising agent at the agency. CAA was considered the most powerful talent agency in the industry, so it thrilled me they were interested. They had enormous clout and would be an asset in packaging a national concert tour. Having them involved would also give me leverage in getting him a meaningful record deal. I signed Richard to CAA, and within a week Stuart called me about interest from noted director, writer, and actor Paul Mazursky in having Little Richard play a minor role in a film he was prepping to direct. My initial reaction was I didn't even know if he could act. He said he was a fan and that he was interested in setting up a meeting. I checked with Richard and he was game, so we put the meeting in motion.

The momentum from the media campaign was building exponentially, and it felt like we were on the precipice of something. I found out that Prince was performing in town, and I knew Little Richard was a fan. I snagged two tickets. I also popped for a limousine to give him the star treatment for one night. The plan was to meet Richard at his hotel and have the limo pick us up there. When I arrived at the hotel, I called to let him know I was there. He said he was dealing with the front desk about a problem but wouldn't divulge anything else. He said he'd be down in few minutes. About ten minutes went by, and he was still upstairs. I called again to see if he was still dealing with the front desk. He said there was a billing issue, and they were threatening him. He informed me that his brother normally took care of his hotel account, but he wouldn't be able to fix the problem until tomorrow. I offered to speak to the hotel manager on his behalf, to see if I could save some time and avoid arriving at the concert too late. As I was walking over to the front desk, an unsettling feeling overwhelmed me. I was setting myself up as a mop to clean up his mess. I advised the woman at the front desk I worked with Little Richard and I understood there was a problem with his account. She calmly stated, yes, there was a problem. They had contacted him several times to settle past due payments. She said they could not extend the payment date again. He would have to vacate his room if he didn't pay tonight. I asked her how much he owed, and she said $3,600. I felt like he had suckered me. I didn't want to set a precedent for bailing him out of financial situations. I thanked her for the details and told her I needed to speak to him. I called and asked if he knew he owed $3,600. He acted surprised and said he didn't know. He reiterated that his brother would be back tomorrow and could settle with the hotel. I told him that wasn't an option. Anyway, I realized that if I gave them my credit card, more than likely, I was risking the proverbial "money gone" scenario. Richard promised his brother would reimburse me the next day, so I opted to trust him. It was one of those moments when you know you're making an idiot move, and you do it anyway. I was now out of pocket $4,000 and still waiting for Richard to come downstairs. And my brilliant idea of having a celebratory date with my client totally sucked—so far. I thought this was a perfect test to see if I could trust him. I also had finished licensing a song deal for him. So in the back of mind I knew if he defaulted on paying me back, I could take it out of the license fee that I had negotiated.

When Richard walked out of the elevator, I was in complete shock. He had completely transformed himself into looking like a rock star again. He had cleaned up his appearance considerably since I first met him. He had been dressing more like a minister, wearing a shaped and trimmed Afro and conservative suits with open-collar shirts. Now, he was rocking a royal blue sequin suit with high-heeled boots, and his hair was a fusion of shiny Jheri curl and curly 'fro. He had on heavy cake make-up and eyeliner. He was also wearing his favorite strong cologne, the kind where the scent arrives before the person. (If he shook your hand, the scent would last all day—I washed my hands profusely and couldn't get rid of it. One time when we were in New York for a television show, Richard, a friend of his, and I were in an elevator on our way up to the studio. The talent coordinator commented, "You guys smell great." I said, "It isn't us, it's just him." Richard laughed and said, "Stop it, Ramon." He had two famous refrains, "Stop it" and "Shut up.") I thought he had done an admirable job of reincarnating his younger rock 'n' roll persona. It turned out to be a fun night. Richard got a lot of adulation, which I could tell made him feel good. The more I got to know Richard, the more I realized that on the surface fame obsessed him, but his real obsession was desperately wanting love. I felt helpless because I knew no matter what I did I wouldn't be able to manifest the level of love he desired.

Once he committed to reviving his rock star persona, his temperament morphed. He wasn't listening as attentively or sticking to the script we had agreed to. Richard was inherently unpredictable, and he followed his instincts with little contemplation or critical assessment. That was one of his gifts as a live performer. In getting attention and taking over a stage or television set, Richard was a master. No matter how much we talked and strategized, once Little Richard got in front of a camera or on stage, it was like a Dr. Jekyll and Mr. Hyde transformation. As soon as it was lights, camera, action, he would veer from the script we had discussed. He'd revert to the same zany persona he had created years ago. When cameras were off, he was calm. He didn't seem to know what triggered his actions, nor could he remember or discuss what he said in any detail.

RICHARD STRIPS TOPLESS LIVE ON A PIANO

The best example of this is when I booked him to be a special guest on the 11th Annual Charlie Daniels Band Volunteer Jam, held at Municipal Auditorium in Nashville, Tennessee, February 2, 1985. Daniels was a prominent country-western star and a fan of Little Richard. He invited him to perform two songs on the show. It was massive, with twenty-four acts performing eighty-eight songs during the nine-hour event. Superstar country group Alabama (a former client); Amy Grant; the actor, singer, and songwriter Kris Kristofferson; and rocker Ted Nugent were some of the biggest stars who joined Daniels. Voice of America broadcast the marathon to a potential worldwide audience of 110 million. Some fifty cable TV systems across America televised the show live on a pay-per-view basis, making it the longest live concert in television history. Also, Showtime taped the entire celebration for a ninety-minute national special that aired later. Little Richard was the only Black artist I can recall who performed. Over twelve thousand packed the auditorium, despite a major blizzard with snow, sleet, and ice. I imagined being there felt like heaven for die-hard country-western music lovers. I think Richard and I may have been the only Black people in attendance—or it just felt that way.

When Little Richard took the stage, Daniels introduced him: "I don't know of anybody in my life who has made as much difference in popular music as this man." Enthusiastic and welcoming applause followed. He captured the audience with his first song. He was wearing an all-white outfit from head to toe, including white go-go boots, and looked every bit like the iconic rock star he had been. After the first song, he received another resounding ovation. Somewhere in the middle of his second song, he stood up to play the piano, which was part of the arsenal of performance antics he had cultivated. He could play just as good standing up as sitting down. To everyone's surprise, he climbed on top of the piano and started stripping. He took off his boots and flung them into the crowd. Then he started unbuttoning his shirt, took it off and was waving it above his head. I'm thinking he is having an epiphany and has lost it. There were cheers and just as many jeers. Everyone was in awe and shock, including me. One of the producers tugged me, asking what's going on. I said I had no clue; it wasn't premeditated. I was just praying he would not take his pants off. Thank God he didn't, but he completed the song bare-chested.

I had only represented two major country artists as a publicist, Mac Davis and one of country music's all-time supergroups, Alabama, when they first started. Both were talented acts, but I wasn't an avid listener of country music, so I felt out of place at their concerts. It was an instinctive feeling, not because people mistreated me. I felt like they were staring at me because I looked out of place. I wanted to say, "I feel you, just trying to do my job." When Richard came off stage, he wasn't responsive to anyone. He didn't say anything about what had just occurred. My thought was to get him dressed and out of the venue ASAP. The crowd reaction was mixed. I wasn't sure if he'd face any repercussions or if anyone would be confrontational. In the limo on the way back to the hotel, I tried to discuss what had transpired, but he wasn't willing to engage. He was stoic and elected not to comment about his actions. The best thing was there was no negative fallout in the media. One review said Little Richard's performance was the highlight of the event.

When we returned to Los Angeles, things started moving forward with Mazursky about Richard's role in his next movie. We had a great meeting with Paul, as they shared mutual respect and admiration. Paul wanted to make it happen and proposed having Little Richard come up with a new song he could perform in the film and put in the soundtrack. I thought the script was brilliant. The stars, Nick Nolte, Bette Midler, and Richard Dreyfuss, were experiencing down periods in their film careers for various reasons. I represented them as a publicist. Richard had been down. So the title, *Down and Out in Beverly Hills*, was symbolically relevant and poignant for all of them.

CHASING A BIOPIC DEAL

While we were completing the film contract, some interest in a biopic surfaced. I had not given a film much contemplation because I knew securing the music rights would be an obstacle. Richard vehemently wanted to see his lawsuit through. We received interest from Jerry Weintraub, a legendary manager and film producer who was representing Eddie Murphy. I knew Jerry and was a publicist for the Carpenters, whom he managed. Sandy Gallin, another powerful manager, was also interested. He was representing Morris Day, the lead singer of the Time, who were protégés of Prince. Both managers wanted their clients to portray Little Richard. Jerry was a seasoned and respected filmmaker, and I knew he could get the project produced. I loved Eddie. He had become close friends with Rick James, who wrote and produced his debut album, *Party All the Time*, which was being released later in the year. Eddie was a celebrated superstar at the time as an actor, film star, and stand-up comedian—but not revered as a singer.

Although Morris Day was not as famous as Eddie (particularly as a film star), I thought he embodied the raw musical talent that Little Richard inherently possessed. Neither were piano players. I also liked and respected Sandy Gallin. He shepherded Dolly Parton's career, and I was confident he could deliver. Both meetings went well. As I had presumed, Jerry and Sandy were both concerned about the costs of acquiring the music rights. They were aware of Richard's lawsuit and knew getting the rights could be a roadblock. I told them I would check into it. Richard was polite during the meetings. I couldn't tell whether either manager had won him over. I needed to check on the music rights and arrange meetings for Richard to meet Eddie and Morris.

I reached out to John Branca, who was Michael Jackson's attorney and one of the most respected lawyers in the industry. We weren't friends, but we knew of each other. My conversation with John was short and sweet. After sharing a minute of pleasantries, I explained why I was calling. He listened and passed on some congratulations for what was transpiring with Little Richard. Then he stated succinctly and frankly that while Little Richard had a lawsuit pending against ATV, he wouldn't grant any of his song rights for a potential film or anything else Richard was doing. The gist of his final salutation was, if Richard dropped the lawsuit, he would work with me to negotiate securing the rights. The call lasted for about five minutes. I already knew that Richard would not compromise and drop the lawsuit. So, instinctively, I realized we would lose both opportunities. I asked Richard, and he responded the way I thought he would. I followed up with Jerry and Sandy to advise them of our predicament and that I needed some more time to sway Richard to reconsider his position.

In the interim, I started pursuing a few record labels, and the response was tepid. However, Charles Koppelman and Martin Bandier, partners in the Entertainment Company, asked about meeting Richard. They had a large independent song catalog and produced artists such as Barbra Streisand, Dolly Parton, Diana Ross, and Cher. They were in the embryonic stages of launching an even larger company, SBK Entertainment World. I thought they would be an ideal fit because they were working with older artists. They seemed genuinely interested, but they wanted to hear some samples of his new musical direction. Unfortunately, Richard didn't have fresh material we could send them and had not defined his musical direction yet. We got a nibble, and they left the door open. We were in the game. I wanted to enlighten Richard and show him the many opportunities he could financially leverage based on the momentum we had generated.

I got a call from veteran and respected producer Suzanne de Passe, whom I had originally met during my tenure at Motown. She was producing *Motown Returns to the Apollo*, a three-hour NBC-TV special that would feature sixty entertainers representing a wide spectrum of pop, soul, and jazz talent over the last fifty years. It would celebrate the fiftieth anniversary of the Apollo and the reopening of the theater, which had been closed to the public since 1976. Bill Cosby served as master of ceremonies, and the show featured a star-studded list of performers, including James Brown, Rod Stewart, Cab Calloway, Sammy Davis Jr., Smokey Robinson, Diana Ross, George Michael, Sarah Vaughan, and Stevie Wonder. Little Richard performed a raucous version of "Didn't Rain," with Billy Preston on piano, and Wilson Pickett and Chuck Jackson joined them.

We flew to New York and stayed at the Berkshire Hotel on East 52nd, which was a popular hotel for artists, musicians, and music industry execs. Richard was scheduled for an afternoon sound check, and the production company was requesting that artists arrive an hour in advance. When we arrived at the Apollo, they were still doing some construction and painting. The work was running behind, so we just chilled in the theater. James Brown was about to start his sound check. Moments before starting, he walked over to the stage manager and told him he needed everyone sitting in the theater to leave—immediately. Richard just laughed and divulged that Brown had been demanding for years that no other artists on the same bill as him be in the audience during his sound check (especially Richard).

After Richard's sound check, we headed back to the hotel, where a bunch of artists had gathered and were talking in the lobby, including the Temptations, whom I had worked with at Motown. They graciously greeted Little Richard and asked him how he was doing, and he said he was doing fabulous. He then told them he was about to sign a major multimillion-dollar record deal—a historic deal. They congratulated him and gave him good wishes. They were heading to their sound check. When we got in the elevator, Richard didn't say a word. The major record deal just was a figment of his imagination. I had grown accustomed to this trait, so I didn't bother asking, and it never came up again. When we got back to Los Angeles, we started focusing on preparing for the film. The production company was sending the pages for the scenes he needed to learn for his first day of shooting.

The film was shooting in Los Angeles at the end of May. *Down and Out in Beverly Hills* was a comedy satire based on the French play *Boudu sauvé des eaux*, which Jean Renoir had adapted for film in 1932. It's about a rich, dysfunctional couple, the Whitemans (Richard Dreyfuss and Bette Midler), who save the life of a suicidal homeless man (Nick Nolte). Little Richard was playing the role of Orvis Goodnight, an aging rock star and one of the Whitemans' well-to-do Beverly Hills neighbors.

HONORING THE SABBATH CRISIS

His first scenes were being shot on a Friday night. Richard's call time was midafternoon. I was at the set to make sure he showed up on time and was waiting for his arrival at his trailer. Richard's scenes were being shot at a house in Beverly Hills. Richard arrived on time, and once he settled in, I went over the scenes and schedule with him. As we were going over everything, he asked me what time his shoot would start. I told him he wouldn't start shooting until it was dark, like around 8 p.m. He immediately responded that he couldn't shoot that late. It stunned me. "What do you mean?" I asked. "This has been on your schedule for two weeks." Out of nowhere, he claimed that he was a Seventh Day Adventist and honored the Sabbath, which prohibited him from working past sundown on Fridays. I was trying to stay calm and told him he should have advised me of any work restrictions before we signed the contract. I told him it was too late to pull out now. He would not budge. He unapologetically said he wouldn't be able to shoot past sundown and asked if they could move up his scene or just reschedule it. I knew neither was possible, but I told him I needed to get in touch with Paul directly. I left the trailer upset.

I got in touch with Stuart first and shared the dilemma that had just fallen into my lap. His response was, "You have to be fucking kidding me." We agreed that we should confer with Paul and get him to talk to Richard. We reached Paul immediately, and he made his way over to the trailer. We huddled outside and explained the predicament. Although it was obvious this wasn't an issue that Paul wanted to be dealing with, he was calm.

I didn't sense he was in any kind of panic mode, but he did need to get the problem resolved. He asked where Richard was, and we told him he was in the trailer.

Paul entered the trailer smiling and acted excited to see Richard. He was instantly warm and sat down across from where Richard was sitting. He started by acknowledging he had just been advised that Richard honored the Sabbath and admitted it surprised him. He explained that he was Jewish but wasn't a dedicated Jew, but understood and respected Richard's religious beliefs and desire to honor the Sabbath. He had zoned in on Richard and captivated his attention. Richard was speechless. He nodded his head, but didn't respond to anything Paul expressed.

Paul explained that God is forgiving. He asked Richard if he agreed, and Richard nodded yes. He also felt God realizes that there are exceptions and times when people must make decisions that he may not approve of. He leaned in toward Richard and said, "If I was God, and I know that's hard to imagine. But, let's just pretend I am. If He was sitting here I think God would say, 'Richard, I understand why you don't want to work tonight, but the right thing for you to do is not let all these people down. You can do this, and I will forgive you.'" Richard was enthralled, and you could see tears cascading down his cheeks. Paul had hypnotized him. We were all mesmerized. Paul had massaged and struck such a heartfelt and emotional chord with Richard. It was magical. I had seen nothing even remotely close. Richard remained quiet for two seconds. In a shaky and quivering voice, he responded, "Paul, I will work tonight." Paul immediately thanked him and reinforced that he was doing the right thing. He promised to do his best to expedite shooting the remaining scenes so Richard could leave earlier. The crisis ended—thank God.

DOWN AND OUT IN BEVERLY HILLS DEBUT

That night Little Richard had several scenes to shoot. One was a scene where the police are responding to a disturbance at the Whitemans' home.

A helicopter is swirling around, shining a spotlight over the area, and sirens are blaring. Little Richard (as Mr. Orvis Goodnight) storms out of his palatial mansion on his front lawn, angry and complaining about all the noise. Little Richard shouts that if he had been the one to call the police, it would have taken them an hour to show up.

Richard was dressed in a silk robe and satin pajamas, and the pants had a drawstring. He was supposed to scream his displeasure and point at the helicopter as soon as he reached his designated spot on the front lawn. Paul called, "Action!" Richard came out yelling. He reached his spot and just as he raised his arm to point at the helicopter, his pajama bottoms started falling. For a second, Richard was trying to grab his pajamas to keep them from falling completely. But he was unsuccessful, and seconds later they fell to his ankles. Paul was yelling, "Cut! Cut!" The entire crew was laughing hysterically, nonstop and loudly. Richard was embarrassed as he bent over to pull up his pants. Paul, laughing, gathered himself and walked over to comfort Richard but couldn't stop laughing. Richard managed a smile and was very apologetic, but everyone knew it wasn't his fault. They called the wardrobe department to help Richard with his pajamas. Once Paul calmed Richard's nerves, he called for a reset of the scene. He double-checked with Richard and asked if he was ready, and Richard affirmed he was ready. Paul yelled, "Action!" As soon as Richard reappeared, everyone started laughing hysterically again. Richard walked toward his spot, tugging at his side to make sure his pants didn't fall again. By this time, the laughter was seismic, and it was sustained even longer. Paul yelled, "Cut! Cut!" The crew was still laughing uncontrollably. He was laughing as well and walked over to talk to Richard again. He urged him to just relax and trust that his pants won't fall again. The scene was reset. Right before Paul was ready to yell action, with no provocation, the laughter erupted again. This time he assertively told everyone to gather themselves and get it together so they could shoot the scene. Finally sanity prevailed. The scene was reset. He yelled, "Action!" Richard came out and this time nailed it. The crew applauded and cheered for Richard, who was smiling and happy. They then shot it a couple more times and moved onto the next scene. Richard's first night shoot ended on a positive note. Driving home that night, I broke into laughter in my car. What a night. It was classic.

They released the film on January 31, 1986, under Touchstone Pictures, a film label distributed by Walt Disney Studios. Richard had also recorded a rollicking gospel-tinged rock 'n' roll song, "Great Gosh Almighty," in the film. It was on the movie soundtrack and was released as a single. It was the last single of Little Richard's career to hit the *Billboard* pop charts, and it peaked at #42. It also charted in the UK. The song captured the perfect fusion of gospel and rock, a combination that could be a viable music direction for him to pursue.

$30,000 FOUND IN LOS ANGELES CAR CRASH

While Little Richard was enjoying his renewed ascension, I learned that he was fielding offers behind my back to avoid paying me a management commission. He had received an offer from Warner Bros. Records UK for a solo record deal. He flew to London without advising me. The day he returned, October 8, 1985, he got in a serious car accident on his way back to the hotel. They reported it happened at 12:05 a.m. Sheriff deputies said he was driving his 1984 Nissan 300ZX, estimated to be going 65–70 mph on Santa Monica Boulevard when he crashed into a telephone pole at Curson Avenue. He was driving alone. After colliding with the pole, he was trapped inside his car for thirty minutes. County firefighters used the jaws of life, a metal-cutting device, to pry him loose. He suffered a broken right leg, broken ribs, and facial injuries. He was listed in serious but stable condition at Cedars–Mount Sinai Medical Center. The next morning, calls about the accident and rumors deluged me. I wasn't aware that he had left the country, was in an accident, and had been hospitalized. I also received a call from the sheriff's office, who said they found a bag with $30,000 hidden under the seat in his car. I later learned that he had signed a record deal and received the money as an advance.

Fortunately, he recovered from his injuries in a matter of days. I spoke to him in the hospital, and he was responsive. He told me how many super-star artists had called or sent flowers. Over the course of his stay, I brought up the money the sheriff's department discovered in the car. I asked him where he got it and why he carried that much cash. That's when he told me about the Warner Bros. record deal, how it was a last-minute decision for him to fly to London. I was more concerned about his health and recovery, but in my heart, I knew I couldn't continue representing him. I had lost all my trust in him as a person. I don't remember when we went our separate ways, but it was within the next couple of months. We didn't have a contract, so there wasn't any definitive expiration date or required legal termination of our business association. In the months after our relationship ended, he received critical acclaim for his appearance in *Down and Out in Beverly Hills*. The film was successful and invigorated the careers of all the featured cast members. He performed on the Academy Awards in early 1986. Later that year, he was one of the ten original inductees into the Rock-and-Roll Hall of Fame. In 1993, he received a Lifetime Achievement Award from the National Academy of Recording Arts and Sciences, and a year later the Rhythm & Blues Foundation honored him with its prestigious Pioneer Award.

When I reflect on my experiences with Little Richard, I remember lots of funny and memorable stories. I failed to achieve all the personal goals I had envisioned for him. But there was a silver lining from a purely historical perspective, I did have a dramatic impact on rejuvenating his career. Historians and music aficionados note that 1984–86 was his enviable third comeback—mission accomplished!

4

YOU CAN CHASE FAME, ACHIEVE IT, AND LOSE IT

During my first year at Rogers & Cowan, I had a voracious appetite to learn as much as possible. I was immediately thrust into ego-infested waters, and I quickly surmised that I was in a sink-or-swim scenario. It was 1977, and Rogers & Cowan was one of the most revered PR firms in the industry. Its client roster was bolstered by many of the biggest names in entertainment. Actors, contemporary music artists, motion pictures, television projects, record labels, film and tv production companies, and Fortune 500 corporations were among their clients. Some were A-list talent at the apex of their fame, others were just holding on or in decline, and a few were desperately trying to make a comeback. However, on some level they were all invested in fueling their fame. I had moved crosstown from Motown in Hollywood to Beverly Hills, hoping to raise my gross income and enhance my professional reputation in the industry.

BLOSSOMING IN A HAVEN FOR STARS

R & C represented many entertainers who had earned global fame, and I embraced the opportunity to work with them. During my first six months at the firm, I started dealing with Paul McCartney on the West Coast. Even though I had not met him or had any direct personal contact with him yet,

I was gaining knowledge just working on his account. I was also interfacing and handling day-to-day activities on other accounts, including James Caan, Nick Nolte, the Carpenters, Peter Frampton, George Benson, Herb Alpert, A Taste of Honey, Marilyn McCoo and Billy Davis Jr, and Daryl Hall and John Oates. Each client posed unique challenges. I was a kid in a candy store, soaking up every ounce of knowledge I could possibly obtain.

In 1977 R & C signed Robert Stigwood, an Australian-born British-resident music entrepreneur, film producer, and impresario. He was best known for managing the legendary Eric Clapton (and his group Cream), the Bee Gees, the theatrical production of *Hair*, film adaptations of *Tommy* and *Jesus Christ Superstar*, and later the monster successes *Grease* and *Saturday Night Fever*, which were released while he was a client of R & C.

Stigwood broke into the British music scene in the 1960s, working under the tutelage of Brian Epstein, who had orchestrated and managed the Beatles, arguably the most famous rock/pop band in the history of recorded music. He signed the Bee Gees to Epstein's NEMS management company, named after the landmark NEMS record store in Liverpool, England, which Epstein owned.

R & C was brought on board to represent Stigwood, the Bee Gees, and his record label, RSO Records (Robert Stigwood Organization), launched in 1973. The Bee Gees were the label's biggest artists, but the roster also included Eric Clapton, Yvonne Elliman, and Andy Gibb, who was the youngest brother of Bee Gees members Barry, Maurice, and Robin Gibb.

Signing this collective of major clients from one primary source was a rare PR coup. The music department handled the Bee Gees on both coasts, and I handled the day-to-day duties on their account in our offices on Bedford Avenue, in the heart of Beverly Hills. The R & C film department would handle *Saturday Night Fever* (1977) and *Grease* (1978). We also represented John Travolta (who starred in both films) and the legendary and flamboyant producer Allan Carr, who coproduced *Grease* with Stigwood.

THE BEE GEES' PATH TO FAME

By 1977, the Bee Gees had already experienced a checkered career that had almost ended in less than a decade. When Stigwood signed them, he proclaimed that the Bee Gees were "the most significant new musical talent of 1967." The group included the Gibb brothers, Colin Petersen, and Vince Melouney. Within the next several years they had achieved a comparable level of stardom in Australia, the UK, and the US, scoring several hit singles, including "Spicks and Specks," "New York Mining Disaster," and the classic soulful ballad, "To Love Somebody," originally written for Otis Redding. After just three album releases, the Gibbs temporarily broke up. All three recorded solo albums. Robin's album (*Robin's Reign*) was the only one released.

The first songs I remember hearing from the Bee Gees were "Massachusetts," "To Love Somebody" (1967), "I've Gotta Get a Message to You" (1968), and "I Started a Joke," which were hits during my final two years in high school. Their harmonies stood out, and their hooks were catchy—but I didn't follow them.

Although Australian, they were part of the "British Invasion," the late-'60s wave of British pop and rock stars who dominated the contemporary pop/rock music scene in America, including the Beatles, Rolling Stones, Jimi Hendrix (who was American but first became a star in the UK), Eric Clapton, the Animals, Donovan, Marianne Faithfull, Herman's Hermits, Tom Jones, the Kinks, the Moody Blues, Dusty Springfield, and the Who.

My favorite artist was Jimi Hendrix. I was also a big fan of the Beatles and the Rolling Stones. When I was sixteen, a friend I played football with invited me over to his house to listen to some records. I had never smoked pot, and he convinced me to try it. I agreed, and we listened to a bunch of records, including Jimi Hendrix's hit songs "Purple Haze" and "Foxy Lady." I was immediately addicted, not to the pot but to Hendrix. I had never heard anyone play electric guitar like that, Black or white. He was exhilarating but cool at the same time. He has been my favorite artist since then. I later developed a fond appreciation for pot.

My mom had just a few jazz records, by iconic singers such as Ray Charles, Dinah Washington, Betty Carter, Harry Belafonte, and Odetta. She played their music incessantly, not every day, but as the primary music in our household. I heard Ray Charles's "Hit the Road Jack" so many times I wanted him to hit the road and "don't come back, no more, no more." I even contemplated breaking the record. Other songs ingrained in my mind were "What I Say" (loved his piano playing), "I Got a Woman," "Georgia on My Mind," and "A Song for You"; Betty Carter's "Stormy Weather" and "Once in Your Life"; and Dinah Washington's classic "What a Difference a Day Makes." Whenever I played Hendrix, she would yell, "Turn that noise down."

No respect.

They were all legendary jazz greats, but I was too naive and pubescent to appreciate the brilliance of their artistry until I got a little older. Once I discovered Hendrix, I began exploring and curating a broader playlist of artists and genres that appealed to me. I became a big fan of James Brown when I heard "Papa's Got a Brand New Bag," "Cold Sweat," "I Feel Good," "Please, Please, Please," "I'm Black and I'm Proud," and "Sex Machine."

I used to practice imitating his dance moves—which I did well enough to get on my mom's nerves. By my late twenties I had amassed a collection of about three thousand records and alphabetized them in stacks that lined the living room floor in my apartment. While I lived in England, I bought plastic covers to protect them. My collection comprised most music genres, including classical, jazz, R & B, rock, pop, dance/disco, rap/hip-hop, reggae, funk, folk—everything except country.

THE BRAINTRUST AND COMEBACK

Initially, I was enthusiastic about working on the Bee Gees account. I was familiar with their level of stardom. They had a seasoned team behind them: Stigwood as their manager, Al Coury as his partner in RSO Records, Dick Ashby, a very amiable and detail-oriented road manager, and Ronnie

Lippin, the label's in-house publicist. They had a layered bureaucracy, which insulated me from dealing with any of them or Stigwood directly. My boss Paul kept me abreast of their inner workings daily. Barry Gibb was the group's spokesperson and managed their internal decision-making. Whenever I was in their company, they acknowledged me, but we only shared salutations and brief chit-chat. I was happy to have a minor role on the team.

Ronnie Lippin became my primary contact. I had to have everything approved by her. For some scheduling issues, I could contact Dick Ashby. Right off the bat, my relationship with Lippin was toxic. We had no previous experience with each other, but we just rubbed each other the wrong way. Over time, I dreaded engaging with her. She made no blatantly offensive remarks, but her tone was consistently condescending. It's unrealistic for everyone you work with to like and respect you, or vice versa. Independent publicists and record label publicists don't always see eye-to-eye. It could have been because I was Black. Didn't matter. When we interacted, I would just summon an extra dose of patience and civility.

When we started representing the Bee Gees, they were in comeback mode. After they hit a rut in the early '70s, Ahmet Ertegun, head of Atlantic Records, their US label, encouraged them to meet with Arif Mardin, an iconic Turkish American record producer. Mardin had produced hits for over thirty years for some of music's most celebrated superstars: Ray Charles, Aretha Franklin, Donny Hathaway, Chaka Khan, Dionne Warwick, Roberta Flack, Patti LaBelle, Diana Ross, Anita Baker, Queen, David Bowie, Bette Midler, Barbra Streisand, and Hall and Oates, to name a few.

He recalibrated their pop style by infusing soul and R & B danceable rhythms into their songs, which featured Barry and Robin's new falsetto lead vocals. They revealed their new sound on "Main Course," the only record Mardin produced for them, which featured the hit singles "Jive Talkin'" and "Nights on Broadway." They followed up that project with a self-produced album, *Children of the World*, released in 1976, which yielded "You Should Be Dancing." The hit song topped the pop and disco charts at

#1 and was a Top 5 hit on the R & B charts. It elevated them to their high-est level of fame yet. The album also included the hits "Love So Right" and "Boogie Child."

The strategic timing for shifting their musical direction was propitious on several levels. It rejuvenated a stagnant career and put them in the forefront of disco, a new music genre that was sweeping the world. It also became the motivation for them to write a handful of songs for the *Saturday Night Fever* film soundtrack.

In a broader context, the shift in musical genres reinforced the fact that fame can happen when you least expect it. You may also have to en-dure moderate failure to achieve it. In the Bee Gees' case, they were willing to step outside of their artistic comfort zone and pursue a different music direction. If they had not failed enough to contemplate pursuing another direction, their career might have completely fizzled out.

A METEORIC RISE IN FULL EFFECT

In the next few months, the Bee Gees' lives and level of fame changed dramatically. They were at the onset of a historic and record-breaking streak as the industry's premier artists. They contributed five songs to the *Saturday Night Fever* soundtrack. The first single, "How Deep Is Your Love," written by the Gibbs, was released in September. The soundtrack album was released November 15, 1977, and the film on December 12. On Christmas day the soundtrack topped the *Billboard* Hot 100 chart.

While *Saturday Night Fever* was climbing the charts, Stigwood was also producing the musical comedy *Sgt. Pepper's Lonely Hearts Club Band* (October–December 1977), which starred the Bee Gees and Peter Framp-ton. Michael Schultz, a talented young Black director, was directing. He had made his debut directing the Broadway production of Lorraine Hans-berry's *To Be Young, Gifted and Black*, which he restaged for television in 1972, and also directed films such as *Honeybaby*, *Cooley High*, *Car Wash*, and *Which Way Is Up?*, starring Richard Pryor (1976). Besides the Bee Gees and

Frampton, the musical also starred Aerosmith, Alice Cooper, Earth, Wind & Fire, Billy Preston, George Burns, Steve Martin, Donald Pleasence, and Dianne Steinberg.

Since they filmed in Los Angeles, I visited the set several times. Michael Schultz was friendly and easy to converse with. There were very few Black directors working in Hollywood, and none on a film of this magnitude, with this level of superstars, a mega-producer like Stigwood, and a $13 million production budget. It was the biggest movie of Schultz's career.

By the end of 1977, the contemporary music landscape was experiencing changes. Prince made his debut with his album *For You*, which had several hits. Michael Jackson had made his film debut in *The Wiz*, and in mid-September, the rap group the Sugarhill Gang released their classic song, "Rapper's Delight." It was the first rap single to become a Top 40 hit on the *Billboard* Hot 100. It was a precursor of the enormous growth and dominant influence rap/hip-hop would have on contemporary music and pop culture over the next several decades.

By the first week in January the album had sold nearly a million records. Their next two singles, "Stayin' Alive" and "Night Fever," also became #1 songs. And they had another #1 with "If I Can't Have You," performed by their label mate Yvonne Elliman, who had starred in Stigwood's *Jesus Christ Superstar*. Over the next nine months they wrote seven #1 records.

The Bee Gees were generating major global media coverage and were one of our most sought-after music clients, along with Peter Frampton, who was still enjoying the success of his multimillion-selling album *Frampton Comes Alive*. They were being inundated with media requests, most of which they weren't willing or able to do. They were a publicist's dream client, and I was getting calls from journalists it would have taken years to access.

One of their hottest months was in March 1978. The week of March 25, five songs they wrote were on the *Billboard* Hot 100 chart and in the Top 10 at the same time: "Stayin' Alive," "Love Is Thicker Than Water," "Night Fever," "If I Can't Have You," and "Emotion." That same month, we secured a *New York Times* article written by the noted music critic John Rockwell, which chronicled their meteoric rise. Rockwell noted, "In some charts the Bee Gees—as composers, performers and/or producers—have four of the top five singles and five of the top 10. It's a dominance unprecedented since the acme of the Beatles' first success in 1964." He added, "The ingredients of the Bee Gees' sound are easy enough to identify, but the 'masons' for their success must inevitably remain more complex and speculative. What Barry and his brothers have done is blend two styles that might have been considered antithetical—disco urgency and lush, middle-of-the-road romanticism."

A CRISIS—BEE GEES ACCUSED OF PILFERING R & B MUSIC

On April 13, 1978, the Bee Gees' and the O'Jays' images were featured on a split cover of *Jet*, with the glaring coverline, "White Stars Cross Over and Get Rich On Black Music." *Jet* is an influential digest-size weekly magazine that focused on covering all aspects of Black news, culture, and entertainment related to the African American community. In 1951, John H. Johnson, the founder and CEO of Johnson Publishing Company, launched *Jet* two years after launching *Ebony*, its popular sister lifestyle magazine. *Ebony* and *Jet* were two of the most prominent and influential Black magazines during the '70s. In 1982 Johnson became the first Black businessman listed on the *Forbes* wealthiest 400 list.

I received an urgent call from my boss about a major Bee Gees problem. I walked over to his office, and he showed me the *Jet* cover story. He asked me to read the article and come back so we could discuss it. He explained that the Bee Gees were seething. They felt themselves wrongfully singled out and victimized. They were seeking a viable solution for redemption and to restore their unblemished reputation. The article was unsolicited. No one at our firm had set it up.

The cover story was written by Ronald E. Kisner, *Jet*'s West Coast bureau chief, and opened with, "No the Bee Gees, Elton John, Billy Joel, Samantha Sang, and Steely Dan aren't Black, but you might think so if you've been tuning in Black radio stations since post–civil rights struggle days. These singing stars and a splattering of some more like the Average White Band and Wild Cherry have managed to make mega hits by draining purses from White and Black communities equally dry."

Later in the article he referred to these artists as "updated Al Jolson's who have Black-voiced-and-tracked their voices masterfully." However, his more scathing remarks disparaged the Bee Gees and their monumental success with their hit songs on the *Saturday Night Fever* soundtrack. He characterized them as "unabashedly thin-veiled mimics."

The Bee Gees had deliberately incorporated R & B music elements into their music, so that aspect of Kisner's claim was correct. However, disco music was gaining steam and becoming the most dominant music genre on contemporary pop radio. As a result, many white artists and Black artists were infusing dance beats into their music to compete with the emergence of disco. Some top disco artists popular in the same period were Donna Summer, ABBA, Gloria Gaynor, Kool & the Gang, Boney M, KC and the Sunshine Band, the Trammps, Chic, Village People, the Weather Girls, Sylvester, Evelyn "Champagne" King, Shalamar, Grace Jones, D Train, Candi Staton, Linda Clifford, and Van McCoy.

The O'Jays were also hot and were enjoying the success of their album *So Full of Love* and their single "Use Ta Be My Girl," which was #1 on the R & B charts for five weeks and Top 5 on *Billboard*'s Hot 100. It became one of their most popular hits. However, while they were superstars to Black audiences, they had not reached the same level of fame with white mainstream audiences—which was not unique to them.

The same was true for most Black artists who had achieved stardom driven primarily by the support of their Black audiences. What the article chronicled was the discouraging truth that white artists like the Bee Gees could become more commercially successful recording R & B music for pop radio than Black artists were. And Black radio stations played music by some major pop stars as well.

I had interfaced several times with Bob Johnson, the longtime editor of *Jet*. He was a respected journalist, loyal company man, and savvy advertising salesman who knew how to leverage and market the magazine's cover story to sell more magazines. After reading the article, I saw that Bob had deliberately targeted the Bee Gees to create a storyline that would be sensational and controversial enough to generate a windfall of magazine sales. He also placated his core Black audience by giving the O'Jays half the cover. It was rare for *Jet* to put anybody white on the cover.

SPIN DOCTOR

Since *Jet* was a Black magazine, Paul sought my recommendation about how we should handle the situation, so as to reduce any further collateral damage and possibly spin the negative into a positive. It flattered me, even though I realized he would not have been seeking my opinion as readily if *Jet* weren't a Black magazine. I was mostly doing grunt publicity work on the Bee Gees, updating their bio and press kit, handling interview requests, and preparing confirmation letters for the few interviews they had time to do.

I felt Paul was testing me to see if I was up to challenge of being a spin doctor. He had already built a lofty reputation for managing celebrity crises, so he could have opted to handle this matter on his own. Having input on a crisis with music's hottest group was a game changer for me. It offered me a chance to upgrade my stock at the firm and with the Bee Gees. It also held some ethical sensitivity for me. The article aptly raised relevant systemic racial issues, which had been ingrained and institutionalized in the music industry for decades.

Yet I didn't know a single Black person who thought the Bee Gees' music qualified as R & B, or any Black radio station that mistook them for being Black. There was no mandate for Black stations to play the Bee Gees. Stations opted to play the group because they had dominated the charts and pop radio consistently for several months. Their goal was to attract some mainstream listeners, raise their Arbitron ratings, and possibly get some ad support from the label. Pop radio played them because they had become global superstars.

My gut feeling was that I didn't see a clear path to vindicate the Bee Gees to their satisfaction. I asked Paul if I could have a little time to contemplate a comprehensive response. I didn't want to propose impulsive recommendations I had not thoroughly vetted. After investing most of my day in formulating my response, I came up with three recommendations to present to Paul:

1. Ignore it. *Jet* didn't have any mainstream appeal and only had moderate circulation within the Black community. It might go unnoticed. If we respond, it could ignite and spread the story even more. We should monitor the situation closely. If the story organically gains momentum, we will reevaluate and strategize an appropriate response.

2. I could draft a letter to the editor and persuade Bob to run it. However, I didn't feel that would generate enough attention to justify doing it. *Jet* devoted a page to letters to the editor called "Readers Rap," but it almost only printed fan letters that praised their articles.

   In fact, in most media outlets, rebuttal letters to the editor and corrections for inaccuracies were usually brief, buried, and never received as much attention as the original article. The Bees Gees had made a conscious decision to insert some R & B music elements into their music. They couldn't be transparent in refuting some charges.

3. We could elevate and platform the Bee Gees in a broader
    context by connecting them directly to the Black community.
    I proposed aligning them with a prominent national nonprofit
    Black civil rights organization, which would include a
    newsworthy charitable donation. This would not happen
    immediately. It would appear as a self-effacing and gratuitous
    gesture. Rather than focusing on the merit of the charges, the
    goal was to change the narrative and do something uplifting
    as humanitarians to show they were sensitive and socially
    conscious. Making a donation to a nonprofit could also be
    written off as a tax credit.

In the short term, I was suggesting we ignore it and implement option 3 when it was optimal and in the Bee Gees' best interest.

The financial part of my recommendation was for them to donate the gross tickets from one of their forthcoming concert tour dates. It would generate national and possibly international media coverage and create long-term residual and positive brand value in the Black community. I also felt I could go back to Bob Johnson and get him to give the Bee Gees a cover story if the organization and the amount of the donation were significant.

There were three organizations that I initially thought might be worth exploring, beginning with the NAACP. However, their membership had declined from five hundred thousand to two hundred thousand, and they were ushering in Benjamin Hooks as the new leader. He was dealing with fallout from the historic University of California reverse discrimination case. Next was Jesse Jackson's Rainbow PUSH organization, which was pressing for a repeal of the landmark *Roe v. Wade* decision granting women the right to have a legal abortion, which made him and his organization less appealing. There was also the National Urban League, helmed by Vernon Jordan.

THE FIX—A BEE GEES AND CORETTA SCOTT KING COLLABORATION

I was intrigued by Coretta Scott King, who was often referred to as "the first lady of the civil rights movement." A year after her husband's death, she set out to honor his legacy by founding the Martin Luther King Jr. Center for Nonviolent Social Change in Atlanta. It operated as a nongovernmental, not-for-profit organization. Mrs. King started formulating plans for the center in the basement of the home where their family had lived until his death. The center's mission was research, education, and training in the principles, philosophy, and methods of Kingian nonviolence.

When Jimmy Carter was elected president in 1976, he joined industrialist Henry Ford II in raising $8 million to help finance the completion of Freedom Hall. Coretta Scott King had earned her stature as an advocate for world peace, racial equality, women's rights, LGBTQ rights, and resistance to the Vietnam War. Simultaneously, she had been spearheading a campaign to establish Martin Luther King Jr.'s birthday as a national holiday, which was being heavily supported and promoted by Stevie Wonder.

Like every other civil rights leader in the '70s, she had detractors. Most notable was the friction between Mrs. King and Ralph Abernathy, Martin Luther King's longtime close friend and partner throughout the civil rights movement. Abernathy served as president of the Southern Christian Leadership Conference (SCLC), the organization they had started together in the late 1950s. The current friction resulted from Mrs. King and Abernathy not envisioning similar goals for developing the center and an ongoing competition for limited funding sources.

I was friendly with one of her sons, Dexter King, and I could count on him to return my calls and vice versa. He was an aspiring entrepreneur and was trying to develop a career in the entertainment business. We had talked a few times about collaborating on projects, but nothing came to fruition. When we connected, he candidly shared that he was enduring a period of estrangement from his family and didn't see eye to eye on the best way to

handle his father's legacy. At the same time, he appeared comfortable being independent and moving in a different direction. He gave me direct
contact information to connect with his mother.

The Bee Gees were planning to release a new studio album to follow up
the success of the *Saturday Night Fever* soundtrack. The release of their fifteenth album, *Spirits Having Flown*, would be supported with their eighth
concert tour. The arena 1979 tour, comprising thirty-eight cities, included
a scheduled late September date at the Omni Arena in Atlanta. The capacity
was just over fifteen thousand. I proposed they donate ticket sale proceeds
from the concert, which would be over $100,000, to the center. They ex-
pected the tour to be a complete sellout. In today's rates, it would be about
$399,000.

While the Bee Gees were in Atlanta, they would invite Mrs. King to
attend their concert and informally meet backstage. Midmorning on the
next day, the Bee Gees would meet Mrs. King at the center. She would
give them a guided tour, and they would both speak at a press conference
attended by major international and national media upon completion of
the tour. The press conference would culminate with the Bee Gees pre-
senting Mrs. King with a giant symbolic check for their $100,000-plus
donation to the center. The "big check" is an old PR gimmick, contrived
and fake, which still works today with most media outlets. Especially if
the principals are famous and the amount is significant.

My altruistic goal was to unite mainstream music's number one artist
with the revered first lady of the civil rights movement, Coretta Scott King,
in a significant humanitarian effort to support the final building phase of
the Martin Luther King Jr. Center for Nonviolent Social Change and its
nonpartisan stance for racial equality, poverty, and world peace. And both
parties would have only had to invest a few hours of their time to make it
happen.

I presented my proposal to Paul, and he liked it. He intuitively felt
the Bee Gees wanted to respond to the controversy in some form, but he
wasn't sure if the donation would be too steep for them. They promptly

committed to my proposal, understanding that I still had to speak with Mrs. King. I was reservedly enthusiastic about leaping over the first hurdle. Now I had to convince Mrs. King. I intentionally waited to call her until I had secured a 100 percent commitment from the Bee Gees.

Reaching Mrs. King took longer than I had envisioned. I initially connected to her assistant, whom I followed up with several times. I advised him that Dexter had referred me, and I clarified that I represented the Bee Gees. Yet I wasn't sure if Mrs. King was familiar with them. People and musical tastes can be like fire and ice. You can't take it for granted they'll know who the most celebrated artists are in every genre.

THE GREEN LIGHT

I confirmed the call. It filled me with anxiety and nervous energy—sweaty palms and forehead. It's Coretta Scott King! I called from my office in Beverly Hills, which was quaint—albeit small. Having one guest made it feel claustrophobic. But it had a large window and a door I could lock. I didn't want any disruptions, so I locked it, sat down, and took a deep breath to gather my thoughts. I rated it as the most important call I had made on behalf of a client.

When she started speaking, she had a deep but calm voice. She spoke deliberately, wasting no words. She was aware of the Bee Gees and glibly mentioned she followed contemporary music. Other than that moment, it was a straightforward business call.

She allowed me to make my pitch uninterrupted. She responded graciously to the Bee Gees' offer and gave me her blessing to move forward. I advised her that a label representative (Lippin) and I would like to set up an in-person meeting to complete all the details, and she said we could work that out with her assistant. I emphasized that I would be her primary contact and would accommodate any of her needs. We talked for less than fifteen minutes. After finishing the call, I jumped out of my chair, did a quick fist pump, and yelled, YES!

I immediately advised Paul of the conversation so he could communicate to the Bee Gees that Mrs. King had graciously agreed to accept their generous offer. Once they reconfirmed their commitment, I planned to draft a comprehensive strategy overview and timeline for every step of the process leading up to the day of the event. The strategy outlined generating media coverage in advance, on the day of, and after the press conference.

The Bee Gees had booked a six-day sold-out concert engagement at Madison Square Garden, on September 7–12. I received a request from Lippin to schedule the in-person meeting with Mrs. King on September 7. Our itinerary for that day included flying from LA to Atlanta, meeting with Mrs. King, and then immediately flying to New York in time to catch their opening night performance. There was also a lavish afterparty planned for the rooftop of the St. Regis Hotel on 55th Street in Manhattan.

I followed up with Mrs. King's assistant. He confirmed she would accommodate the requested date/time for the meeting and said the meeting would most likely be held at the historic Ebenezer Baptist Church, on Auburn Avenue, in the fourth ward. It was the segregated area where King grew up. His father had been a pastor at the church, and he assumed the role when his father died. It was just two blocks from where the center was being built. They planned to include a tour of the center as part of our itinerary.

THE FIX FALLS APART

A few weeks before our scheduled meeting with Mrs. King, Paul buzzed me to come to his office. He told me the Bee Gees had reconsidered the amount of their donation. I immediately said, "You're kidding, right?" I reminded him we had already issued the press release saying they were donating proceeds from the Atlanta concert. He said it was out of his hands. They were reducing the donation to $30,000.

I felt blindsided; I was livid. I was Mrs. King's only contact and had acted in good faith. She had put her trust in my word. The fact that I could not honor that commitment made me feel like I had betrayed her, which left me miserable. Plus, he said that I had still had to go to Atlanta with Lippin to complete the details. My intuitive sense was that she might not meet with us at all. After I explained the circumstances to Mrs. King's assistant, he advised me that she had agreed to take the meeting.

I was dreading the flight to Atlanta. The only upside was that I was going to be flying first class, which for me was a real treat. Different travel agencies booked our tickets. I boarded first. When Lippin boarded the plane, we discovered they had assigned her the seat next to me. Neither of us was happy about it. We were sitting in the smoking section, which she apparently failed to notice.

Once we were in the air, I reached into my pocket to grab a cigarette. She freaked out and started ranting that I couldn't smoke. Once I explained that we were in the smoking section, she pleaded with me not to continue smoking. She said she was allergic to smoke, and it would make her feel nauseous. Even though I desperately wanted to smoke just one cigarette, I didn't want to risk her vomiting for the duration of the flight. So, out of courtesy, I acquiesced. It was all quiet on the western front. We barely engaged for the rest of the flight.

When we arrived in Atlanta, we went straight to Mrs. King's office, which wasn't anything elaborate. It was a small space with walnut-paneled walls and a lot of walnut furniture, primarily desks and chairs. Her assistant told us that Mrs. King was running a little late. I viewed it as a red herring, and I could sense Lippin was fuming. After we had waited for about twenty minutes, he came back and conveyed that Mrs. King sent her sincere apologies. She was in a meeting that was running considerably longer than expected.

This trip was turning into a disaster, and I didn't have any way of altering the outcome. We had allowed an hour for the meeting and were facing a time crunch to make our flight to New York. Her assistant was very polite and apologetic, but his messages were not reassuring. Lippin was no longer smoldering—she was furious. And rightly so. Keeping us waiting for nearly an hour was disrespectful and rude.

I took her assistant aside and asked him point blank if she was coming or if we could talk to her on the phone. He reiterated that she was coming but wasn't reachable by phone. I shared his feedback with Lippin and suggested we wait for fifteen or twenty more minutes. She agreed to wait. Mrs. King never showed up, and we had to leave. I was disappointed and felt like a sacrificial lamb. Lippin was beside herself and had a personal "how dare she" attitude emblazoned on her red face.

Now I had to endure another flight with her. In a few hours, the Bee Gees and their brain trust would confront me. I started imagining how the Christians must have felt going to battle in the Coliseum against those fierce lions. On the flight to New York, I wanted to get drunk, but it would have exacerbated the situation. There wasn't much I could say. They had reneged on the amount of the contribution, offering no explanation, and Mrs. King had stood us up, offering no apology. They could rescind the $30,000 or honor it. My plan was to let Lippin carry the meeting and explain what had happened. I didn't want to give her the opportunity to counter or cast dispersion to the team about my interpretation of what had transpired in Atlanta.

The meeting was held in an enormous suite at the St. Regis Hotel. The Bee Gees, Dick Ashby, and I think one or two other people from RSO Records were in attendance. The room was dimly lit. They had moved several traditional colonial-style chairs around to accommodate everyone. While luxuriously decorated, it didn't suit my tastes, I felt.

Lippin kicked off the meeting and gave her account of what had happened. It was accurate, with minimal embellishment, except her belief that based on Mrs. King's actions, she didn't deserve the $30,000 donation. Once she finished, I spoke and endorsed her explanation of what had transpired. I reaffirmed that Mrs. King had committed to the meeting. I shared my displeasure and advised them I planned to get a firsthand account from Mrs. King. If what transpired had altered their decision to make the donation, I would advise her accordingly.

Everyone in the room felt justified reducing the donation except me, but I didn't want to throw more coals on the fire. In that moment, I didn't care what they decided. I wanted to stay focused on minimizing any further collateral damage. The meeting was brief, at least in terms of my participation. After I spoke, they thanked me, promising to discuss among themselves and get back to me. I exited the room, feeling derailed, like I had been in a train wreck.

I relaxed in my hotel room for a bit and called my boss to fill him in about everything. I went to the concert at Madison Square Garden, which was an enormous success. Then I attended an elegant and swanky afterparty on the rooftop of the St. Regis New York. I had been to New York several times and knew about the St. Regis, but the room rates were considerably above my pay scale.

The atmosphere and decor resembled an upscale nightclub. Lots of leather-clad partiers. Men wearing open-collar, half-buttoned shirts, women scantily dressed in outfits that looked like someone had glued them on. The guests were in a festive mood, dancing and drinking top-shelf drinks at the open bar and fancy buffet. I didn't know most of the people, and I wasn't in a partying mood, but it beat sitting alone in my hotel room.

I had distanced myself from the people who were crowding around the dance floor. Out of nowhere, Robert Stigwood appeared. I had officially met him before. He reintroduced himself and used my first name. He then thanked me and said he was aware of all my hard work on behalf of the Bee Gees. It shocked me. He was holding a drink and looked red-faced and tipsy, and he was slurring his words. He said he was hosting a party on his "yacht" later and invited me to come. The gesture flattered me.

I thanked him and asked who was going to be there. He looked straight at me, smiled, and said, "Just you and I!" I paused for a moment and dug deep to prevent myself from laughing. It was more laughable than offensive. I had finally chilled and put the events of the day behind me—and now I was getting hit on by one of the most powerful men in Hollywood. I had a little smirk on my face, and said, "Sorry, but I'm not interested." He remarked, "Are you sure?" I responded, "Yeah, it's not happening." He said okay and walked away. I didn't realize he was gay, but it didn't bother me. I didn't feel threatened. His timing sucked. I kept it to myself. It was a surreal ending to a stressful and awful day.

THE SETTLEMENT AND DISCO SILENCED

When I returned to LA, Paul told me the Bee Gees still wanted to donate the $30,000. I had not heard from or connected with Mrs. King since she stood us up. I called, and this time her assistant connected us. She apologized for missing the meeting and said heavy traffic had delayed her. I thanked her for the apology and noted a simple courtesy call would have been considerate. She explained she wasn't happy about the Bee Gees' decision to change the amount of their donation at the last minute, and she couldn't allow the Bee Gees to "pimp" her husband's name, which she expressed in a calm and stern tone.

I apologized to her and reaffirmed that I understood and respected her views. I was honest and told her they had caught me off guard and failed to give me a forewarning. I recommended she accept the $30,000 with no strings attached. She would not have to meet or take any photographs with the Bee Gees. They also weren't seeking any additional media coverage. She agreed to accept the donation. We ended our conversation on an upbeat note.

Once the Bee Gees and King project was closed, Paul agreed to take on the added responsibility of dealing with Lippin, which was an immense relief and weight off my shoulder. I continued to contribute to our team on the account.

THE FINAL LEG

In May 1978, we had announced that Stigwood, the Bee Gees, David Frost, and UNICEF would join forces to launch The Music for UNICEF Concert: A Gift of Song, an idea crafted by Stigwood. It came to fruition on January 9,

1979, and included a major concert held at the General Assembly in the United Nations and broadcast on NBC. The live event would mark the beginning of International Year of the Child in 1979 and raise funds to support UNICEF's world hunger programs for children. The concert was also broadcast worldwide to over seventy countries.

Joining the Bee Gees as guest performers were ABBA; Rita Coolidge and Kris Kristofferson; John Denver; Earth, Wind & Fire; Andy Gibb; Olivia Newton-John; Rod Stewart; and Donna Summer. David Frost served as host with help from Henry Winkler, Gilda Radner, and Henry Fonda. Each artist agreed to contribute the royalties from one song to the fund.

A few days later on January 12, 1979, the prestigious Hollywood Walk of Fame honored the group with a coveted star. I had worked on several of these ceremonial events, but in terms of the fan turnout and level of sheer hysteria, the Bee Gees' installation was mayhem.

Their star is at 6845 Hollywood Boulevard, a little over a block from the legendary Grauman's Chinese Theater. Normally the adjacent streets are blocked off. The crowds vary in size, but the Bee Gees crowd was considerably larger than normal. It's usually about a thirty-minute ceremony, and it started around 11 a.m. As they completed the star unveiling ceremony, fans broke through the protective barriers. The security team immediately escorted the Bee Gees to their limo.

As the driver pulled off, hundreds of fans blocked and engulfed the limo so that for about three blocks it could move no faster than five miles per hour. They were screaming, "We love you!" and directing their love to their favorite Bee Gee by name. Fans tapped on the limo and tried to get the Bee Gees to roll down the windows to autograph pictures, records, and other memorabilia. It could have gotten unruly, but there was no violence, nobody got hurt, and the crowd finally peacefully dispersed.

In February at the Grammys, disco dominated the awards. The Bee Gees swept the Grammy Awards, winning five major awards for the *Saturday Night Fever* soundtrack, including Album of the Year, Song and Record of the Year ("Stayin' Alive"), Producer of the Year (Non-Classical with Albhy

Galuten and Karl Richardson), and Best Pop Vocal Performance by a Duo or Group with Vocals ("Stayin' Alive"). My client, A Taste of Honey, won the Best New Artist Grammy Award thanks to their smash hit "Boogie Oogie Oogie" (defeating Elvis Costello, the Cars, Chris Rea, and Toto).

Later, while attending a black-tie industry event in Los Angeles, I spotted Coretta Scott King sitting with just a security guard and a few people surrounding her. Seated in a high-back Queen Anne chair wearing a lovely gown, she looked regal. This was a serendipitous moment that I couldn't pass up. I walked over to her and said, "I'm not sure if you'll remember me, but my name is Ramon Hervey II," and before I finished, she interrupted, smiled, and said she remembered me. I let her know I enjoyed meeting her. I apologized again for what had transpired. She was very warm and engaging. We only chatted for a few minutes. It was the highlight of my evening and a few moments I've always treasured.

A COLLISION OF SUPERSTARS

Riding on the wave of global success achieved with "Saturday Night Fever," Stigwood planned to release the film *Sgt. Pepper's Lonely Hearts Club Band*. When the initial deal and production started, Frampton was hotter than the Bee Gees, but by the release date, the Bee Gees had far exceeded Frampton in popularity. Since I worked with both, I knew it was causing some in-house friction between Stigwood and Dee Anthony, Frampton's manager, who felt Frampton still deserved top billing.

On the day of the premiere, July 24, 1978, Paul told me we needed to split up the responsibility of covering the Bee Gees and Frampton. Stigwood had insisted he handle the Bee Gees throughout the evening. That left me to handle the already much-chagrined Dee Anthony and Peter Frampton. My relationship with both had been copacetic. No ruffled feathers from either side. But Dee could be brash, tough, and short-tempered if provoked. Because of the wrangling I knew had been going on, I was prepared for an icy evening.

A publicist's duties on a major movie premiere night are to coordinate the artists' arrival at the theater, greet them once their limousine has pulled up, escort them through the red carpet area, coordinate interviews with key media stationed along the red carpet, organize photo ops with paparazzi in front of step and repeat banners, and stay by their side while they're schmoozing with friends and other celebrities. That normally happens in the lobby area of the theater. Then you escort them to their seats. You do the same when they're ready to exit.

The premiere was at the futuristic geodesic Cinerama Dome on Sunset Boulevard just west of Vine Street. It had opened in 1963 as the only concrete geodesic dome and had the largest contour motion picture screen in the world (thirty-two feet high and eighty-six feet wide). It was also the first new movie theater in Hollywood in thirty-three years and had become popular for film premieres and with local fans and tourists.

When Peter and Dee arrived, it was just like I envisioned. Dee was icy cold and barely acknowledged my presence. Peter was cordial and easy-going, which was his normal demeanor. I escorted them through the red-carpet area, and Peter accommodated talking to media and taking photos. As we were walking to their seats, Dee curtly asked, "Where's Paul?" I told him I had not seen him yet. He clearly was upset that Paul wasn't present and added, "Tell him to call me when you see him." I realized then that Paul had not advised him he would be with the Bee Gees.

I breathed an enormous sigh of relief as I walked away. It could have been worse. The movie was horrific, and the gigantic screen made it even worse. The only redeeming part for me was Billy Preston's performance. I was a big fan and had seen him perform live at Wembley Stadium as the opening act for the Rolling Stones while I lived in London, and I thought he blew them away.

I felt bad for Michael Schultz, but I couldn't stomach it, so I meandered in the lobby, waiting for it to end. While I was pacing, Gil Friesen, who was president of A & M Records, walked up to say hey. He thought the movie was awful, and as I walked away, he said, "I'm embarrassed to be in the record industry." The media critically pulverized the movie as a disaster, but it was commercially successful enough to make a little more than the budget. Dee and Peter's exit went smoothly. It wasn't a fun evening, but fortunately it was over.

The *Saturday Night Fever* soundtrack sold over forty-five million records worldwide and is the second-biggest selling soundtrack of all time, after the soundtrack for *The Bodyguard*. It held the #1 slot on the *Billboard* Album charts for twenty-four consecutive weeks and stayed on the *Billboard* Album charts 120 weeks, until March 1980. Their thirty-eight-city tour grossed over $10 million and was the most extravagant ever. They extended their engagement in Atlanta to two days, September 29–30. They sold out both nights (31,951 seats) and grossed $455,315.

FAILURES AND LESSONS

By the end of 1979, the Bee Gees' phenomenal nearly two-year run as the most famous disco artists ever came to a screeching halt. There was a historic industry-wide backlash to disco music that virtually shut it down as a mainstream music genre. Pop radio stations abruptly refused to play any disco artists, labels stopped signing and promoting them, live performances dried up, and its mainstream popularity took a cataclysmic dive.

No group suffered more than the Bee Gees, who lost their lofty perch as the face of the genre. They didn't stop recording, but they never achieved the same level of success again. They are credited with selling over 120 million records over the span of their long career.

In retrospect, working with the Bee Gees was a watershed moment for me. It helped build my professional confidence and belief that I could compete with other publicists who were more seasoned. Even though I didn't develop relationships with any of the Bee Gees, it gave me a chance to contribute to their ascension as the most successful artists in contemporary music at the pinnacle of their fame and career.

I have never repeated that feat with any other music client I've managed or represented as a publicist for over thirty-five years. I learned about the fragility of fame and how fleeting it can be—how you can chase it, never achieve it, suddenly achieve it when it's least expected, and then lose it again through no fault of your own.

The Bee Gees' talents as songwriters and artists weren't in decline; they were victims of an unfortunate and unprecedented shift in the value of the music genre that made them famous. It forced them out. Having an inside view of their rise and fall forever influenced my perception of fame and how to treat it. Fame is a joint venture between the celebrity and the public, and when the public decides you aren't relevant anymore, it's an ominous task to convince them otherwise.

The most valuable lesson I learned is that mixing famous artists and famous humanitarians or organizations only works when both parties have a vested and passionate interest in the partnership and the cause. The Bee Gees didn't have a vested interest in supporting Coretta Scott King and the King Center. Coretta Scott King didn't have a vested interest in the Bee Gees.

5

FAME BEGETS FAME—
THE MORE YOU GET,
THE HARDER IT IS TO MANAGE

When you've devoted half your life to working with famous people, it's unavoidable that you will rate one client's level of fame versus another. I've represented Paul McCartney as a solo artist, Michael Jackson as a member of the Jacksons, Richard Pryor, Bette Midler, Quincy Jones, the Bee Gees, and a few others who have attained enormous levels of fame. I'm not sure who is regarded as the most famous. There is no exact science or analytical data one can use to make a valid assessment. It's subjective, predicated on personal bias and how one defines fame. I've always been more intrigued about how one attains fame, what people do with it once they have it, and how long they are able to sustain it. Fame is simply a by-product derived from achieving success. Not all successful people become famous. Not all people who attain fame can sustain the success that triggered their fame. There's no guaranteed recipe for success, but some prerequisite ingredients that are helpful to possess are an abundance of talent, creative vision, quality products that can be commercially exploited, a savvy professional support team, perseverance, patience, flexibility, charisma, passion, public acceptance, opportunistic timing, and an exorbitant dose of luck.

I've studied the unique success stories of all my clients, as well as many other celebrities that I never represented. Fame is not ubiquitous, and every story is unique. One story that has fascinated me is the unprecedented success story of Quincy Jones. He possesses vintage fame, which has aged, matured, and grown exponentially over a career that spans nearly seventy years. As an African American, he has singularly had more influence in all facets of the entertainment business than anyone ever, including his peers, present-day stars, and his predecessors. He achieved fame while his generation endured overt systemic racism, social injustice, and Jim Crow laws, in an industry that has perpetuated negative racial stereotypes and institutionalized racial inequity and discriminatory employment practices in every facet. Despite those immense roadblocks, he has left an indelible imprint of success as an artist, musician, songwriter, composer for motion picture and television, conductor, arranger, record producer, motion picture and television producer, and record executive. He founded production companies, record labels, film and television production companies, magazines, and his own digital jazz network, and he created an immense amount of memorable entertainment content in every medium.

A GLANCE AT QUINCY JONES'S LEGACY

When I met Quincy, he was forty-five years old. He had already amassed considerable success as an arranger and composer for film and television, a conductor, a jazz instrumentalist, a record producer, and a record executive. He had attained a respectable level of fame within the industry, but he had also achieved a level of pop culture fame and amassed considerable wealth. In fact, he had just touched the surface of the mega-fame he would achieve a decade later. There are books and documentaries (*The Autobiography of Quincy Jones*, published in 2001, and a documentary titled *Quincy*, released by Netflix in 2018) that aptly chronicle his personal saga and his multitude of achievements, honors, and awards—which are staggering. The trajectory of his success, especially at the time he achieved it, is remarkable. I can't take an iota of credit for contributing to or spiking his fame.

The project I initially worked on with him may have added about thirty seconds to his fame. And that might be a generous estimation. However, our initial interaction was serendipity for both of us in unique ways. It's impossible to understand and appreciate his success story without examining his immense body of work.

Quincy came to prominence in the 1950s as a jazz arranger and conductor. In 1953, at nineteen, he toured throughout Europe with the jazz bandleader Lionel Hampton and played trumpet in the Hampton Orchestra. While on tour, he displayed a natural gift as an arranger. He moved to New York City, and before he turned thirty, he had collaborated as an arranger, musician/trumpeter, or conductor with many of the most revered jazz artists of his generation, including Dizzy Gillespie, Ray Charles, Frank Sinatra, Harold Arlen, Miles Davis, Count Basie, Elvis Presley, Billy Eckstine, Ella Fitzgerald, Shirley Horn, Peggy Lee, Nana Mouskouri, Frank Sinatra, Sarah Vaughan, Gene Krupa, and Dinah Washington. His solo recordings included "Walking in Space," "Gula Matari," "Smackwater Jack," "You've Got It Bad Girl," "Body Heat," "Mellow Madness," and "I Heard That!!" In the '60s, he was prolific and broke racial barriers as an African American arranger and composer, a feat that remains unparalleled in the motion picture and television industry. He is unequivocally the GOAT in that arena.

Quincy realized that becoming a successful young jazz musician and working with some of the best jazz musicians in the world was an extraordinary artistic and personal experience, but jazz musicians were all struggling financially. Historically, many jazz musicians went to Europe because it was more lucrative, and they were respected and appreciated more as people. In those days, Black jazz musicians touring in the US weren't allowed to stay in most hotels or even eat in the same nightclubs in which they were performing. They were forced to eat and sleep on the bus. His foresight to understand that paradigm, diversify, and exploit his other artistic gifts as an arranger and composer would pay huge dividends in the next phase of his career.

In 1961, Quincy became a vice president at Mercury Records, becoming the first African American to hold that position at any record company. Director Sidney Lumet later hired him to compose music for *The Pawnbroker* (1964), the first of some forty major motion picture scores he would pen. From 1965 to 1978, Quincy wrote thirty-three film scores, including many classics: *Mirage*; *The Slender Thread*; *Walk, Don't Run*; *The Deadly Affair*; *In Cold Blood*; *In the Heat of the Night*; *Mackenna's Gold*; *The Italian Job*; *Bob & Carol & Ted & Alice*; *Cactus Flower*; *The Out-of-Towners*; *They Call Me Mister Tibbs!*; *The Anderson Tapes*; *$ (Dollars)*; and *The Getaway*. In addition, he composed "The Streetbeater," which became the theme music for the television sitcom *Sanford and Son*, starring his close friend Redd Foxx, as well as the music for other TV shows, including *Ironside*, *Rebop*, *Banacek*, *The Cosby Show*, *Roots*, and *Mad TV*. At thirty-five, Jones and his songwriting partner, Bob Russell, became the first African Americans nominated for an Academy Award for Best Original Song, for "The Eyes of Love," from the film *Banning*. During the mid-'60s, he also produced a half-dozen pop hits for the UK pop star Lesley Gore, including "It's My Party" (US #1), "Judy's Turn to Cry," "She's a Fool," "You Don't Own Me," "Look of Love," and "Maybe I Know."

He kicked off the '70s by becoming the first African American to be named musical director and conductor of the Academy Awards ceremony and telecast. In 1974, at forty-one, he had a life-threatening operation to correct a brain aneurysm. He launched Qwest Records in 1975 with Warner Bros. Records (Warner Music Group), with albums by George Benson and Frank Sinatra. In 1978, he produced the soundtrack for *The Wiz* and met Michael Jackson for the first time. He was forty-six, and over eight years (1979–87) they collaborated on three albums, which dramatically bolstered and surpassed the level of fame either had previously achieved. Those projects revolutionized contemporary pop music and dominated the world music scene for nearly a decade. Jackson's history-making albums were *Off the Wall* (1979, sold over 20 million copies), *Thriller* (1982, sold 60 million copies and became the highest-selling album of all time), and *Bad* (1987, sold 45 million copies). In 1985, Quincy produced and conducted the legendary live recording of the charitable song "We Are the World" (written by Jackson and Lionel Richie), which featured forty of the world's most renowned recording artists. It raised millions of dollars to provide relief for victims of famine in Ethiopia. He has produced many major live music and network television events for worthy causes, presidential candidates, and presidents throughout his career. He has received eighty Grammy Award nominations, the most in the industry, and won twenty-eight. He was the recipient of a Grammy Legend Award in 1992. He is enshrined in the Rock & Roll Hall of Fame. *TIME* named him one of the most influential jazz musicians of the twentieth century. In 1995 he was the first African American to receive the Academy Awards' Jean Hersholt Humanitarian Award. He has tied with sound designer Willie D. Burton as the second most Oscar-nominated African American, with seven nominations.

What distinguishes Quincy and other famous people of his ilk is his capacity to be a quintessential multitasker, his drive, passion, expansive network and access, diversity, range of talents, and sense of inclusion. He also exudes an uncanny charm that can break through global cross-generational, racial, and cultural mores. He is human-friendly, which has never been the prevailing mode of operation in our industry. Whether you're gentile, Jewish, Black, Latino, Asian, European, LBGTQ, rich, poor, a hip-hop artist from the hood, a celebrity, or an artist from the jazz, pop, R & B, rock, country, gospel, punk, or alternative fields, Quincy will find common ground to communicate. It's his endearing aura, compassion, fallibility, and indomitable spirit that make him such an extraordinary person.

Hopefully now you can imagine why I might be understandably excited and intimidated when I found out I might meet and work with Mr. Quincy Jones.

BREAKING INTO THE BIZ YOUNG AND BROKE-ASS

I was a young, broke-ass, struggling publicist trying to navigate my way through one of most renowned entertainment public relation companies in the business. It was 1977, and I had just started working at Rogers & Cowan. At that point, actors and actresses were treated like employees whose rights and careers were contractually owned by the studios that hired them. R & C revolutionized the industry by disrupting the studios' exclusivity and siphoning top talent to promote their careers independently. By the time I arrived, Rogers & Cowan was one of the most powerful entertainment PR companies in the industry. They represented film and television stars, contemporary music artists, directors, producers, film companies, production companies, record labels, corporations, industry executives, and the whole gamut of top echelon talent and entertainment entities in the business. I think they had fifteen to twenty account executives. I discovered that there were no Black account executives or employees working in their Beverly Hills office, located in the heart of Beverly Hills at the corner of Bedford Drive and Wilshire Boulevard. It wasn't a high-rise building, just moderate, with underground parking, and R & C occupied one full floor.

I was almost a year into working as a writer and publicist at Motown Records when they laid me off. My boss, Bob Jones, was one of the few Black publicists who had ever worked at R & C. He offered to set up a meeting for me to meet the head of the contemporary music division, Paul Bloch. His motivation was to help me make some side income until Motown could rehire me. He knew that Rogers & Cowan hired freelance writers to work on projects, writing bios, press releases, and so on, and paid competitive fees to writers. Bob advised me that Paul had agreed to meet me—with no guarantees.

DRIVING TO ROGERS & COWAN WITH NO REVERSE

They set up the meeting at 7 p.m., which meant he was squeezing me in after work hours. I wore a suit and tie and headed over in my jalopy, a maroon 1965 Dodge Dart that always drove like it was gasping its last breath. It had an oil leak, which often caused an emission of billowing smoke—much to the chagrin of every car I passed. It belonged to my youngest brother,

George, who had been accepted to West Point. I direly needed some wheels, and it was just sitting at my parents' house, so I took it. It was an automatic and a verifiable lemon. Over the two months prior to my meeting, the reverse gear was inoperative. I had been saving up to get it repaired. So everywhere I drove I had to figure out a place to park on the street where I could exit without having to use reverse. That became an ominous and frustrating task—which I abhorred. Driving without reverse eliminated parking garages—which I couldn't afford either. That night, I parked on the street, within reasonable walking distance from R & C's office. I entered the office building and took the elevator up, rang a buzzer, and Paul let me in. The offices were desolate, with no one in sight.

Paul was an interesting character, White, bald, a little taller than me, severely tan, overweight, a fast talker, hyper, slightly scattered, but engaging. It wasn't your typical question-and-answer interview. He did most of the talking, and I felt that he was only meeting me as an obligatory favor to Bob. The meeting lasted about thirty minutes. He was noncommittal. He stated he didn't have any present need for a writer and would call me if an opportunity came up. I walked away feeling somewhat deflated, but I wasn't desperate. I wasn't looking for a full-time job, just an opportunity to make some money.

While I was walking back to my car, I started pondering other options. I doubted I'd ever hear from Paul. As I approached my car, I realized that I had screwed up and allowed enough space for a car to park in front of me. That was a red code violation—an idiot blunder. The only way out was to open the driver's side door and push the car back far enough to drive out. Luckily, there wasn't a car behind me. However, being a Black guy in a suit pushing a jalopy at night in Beverly Hills was not a good look. There was also a minor incline, which made pushing the car more challenging. I tried several times. I was sweating profusely and had barely moved the car a few inches. A random white guy walked by and inquisitively asked, "Are you having some trouble with your car?" I thought it looked obvious, but I didn't want to scare him off. So, I lied and pretended I didn't know it was not working, "Yeah, my reverse gear doesn't seem to work, so I'm trying to push my car out of this space." Thankfully, he offered to help. Using his leverage to push from the front of the car, I could drive away. It was a humbling adventure and subtle reminder that I needed to remain resilient.

I'M HIRED FOR A PAUL MCCARTNEY PROJECT

About three weeks later, I got a call from Paul Bloch. He said he wanted to hire me to work for three weeks on a writing project for Paul McCartney. I knew of only one Paul McCartney. For clarification, I asked, "The Beatles' Paul McCartney?" He responded yes. I discovered that Paul had a vast publishing company, MPL Communications (McCartney Productions Ltd.). Founded in 1969, it is the umbrella company for his business interests.

Besides handling McCartney's post-Beatles work, MPL is one of the world's largest privately owned music publishers through its acquisition of other publishing companies. The Beatles broke up in 1970, and McCartney was in the seventh year of his solo career, while expanding his business interests into other areas. He owned the music catalog of the legendary rock 'n' roll star Buddy Holly and was putting together a special Buddy Holly Week to celebrate the rocker's life and music. My assignment was to craft a press kit to comprise text content on Holly, his catalog, and all the events that were being scheduled throughout the week. Bloch arranged for me to have office space so I could access files and documentation to create the text content. I never spoke to McCartney directly. I created a dummy sample quote that I wanted to include in the press release about the week. The office space was compact but self-contained and next to Bloch's office. It was available because the account executive who occupied it was away on vacation. All I had was a desk and a typewriter, and there were no fax machines or computers yet.

I finished creating the text and brand materials in about four days. Paul was ecstatic, and McCartney apparently was impressed. I was a little hesitant to turn it in because I didn't want to risk losing the balance of the three weeks' income we had agreed upon. Several days later, while I was waiting to get my next writing assignment, I received a call from Paul. Instead of giving me another project, he offered me a full-time job. R & C was offering me $250 a week, $50 more than Motown. I would report directly to Paul and work on all his existing clients. It would be an interesting transition moving from an essentially all-Black company to a white one, but I didn't view that as a deterrent. In fact, I was thrilled. I wanted to learn and prove I could compete on every level with the best in the business. Intensely motivated, I welcomed the challenge. I thanked Paul for the offer and told him that out of courtesy I wanted to speak to Bob before making a commitment. Bob was cool and gave me his blessing.

SURVIVAL OF THE FITTEST

Once thrust into the Rogers & Cowan environment, I discovered that the company was permeated with an even more cutthroat survival-of-the-fittest mentality than Motown. It didn't take long for several naysayers to show they weren't receptive to someone like me infiltrating their inner sanctum. Some clandestinely maneuvered behind my back to undermine me over the tiniest of errors. For example, if I had made a typo in a press release, instead of pointing it out to me, they would circle it and send it to a superior to review. I was treading in shark-infested waters, but it made me more disciplined and determined to achieve perfection and produce error-free content.

Buffering your level of trust in an unfamiliar business environment is essential. Not everyone is your enemy. Not everyone is an ally. If you want to survive and grow, you must learn to differentiate one from the other. I was more focused on how the R & C financial system worked, how much the VPs and top account executives grossed annually, and how they calculated bonuses. Most of the major service companies in the entertainment industry routinely paid executives an annual salary plus a percentage of the gross client fees or revenues they brought to the company. R & C required a minimum monthly retainer fee of $3,000. If the artist was signed for a six-month term, that would be $18,000. The signing percentage for R & C was 10 percent.

By building a client base of five to ten clients, I could add a respectable stipend to my annual income. Public relations companies, personal managers, talent agents, business managers, and accountants all used incentive-based deals for signers. Naturally, when you're a signer and are contributing moderately to the company's bottom line, you accrue leverage and clout that can lead to raises in your annual salary, stock options (if available), a higher entertainment expenditures budget, more vacation days, healthcare, and so on. I understood that I was a virtual unknown. It committed me to work overtime, becoming a magnet, a sponge, grabbing every ounce of knowledge I could in meetings, lunches, dinners, anywhere I might be exposed to data and to take mental notes that I could log and use whenever applicable.

PAUL BLOCH TAKES ME UNDER HIS WING

I hunkered down and did my best to deliver for Paul's clients. As he and they became more comfortable with me, Paul slowly positioned me to take over as their responsible day-to-day contact. Paul didn't divest himself from them completely. Some he had represented for years. Sliding me into the day-to-day role just gave him some freedom and latitude. Paul was a prolific signer—celebrities loved his bigger-than-life persona and unbridled enthusiasm. He had some splendid ideas, but he didn't write. He wasn't an exceptional administrator or particularly organized.

However, he was a people person with an A-list Rolodex of top-tier media editors, journalists, and industry kingpins. He was a hard worker and dedicated to R & C. And he legitimately championed me. He openly established me as his right hand, and not in a disparaging manner. To his clients he reinforced that we were a team and stressed that they were getting more service—not less. And it worked. Some clients I worked closely with in my developmental stage included Bette Midler, James Caan, Nick Nolte, the Bee Gees, Peter Frampton, Herb Alpert, football Hall of Famer Jim Brown, Dudley Moore, Donald Sutherland, Elliott Gould, Tony Bennett, Priscilla Presley, the Carpenters, and Paul McCartney. At one point, if certain clients called him, he would say something like, "Bette called, is there anything I need to know about?" I would tell him, "As far as I knew everything is cool. Maybe she just wants to say hi or pick your brain." I would usually give him a synopsis of where things stood and update him on all the client's current activities.

SIGNING QUINCY'S *THE WIZ* SOUNDTRACK

It was 1978. I had been there for almost a year and had not signed a client yet. I received a call from a friend of mine, Dorene Lauer, who was a publicist at MCA Records. MCA was releasing the soundtrack album for *The Wiz*, the motion picture musical remake of the classic *Wizard of Oz*. Quincy Jones had produced the soundtrack. She wanted to know if I'd be interested in representing the soundtrack. For me that was an "are you kidding?" question. I was definitely interested. Quincy Jones! My only concern was how accessible Quincy would be for doing media interviews and whether any of the cast members would be available. She wasn't sure nor could she speak for any of the cast members (which included Diana Ross and Michael Jackson). They had advised her that Quincy would support promoting the soundtrack, but she didn't know the extent of his availability. I offered to submit a PR campaign proposal for the project that MCA could present to him. If he liked it, then I had the inside lane to get the account. In the interim, she promised to send me a copy of the album. *The Wiz* soundtrack album was based on the 1978 film adaptation of the Broadway musical. Although the film had been produced for Universal Pictures by Motown Records' film division, MCA Records released the soundtrack as a two-LP collection (Universal was owned by MCA at the time). Quincy Jones was the principal producer, and the album featured a few non-film synced cast performances by the stars of the film, including Diana Ross, Michael Jackson, Nipsey Russell, Ted Ross, Mabel King, Theresa Merritt, Thelma Carpenter, and Lena Horne. The artist performances on the soundtrack were prerecorded and were not the same as the performances depicted in the film. The album comprised songs from the original 1975 Broadway musical by Charlie Smalls and Luther Vandross. Quincy, Nickolas Ashford and Valerie Simpson, and Anthony Jackson wrote new songs for the soundtrack. I later represented both Luther and Nick Ashford and Valerie Simpson. The album was impressive. I thought Quincy had done a magnificent job of getting the most out of all the artists. That was a rare gift that distinguished him from his peers.

Unfortunately, the media narrative on the film, and especially the casting of thirty-three-year-old Diana Ross in the lead role of a young Dorothy, had been disastrous. That Berry Gordy and Motown Productions were producing the film compounded it. Gordy had secured the film rights for the Broadway production of *The Wiz* in 1977. It starred the much younger R & B singer Stephanie Mills as Dorothy. The play, which featured an all-Black cast, had premiered at the Majestic Theatre in 1975 and won seven Tony Awards, including Best Musical. Mills, who was eighteen years old, didn't get nominated for a Tony Award, but she had a #1 R & B hit with the song "Home." The role turned her into a star. When Gordy secured the film rights to the play, he signed Mills to play Dorothy. Then Ross found out Gordy had secured the rights, and she asked him if she could play the role of Dorothy. Gordy told her she was too old to play the role. Ross persisted and enlisted producer Rob Cohen to finance the production, contingent on Ross playing Dorothy. Gordy reversed his position, and Ross got the role. Joel Schumacher reworked the story written from William F. Brown's Broadway libretto. In the revised story, Dorothy was a shy, twenty-four-year-old schoolteacher from Harlem. In a magical dream sequence, she lands in a fantasy urban oasis, the Land of Oz incarnation of New York City. Cohen produced, Sidney Lumet directed, and the film starred Diana Ross,

Michael Jackson, Nipsey Russell, Ted Ross, Mabel King, Theresa Merritt, Thelma Carpenter, Lena Horne, and Richard Pryor.

When they cast Ross, the media treated her harshly, berating her for being too old. The public outcry was that she didn't deserve the role—and that Mills had earned the right to play Dorothy. It became a lightning rod for negative press that continued to shadow the project. There was no way to tell if negative press would generate a media backlash against the soundtrack, but it seemed highly unlikely that Ross would do any interviews.

When I drafted my publicity campaign proposal, I presumed I might get Quincy to do ten to twelve major media interviews. That was a safe and predictable number for a lot of celebrities in terms of the time they would give to support one-off projects. However, for music artists promoting albums, that was a low number. Most artists are expected to invest considerable time in hawking their projects to radio stations, TV (if it's available), major metropolitan newspapers, Black publications and newspapers, live performances, industry events, listening parties, award programs, and promotional tours—a plethora of PR and promotional activities. There were, however, ways to circumvent this restriction and reach many media outlets simultaneously with just one interview.

In those days, radio was the most powerful media platform for Black or urban music projects and had the power to break and sustain records. If you couldn't get a played on Black radio, that was the kiss of death for your project. One of the most influential American syndicated radio networks in the country at the time was Westwood One. Founded by Norm Pattis, it syndicated many programs to its radio affiliates, which at the time counted several hundred. It had a popular Black program director, Walt Love, who had been supportive of most of my urban clients. I pitched him on a two-hour syndicated radio special dedicated to Quincy, to talk about the *Wiz* soundtrack and his overall career.

The beauty of the special is that we provided the content to Westwood One and gave each station the latitude to integrate one of its own on-air personalities into the special to ask the questions and give the appearance he or she was talking to Quincy. Or they could pull segments from the special and program a shorter special. Stations also had the option to pitch sponsors on the special, without having to pay Quincy or MCA Records.

Content is king, and my goal was to generate free exposure on major market urban stations during peak and prime-time hours. I also proposed sending a canned feature to the top fifty Black newspapers in the country. Many couldn't afford to keep writers on salary, so often the story was credited to the publication's entertainment/music writer so it would have more local appeal. The campaign also included pitching major metropolitan newspapers like the *Los Angeles Times*, *New York Times*, *Chicago Tribune*, and top music publications like *Rolling Stone*, *Billboard*, and *Interview* Magazine. Once a project starts percolating with the public and media, additional spontaneous media opportunities arise.

MEETING QUINCY

Doreen told me Quincy liked the campaign, and MCA committed to retain my services. Quincy expressed interest in meeting me and agreed to do the interview for Westwood One. He invited me to do it over lunch at his home. He lived up in the hills on Stone Canyon Road, a long, winding, and rustic road off Sunset Boulevard in Bel-Air, one of the most expensive and coveted residential areas in Los Angeles. The lower part of Stone Canyon wrapped around the Hotel Bel-Air. Lush landscaping surrounded the hotel, allowing for just a momentary peek-a-boo as you continued up the road. I was feeling a little nervous anxiety about meeting Quincy for the first time and interviewing him.

The road was curvy, and his house was higher than I imagined, which abetted me in restoring a sense of calm. When I arrived, I parked on the street. I rang the doorbell, and his wife, Peggy Lipton, answered the door. I wasn't expecting that, but she was gracious and took me to a patio area next to the house. She served freshly made lemonade while I waited briefly for Quincy. Quincy was just as warm and welcoming. Once he sat down, I felt instantly relaxed. He had a peaceful aura and was charming and conversational. We talked briefly about our personal lives, and he noted that he was familiar with me and my background, and that he had been looking forward to our meeting. He also shared some insight about his life-threatening brain aneurysm operation in 1974, which he described as a harrowing and life-altering experience. He had married Peggy Lipton that same year. He was candid and transparent, which I discovered later was an inherent part of his personality—at least with me. We talked for over two hours, and I recorded most of it for the interview. He was exceptional, and he shared a lot of behind-the-scenes anecdotes and insight about recording the album and working with the cast members. He was a consummate professional and understood the content that would appeal to urban radio.

Once the campaign took off, I got the USC Trojan Marching Band, one of the most celebrated in the country, to feature several songs from the soundtrack during one of their upcoming halftime shows. Fortunately, they agreed to do it during the halftime show of the legendary USC–Notre Dame annual rivalry game. In addition, they agreed to let Quincy come on the field to conduct the band. That game perennially was one of the most watched NCAA games of the college football season.

In 1978, it featured Notre Dame quarterback Joe Montana against USC's star running back, Charles White. In an exciting, contested battle, USC hit a late game-winning field goal to edge Notre Dame 27–25. The win enabled USC to share in the national title. I was an enormous USC fan, so I was ecstatic about the way the game ended. Before the game, they invited Quincy, his right hand Ed Eckstine (who was the general manager of Quincy Jones Productions), and me to attend one of the traditional USC Boosters game-day brunches, which was a surreal experience. The boosters, all adorned in USC merchandise, reflected a world that I had read about, heard about, knew existed, but had never experienced firsthand. Quincy seemed pleased, and it was a fun day.

The only downside was that he received little on-camera time conducting the band. The station cut away from the band's performance sooner than expected to give updates on other college game day scores. Days later, Ed brought it up on a phone call with some disdain. I shared the same disappointment, but they had not given me a guaranteed amount of on-air time upfront, and I didn't promise such. Live network television is a crapshoot, and it's not something USC or I could control—even for Quincy. I listened and accepted the criticism and left it at that. Quincy mentioned nothing to me directly about it. In terms of the bigger picture, it delivered another opportunity to create media attention for Quincy and market the soundtrack.

The Wiz was the first client I signed to Rogers & Cowan (and I got my first signing bonus). I admired and respected Quincy enormously, so meeting and working with him was extremely gratifying. I never told him I was a virgin because I was too busy trying to impress him. It sparked a lasting friendship and business association with him that I've always cherished. For Quincy, it had also been quite serendipitous. It marked the first time he met and collaborated with Michael Jackson and became the genesis for their historic and record-breaking recording artist–producer collaborations. They considered the soundtrack a success. It earned gold certification (five hundred thousand copies) in the US. It yielded several hit singles, including Jackson's "Ease on Down the Road," and Diana Ross's version of "Brand New Day (Everybody Rejoice)." "Brand New Day" was also a #1 single in the Netherlands, and the album sold well in several European territories and Australia. The media panned the film. It never recouped its production costs and was considered a flop.

QUINCY OFFERS ME A JOB

A few weeks following my engagement term on The Wiz, Ed Eckstine called me. My initial thought was that he had a problem with something I did. That was not the case. He said he was calling on behalf of Quincy, and that Quincy had enjoyed working with me and liked the way things went on the

Wiz campaign and wanted to offer me a job working at Quincy Jones Productions. Jerry Moss and Herb Alpert, founders of A & M Records, had acquired Quincy's company. His offices were on the A & M Records lot which was a historical landmark once owned by Charlie Chaplin. I represented Herb Alpert and had been on the lot many times.

I did not see that coming at all. I felt flattered, but it surprised me that Quincy didn't make the offer directly. Ed and I knew each other, but we weren't buddies. I thought things were cool between us. Ed was in charge, and even though he intimated I'd be working for Quincy, I interpreted that to mean I would have two bosses. It was Quincy Jones, but it didn't feel like an optimum scenario.

It wasn't about them; it was about me. I was just getting my feet wet at R & C and didn't feel I had accomplished anything substantive yet. I had already started contemplating my next move, which would be to launch my own company. I had given myself a two-year window to do that—so I declined. After *The Wiz*, I stayed connected with Quincy as a friend and worked indirectly with him on several entertainment projects. I don't know if he had a "friends list," but he invited me to many fun personal events and some of his birthday parties, and I still get gifts and family holiday cards from him. His holiday cards always include a thought-provoking message with lovely symbolic imagery or family photos.

One of my favorites that I hang in my office is a color closeup of just his hands clasped together, with the words *LOVE, LIVE, LAUGH, GIVE* inscribed individually on the borders of the square. Another year, he surprised me with a birthday present of a classic live performance shot of Jimi Hendrix, my favorite artist of all time. I had no clue he knew when my birthday was or that I was an avid fan of Hendrix.

His birthday parties are legendary. Many Hollywood luminaries who were his friends attended them. I attended two, one that was very intimate and one that was spectacular, oozing with pomp, grandiose catering, and an abundance of celebrities and glamorous in-crowd folks. To put it mildly, Quincy seemed to know everybody, and if he invited people to party with him, they turned out. I was invited to his fifty-fifth birthday celebration, which I attended with my wife, Vanessa Williams, who was pregnant with our first child. It was an intimate gathering he hosted at his home.

There may have been fifty to seventy-five family members and friends there—a mix of celebrities, actors, and artists. Guests included Robert DeNiro, Gregory Peck, and Barbra Streisand, all of whom I chatted with briefly but not long enough to be intrusive. Robert DeNiro was engaging, and we talked the longest. Michael Jackson walked in cradling his best young friend at the time, Emmanuel Lewis, who starred as a child in a Burger King Whopper commercial and in the hit TV series *Webster*, in his arms while greeting Quincy and a few people in the entry foyer area. They went upstairs to watch television and chose not to mingle with guests, so I never got a chance to chat with Michael before leaving. Neither reappeared before we left. I felt privileged that Quincy had invited me.

He also invited me to another celebration, held in a palatial estate in Beverly Hills. It was an extravaganza, a fancy dress affair, lavishly catered, with bars and buffet food stations neatly positioned throughout the property. There had to be five hundred to a thousand partygoers. It felt like a celebrity amusement park. The grounds were oozing with a bevy of Hollywood's most celebrated stars, affluence, wealth, and a multicultural and cross-generational mix of the happening folks. Quincy seemed overwhelmed and said it wasn't his idea. His lady friend had put it together.

QUINCY AND MICHAEL BUILD BOND WITH ANDRAÉ CROUCH

During Quincy's run as a producer with Michael Jackson, I was managing contemporary gospel music legend Andraé Crouch. Andraé was a seminal artist and pioneer in gospel music as songwriter, producer, arranger, and performer. His vocal choir arrangements were phenomenal. Quincy adored him and used him and the Andraé Crouch Choir on many of his recordings and projects. Michael Jackson featured Andraé's vocal arrangements and choir on his classic hit "Man in the Mirror" and on several other recordings. Quincy also used Andraé and his choir for *The Color Purple*. One of Andraé's best friends and favorite lead singers, Táta Vega, performed all the songs for Margaret Avery's character, Shug Avery.

One of the most memorable highlights of those collaborations between Quincy, Michael, and Andraé happened when they asked Andraé to put together a twenty-six-member choir to perform "Man in the Mirror" on the 30th Annual Grammy Awards in 1988. The performance lasted seven minutes and twelve seconds. Michael was stupendous. Besides the choir, he also featured Andraé, Andraé's twin sister Sandra, Táta Vega, and Siedah Garrett (who wrote the song) on stage with him. The performance received a rousing standing ovation. Michael and Quincy were pleased.

QUINCY INVITES ANDRAÉ TO PERFORM AT MONTREUX JAZZ FESTIVAL

In 1993, Quincy booked all nineteen days of the Montreux Jazz Festival, held annually in Montreux, Switzerland. Montreux is a quaint Swiss town (pop. about 25,000) on the shoreline of Lake Geneva at the foot of the Alps, about forty miles from Geneva. Quincy was close friends with Claude Nobs, who founded the festival in 1967. He is credited with helping Nobs curate and develop the festival into the second-largest and one of the most influential music festivals in the world. Quincy asked Andraé to headline a special first-ever gospel night and to perform with the Atlanta Super Choir, which comprised about forty members. It was one of his most prestigious festival appearances of his career.

QUINCY CALLS TO GET MY SISTER FOR *THE FRESH PRINCE OF BEL-AIR*

During the same year, Quincy reached out to me, which wasn't really a regular occurrence. Whenever he needed to get in touch with me, one of his assistants would reach out on his behalf. So, I was thoroughly surprised he called me directly. We caught up for a minute or two, and then he explained that he was calling about my youngest sister, Wini Hervey. He reminded me that his show, *The Fresh Prince of Bel-Air* (launched on NBC-TV in 1990) was about to end its first season. They were making an executive producer/showrunner change in the show—and he wanted to hire my sister. The series starred hip-hop artist Will Smith, making his television debut as a lead actor in the series. He portrayed a street-savvy, troubled teenager who had grown up in the hood in West Philadelphia. To keep him out of trouble, they sent him to live with his wealthy uncle and aunt in their Bel-Air mansion.

Wini was a young, seasoned, successful writer and producer who had worked as a writer for the Garry Marshall Company (on the sitcoms *Laverne & Shirley, Mork & Mindy*, and *The New Odd Couple*). She also worked as a writer and producer for *Benson*, *The Cosby Show*, and *The Golden Girls*, earning an Emmy Award for Outstanding Comedy Series in 1987. CAA represented her, and I wasn't fulfilling any business role for her. I think Quincy just wanted me to put in a kind word for him. He asked me what I thought it would take to get her interested, and I said, "Pay her and make an offer she can't refuse." He laughed, and I promised I would pass on his interest and mention that he took the time to reach out.

I thought it would be a significant opportunity for her to be a showrunner and work with Quincy. The ratings for the first season had fallen considerably short of the network's expectations, so whoever came in would have to resurrect the series to keep in on the air. There was also a glaring and inequitable shortage of Black female executive producers and showrunners in television, so I felt it would be a tremendous boost to her career. I love my sister dearly, but as a doting brother, I made it a point not to infringe on or try to dictate her professional decisions. When we spoke, I made it clear I was just delivering a message from Quincy. After some negotiating, she agreed to accept Quincy's offer, and she served as executive producer of *The Fresh Prince of Bel-Air* for two seasons (1992–93), both of which produced a spike in the show's ratings. I was happy that the deal worked out. I visited the set several times just to show support.

In my blatantly biased opinion, it was a smart move by Quincy to hire her, and she received a lot of residual value from a prestige perspective, which financially helped move her career forward. After she left, the series lasted for three more seasons, ending in 1996.

Probably the thing that amazed me the most about Quincy was that he never limited himself to one area of the business. He was multifaceted and could multitask better than anyone I knew. Whenever I thought I had become insanely busy and was at my wit's end, I would think about him, and it would make my level of stress feel like child's play.

When we ran into each other at an event or a rehearsal where we could talk, he ran through a list of at least two dozen projects he was working on. He might also share some family stories, his dating scenario, or views on the industry, current news, or social and political issues that he was happy or had misgivings about. Once, while seated for a rehearsal, we were talking about dating; he shared a story about his entire family conspiring to force an intervention to convince him he was too old to have a relationship with a twenty-four-year-old woman. He said it shocked him that they had the nerve, and he used "nerve" emphatically, to tell them how he should live his life.

He also cursed incessantly—MF this, MF that—and as he was recapping the story, he was getting all riled up, like it was happening in real time. As I recall, the gist of what he expressed was, "I love them and I know they were trying to look out for me, but I told them they need to mind their own business." The rant went on for a few more minutes. He was dead serious, but he also inserted the right measure of comic relief to make it funny.

Throughout my tenure as Andraé Crouch's manager, Quincy and I connected from time to time while he was producing Michael Jackson's albums. Andraé was active as a songwriter, producer, arranger, and live performer throughout his career, but for seven years, between 1986 and 1993, he didn't release an album. Quincy had reached out to me because he heard that Andraé had not been feeling good. During our telephone conversation, I told him Andraé was feeling better and would be fine. He also asked what was going on with his solo career. I told him, Andraé tells me he's writing all the time, but he hoards his music. He rarely let me hear any finished tracks. I was frank and honest and explained that I didn't feel he was motivated to make an album or sign with a record label.

I also advised him that we had some preliminary discussions with a few labels, but Andraé didn't think they were the right fit. Then he said, "Let's get him to sign with Qwest," and that he'd love to have him on the label. I wanted to make this happen. Later that day, I called Andraé to share the news, and he was legitimately excited. At that moment, I only had his verbal word, but he said someone would be in touch with me. Within a week, I heard from the head of the label, and we started negotiations on a record deal. I was effusive with joy. Quincy was giving Andraé a chance to rejuvenate his recording career, which had been in the doldrums far too long.

I was determined to make sure we didn't waste this golden opportunity and let him down. Quincy had launched Qwest Records as a joint venture with Warner Bros. Records in 1980, which he did while having contractual obligations to A & M Records for Quincy Jones Productions until 1981. The label's first release was George Benson's album *Give Me the Night* (shared with Warner Bros.). I was Benson's publicist when it came out. Some other Qwest artists included Frank Sinatra, Patti Austin, Tevin Campbell, Radiance, the British post-punk bands New Order and Joy Division, gospel artists the Winans and singer Táta Vega, and the jazz artist Robert Stewart. Andraé's first album on the label, *Mercy* (1994), won a Grammy Award for Best Contemporary Gospel Album, which provided a level of vindication that Quincy's risk and investment had paid off. Andraé recorded two other albums for the label, *Pray* (1997) and his first holiday album, *Gift of Christmas* (1998), which featured guest appearances by Chaka Khan, Yolanda Adams, Patti Austin, and Kirk Whalum, among others. Qwest closed in 2000.

During Andraé's run at Qwest, I was also managing Vanessa's career and Kenny "Babyface" Edmonds. Vanessa and I were trying to balance our business relationship, our marriage, and being parents of three single-digit children, Melanie (nine), Jillian (seven), and Devin (three). Both our careers were flourishing, but our marriage was hemorrhaging. The fabric of the relationship was bursting at the seams. She was enjoying the success of one of the biggest hits of her career, "Colors of the Wind," written by Alan Menken and Steven Schwartz. It was the theme song for the hit Disney movie *Pocahontas* and reached the Top 10 on the *Billboard* Pop chart. It also received an Academy Award nomination for Best Original Song, as well as Golden Globe and Grammy Award nominations. The song ended up winning all three awards. Quincy was producing the Oscars telecast, marking the first time in history they had given an African American that role. He was planning to feature performances of the five Best Original Song nominees in the telecast, so Vanessa was invited to perform. I had negotiated the deal and normally would accompany her for a major appearance like the Oscars. However, rumors were rampant about our marriage being on the brink. To divert media attention and keep our distance, I stayed home in New York with our children.

On the day of her rehearsal, I got a call from Quincy. We usually talked about business. This time we were having a casual conversation, which went on longer than usual. I wasn't sure why he was calling, so I just asked if he needed me to do something for him. He noted that he didn't need me to do anything. He was just calling to check in and see how I was doing. He expressed concern and commented that he had been there several times and understood. He encouraged me to hang in, and said that we'd figure things out and get through it. I thanked him for taking the time to call. It was unexpected but such a generous and warm gesture on his part. It still amazes me anytime it drifts into my consciousness.

I haven't been in personal contact with Quincy in quite a while. I've seen him out at a few industry events in Los Angeles and New York, and we've exchanged brief hugs. I've tried to emulate his work ethic, and I remain appreciative of the opportunities he gave me over the years, his encouragement, his mentorship, his humorous and enlightening stories, and the times I was in his presence—lots of great memories that I'll continue to covet.

6

DON'T OBSESS ABOUT BECOMING FAMOUS— OBSESS TO BE YOUR BEST

Fame has siren-like powers that can lure artists obsessed with chasing it into believing they've transcended to a higher plateau of entitlement. In fact, if an artist has an addictive personality and is self-obsessed, getting intoxicated by fame can trigger an insatiable desire. It becomes embedded in their consciousness, running through their veins and ballooning their ego to nonsensical proportions.

Obsession with fame fueled by an addiction to drugs and alcohol can cause some individuals to believe they are invincible. It's harder for them to become satisfied with normalcy as they develop an inflated sense of self-worth. In many cases, they also alienate the people closest to them, who played significant roles in supporting and assisting their ascent to fame.

Most of my clients had experienced a moderate level of fame before I represented them. Though still chasing it, they had learned that fame requires an appropriate measure of humility. It neither empowers nor gives one the permission or right to disrespect, humiliate, or denigrate anyone—or to consider yourself above others, especially the law. By today's standards, artists or celebrities who sexually or emotionally harass others, or are misogynistic, abusive, inebriated on drugs or alcohol while working, rude, or inexcusably and persistently late can suffer severe ramifications from the media, exorbitant fines, arrest, or loss of employment.

From 1977 through the mid-'80s, I represented Rick James, an immensely talented musician, songwriter, producer, arranger, and performer from Buffalo, New York. I was new to Motown, and he had just been signed to the label. He was twenty-nine and recording his debut album. Over the previous decade, he had become a journeyman songwriter, singer, and producer with a checkered and turbulent past. He didn't have any hits under his belt, and he had not accrued even a nominal level of fame. But you couldn't tell him that.

Rick exuded an aura of swagger, arrogance, and entitlement—his view of what it meant to be a bona fide star. He strutted down the hallways like he owned the label. His goal wasn't just to show up—he arrived. He liked creating shock waves throughout the building. Rick dressed in his version of rock star garb and loved attracting attention and making an impression.

You must believe you're a star to create that perception, and that was one of Rick's strengths and gifts. He innately knew what it took to grab people's attention. But it's just as important to know when tempered moderation is a better option. Exuding confidence is a plus; flaunting self-obsession is a flaw. Rick was ineffectual in maintaining that balance throughout his career.

RICK'S ROOTS

Rick had been around famous musicians and artists since his single digits. They undoubtedly helped influence and shape his persona. He acknowledged that he didn't have a traditional childhood, which ultimately affected his formative years as a musician.

He was born on February 1, 1948, in Buffalo, New York, one of eight children. His mother, Mabel Johnson (née Sims), danced professionally with the Katherine Dunham Troupe but gave up dancing and became a numbers-runner to support her family. Rick's father, James Ambrose

Johnson Sr., was an autoworker who left the family when Rick was ten. I met his mother a few times and remain friends with one of his brothers, LeRoi Johnson. LeRoi managed Rick from 1981 to 1991 and built a successful career as a lawyer and artist/painter. I never met any of his other family members.

While hanging out with his mother, he met such legendary artists as John Coltrane, Miles Davis, and Etta James. She took him to the bars on her collecting route where they performed. Prior to dropping out, he attended Orchard Park High School and Bennett High School. At an early age Rick started taking drugs and engaging in sex, got busted for burglary, and was sentenced to time in jail. To avoid being jailed, at fifteen he lied about his age and enlisted in the US Navy. That decision led to desertion, court martials, becoming a fugitive, several sentences to hard labor, and ultimately serving five months at the Portsmouth Naval Prison in Kittery, Maine.

After he fled the navy, he moved to Toronto, which became his haven and where the genesis of his development as an artist took hold. He immersed himself in the Toronto music scene, and between stints in Toronto and LA, he joined several groups over the span of a dozen years. His musicians' network included the notable young rock upstarts Levon Helm, Joni Mitchell, and Neil Young.

During his first year in Toronto he formed the Mynah Birds, a rock, soul, folk, and fusion band. The Canadian affiliate label of Columbia Records signed them and released one single, "Mynah Bird Hop" / "Mynah Bird Song" (1965). Neil Young eventually joined one of the band's configurations. Since Rick was a fugitive, he used aliases to avoid being caught by military police. So as Ricky James Matthews, with Young in the band, they traveled to Detroit and started cutting some tracks for Motown. While there, he met Marvin Gaye and Stevie Wonder, who both were major musical influences and heroes to him. Wonder advised Rick his name was too long and recommended he change it to Ricky James.

The Mynah Birds were close to signing with Motown, but when the label found out he was AWOL from the military, it fell through. Throughout the early '70s, he jumped from band to band between Toronto and LA, performing in Heaven and Earth (later changed to Great White Cane), Hot Lips, and Mainline, and had a few singles released. He was active but not gaining much traction.

In 1976, at twenty-eight, after being away from home for thirteen years, he moved back to Buffalo. He quickly formed another group with several Buffalo-based musicians, which he named the Stone City Band. He decided to pitch the band to Motown, and they signed in 1977 with Gordy Records, which was one of Motown's imprints. They began recording their debut album in New York.

MEETING RICK

Rick and I were like passing ships in the night. When he was on his way into the Motown family, I was leaving to seek greener pastures. I left before his debut album was released, but I thought his album had a lot of potential. His multitude of talents impressed me. He sang and was an adept musician on all the principal rhythm instruments: guitar, keyboards, synthesizers, drums, and bass. He wrote songs with strong melodies, risqué lyrical themes, and catchy hooks. On top of that, he was a talented producer and arranger (for vocals and horns) who had an expert eye and ear for talent.

Rick's sound was lush, full-throttle, a distinctive blend of funk, R & B, soul, rock, and pop. The Stone City Band was a tight and skilled collective of musicians who aptly complemented each other. After I left Motown, I followed Rick's career trajectory and listened to his albums. I was a legitimate fan of his music and talents—but not of his antics.

RICK DEBUTS

Motown released Rick's debut album, *Come Get It*, on Gordy Records in April 1978. It yielded the chart hits "You & I" (#1 R & B, #13 Pop) and "Mary Jane" (#3 R & B). This homage to marijuana became one of his signature songs. The album was certified gold and made it to #13 on *Billboard*'s Top 100 Albums chart and #3 on the R & B chart. Rick had finally wedged one foot in far enough to crack open the door of fame. It was a testament to his resilience and determination to move his artistry to a higher plateau and reap the adulation he desperately craved for his talents.

His sophomore album, *Bustin' Out of L Seven*, came out just eight months later, in January 1979. The album's first single, "Bustin' Out (On Funk)," peaked at #8 on the R & B charts but only reached #71 on the Pop charts. But the album, which peaked at #2 on the R & B Albums chart, sold one million copies to become his first platinum album.

Behind the scenes, Rick was writing, producing, and recording other projects—most notably for his Stone City Band and for a young soulful white "sanger" with a torching soprano voice whom he took under his wing, Teena Marie. He wrote and produced her debut album, *Wild and Peaceful*, which Motown released in March 1979. He sang a duet with Teena, "I'm a Sucker for Your Love," which was the album's first single and peaked at #8 on the R & B charts.

Even though the album was unapologetically R & B laden, Motown was afraid they might get backlash for releasing a white female singer who sounded Black. Initially, they decided not to include an image of her in the album package—so consumers would presume she was Black. That strategy proved ill-fated once they performed the song on *Soul Train*, making Teena one of a just a handful of white artists to perform on the show.

RICK AND I JOIN FORCES

After the release of his second album, Rick hired me as his publicist. His momentum, level of stardom, and fan base had markedly grown, and he was driven to become a megastar. He also aspired to build his own production entity and empire writing, producing, packaging, and developing other artists and bands, as well as writing and producing material for established stars. His mission was admirable, and he had the talent to do it, but he wasn't sensitive to strategic planning. He tended to try to bully things into happening instead of being patient and giving each project the space to be commercially exploitable.

I thought, with the right guidance, Rick and the Stone City Band had the potential to become the Sly and the Family Stone of his generation. Sly fused and bridged funk, rock, R & B/soul, and pop and became one of the most influential Black male crossover superstars (and bands) in the late '60s and '70s. I was a huge fan and saw him perform live—forty-five minutes later than his designated showtime at the Long Beach Auditorium, in Long Beach, California. He was so late several fans near my seat were pissed off and complained their drugs were going to wear off before he hit the stage.

Rick enlisted Shep Gordon, one of the most powerful managers in the industry, to manage him. Shep revealed in an interview with Questlove that when they initially met, Rick introduced himself as "the baddest motherfucker you ever came across in your life." Shep managed Alice Cooper, Maurice White, Blondie, Mtume, Pink Floyd, George Clinton, Raquel Welch, Groucho Marx, and the Pointer Sisters, to name a few.

He put together the "Rick James and Stone City Band Fire It Up" tour, which comprised forty-three engagements and ran for nine weeks starting in late November, then started up again from January through early May in 1980. The tour dates were a mix of five thousand– to ten thousand–seat capacity theaters and arenas, and followed Motown's release of Rick's third album, *Fire It Up*, on October 16, 1979.

During his peak years, Rick was a huge live concert attraction. His shows weren't just concerts; they were events. He usually sold out in most of the top urban markets, such as New York, Los Angeles, Oakland/San Francisco, Philadelphia, DC/Baltimore, Dallas, Houston, Chicago, Detroit, Cincinnati, Cleveland, Charlotte, Atlanta, and Miami.

The audiences were a mix of predominantly Black funksters and R & B fans, and a smaller percentage of white funk fans who came to party and cut loose. Many were high on something and wore curated "anything goes" fashion with tight-fitting leather pants or tight dresses, furs, high heels, and high boots. There were no rules. Whatever you partied in—funky, flashy, sexy, or sleazy—and wanted to show off and not blend in was acceptable. Rick's core fans didn't end their night after the show—they started it there. I attended a bunch of his concerts, and the audiences provided ample eye candy.

THE RICK VERSUS PRINCE WAR BEGINS

Shep was looking for an opening act that would add some media buzz to the tour and enhance ticket sales, and he chose an up-and-coming twenty-two-year-old Black funk and soul singer from Minneapolis, Minnesota, named Prince. Warner Bros. released Prince's debut album, *For You*, on April 7, 1978, but it wasn't a commercial success. They followed up with his self-titled second album just three days after Rick's, on October 19, 1979. Prince wrote, produced, and arranged the entire album. The heralded long-time *Village Voice* music critic Robert Christgau reviewed it for his Christgau Record Guide: "This boy is going to be a big star, and he deserves it." He launched his first headlining club tour of thirteen dates right before joining the "Fire It Up" tour.

On paper, it seemed like an optimum pairing. Prince was twenty-one, and Rick was thirty-one. They were both self-contained funksters and guitarists fronting skilled bands and were pushing the envelope with their stage personas and lyrics. Their first show together was on February 22 in Fort Worth, Texas, and it wasn't long before they became warring antagonists stoking their egos by slighting each other in the media. Rick was doing most of the bashing, calling Prince a "punk-ass bitch," accusing him of stealing his mic moves and funk sign and incorporating them into his show. Prince was only doing seven or eight songs in his forty-minute set, compared to Rick's two-hour set, but Prince's show was electric and charged up. He was also building momentum from the release of "I Wanna Be Your Lover," the lead single from his new album. It had been released a month before the beginning of the tour and had climbed to #11 on *Bill-board*'s Pop Singles chart. Prince's rising stardom and critical acclaim infuriated Rick. The more attention Prince got, the more Rick lashed out at him in the media. Once the trash-talking spread throughout the industry, the tour earned the title "the Funk Battle."

Unfortunately, Rick had become the lead antagonist and was losing the battle in the minds of audiences, concert reviewers, and the media. One of Rick's most vitriolic personal slams appeared an interview with *Rolling Stone*. He vented, "I can't believe people are gullible enough to buy Prince's jive records. . . . Prince is a mentally disturbed young man. He's out to lunch. You can't take his music seriously." I've never been a fan of artists exposing and escalating beefs via the media. It's not a good look, and the one who is fueling the spat usually suffers the most damage. And both are getting pimped as fodder by the media.

I tried to convince Rick to take the high road. He was ten years older and had given Prince access to his platform. Prince spiked ticket sales, which ultimately generated more revenue for Rick than for Prince. I urged him to just take credit for recognizing Prince's talent and giving him a break. His rants were getting stale, and he needed to change the narrative. He listened and responded with his usual diatribe of expletives about Prince and didn't heed my advice. Rick's inability to sublimate his ego in critical situations when he had more to gain by doing so was a crippling weakness that hindered his image and fame.

Fire It Up reached #34 on the Pop charts and #5 on the R & B charts and was certified gold. The album's lead single, "Love Gun," reached #13 on the R & B chart. Prince's album peaked at #22 on *Billboard*'s Pop Albums chart and at #3 on the R & B Albums chart. Months after its release, *Prince* was certified platinum, having sold a million copies.

A couple of months after they completed the tour, Gordy/Motown released Rick's fourth album, *Garden of Love*, on July 16, 1980. It was a significant departure from the hard-driving, punk-funk, danceable songs that embodied his initial three albums. However, it was one of his most personal efforts, comprising mostly laid-back funky ballads. It only yielded one hit single, "Big Time," which peaked at #17 on *Billboard*'s R & B Singles chart and #38 on the Dance chart.

Hardly anyone ever mentioned the lyrical content of "Big Time," but I felt it subtly framed his self-perspective, obsession, and insecurities about chasing fame and what it meant to him. He infers that fame is a crazy game that he had to play. But after achieving it he reveals in the first verse, "And now I got my wish, I don't know if I can handle it."

The song was prophetic, an omen for his short-term and long-term future. From a commercial perspective, *Garden of Love* underachieved, though it sold five hundred thousand copies and went gold. It reached #17 on the *Billboard* R & B Albums chart and fizzled out at #83 on *Billboard*'s Top 200 Albums chart.

STREET SONGS

I had worked with the Bee Gees at the peak of their fame in 1977, but I was much closer to Rick when he was on the precipice of experiencing the height of his fame in 1981. Rick had been recording his "punk-funk for life" album, which he titled *Street Songs*. Besides writing, producing, and arranging it, he played bass, drums, guitar, horns, percussion, and timbales on the record. He loaded it up with a slew of celebrated guest artists and musicians, including Stevie Wonder, who played harmonica on "Mr. Policeman," a no-holds-barred indictment of police brutality, and "Fire and Desire," a duet with his protégé, Teena Marie, the most socially relevant song he had recorded.

Other guest performers included the Temptations (Dennis Edwards, Melvin Franklin, Richard Street, and Otis Williams), the Mary Jane Girls, Ja'Net Dubois and Lawrence Hilton-Jacobs (background singers), saxophonist Gerald Albright, drummer Narada Michael Walden, and the Stone

City Band: Levi Ruffin, synthesizers; Tom McDermott, guitar and percussion; Danny LeMelle, alto and tenor sax; Oscar Alston, bass; Clifford J. Ervin, flugelhorn; John Ervin, flute; and Fernando Harkless and Roy Poper, trumpet.

I thought it was the best album he had recorded. It sounded like it had tremendous crossover potential. Rick had become popular as a Black artist within the Black community and media, as well as music industry publications, but he wasn't on the radar of most mainstream media and audiences—meaning white people.

He was loyal and had a heartfelt respect and appreciation for the Black community and the Black media (radio, television, and newspapers) that supported him. He was especially grateful to Don Cornelius and *Soul Train*, who had embraced his notoriety and consistently booked him to support all his previous albums. But he wasn't happy and didn't want to settle for being just a Black success story. He sought more fame and wanted to bask in the milk-and-honey land of pop superstardom.

Every Black artist faced the same challenge, but Rick was less shy about vocalizing the flagrant racial disparities that existed in the industry. Black fame just didn't measure up to white fame on almost any level—especially in adding more digits to your bank account. He hired me to generate more mainstream media coverage for him, and I thought *Street Songs* would help accomplish that goal.

The album's debut single, "Give It to Me Baby," immediately climbed the charts. It became a #1 song on the R & B chart and stayed on top for five consecutive weeks. On the *Billboard* Hot 100, it only reached #40. The song showcased Rick's patented infectious funk and became popular in the clubs, reaching #38 on the charts. A provocative R-rated video supported the single, depicting him coming home late at night to seduce his lady. It was an auspicious beginning that set the tone for the rest of the project and became a go-to track on my personal playlist.

The song embodied the exact image Rick wanted to portray, which he captured in the album cover photo. His over-the-shoulder curly dreads, a tight black leather outfit with red thigh boots, a guitar straddling his body while he leaned against a streetlight pole on a vacant street late at night. It exuded his brazen, flamboyant, macho, sex-symbol persona. Rick was savvy about looking every bit the superstar and played it to the hilt whenever he could. His hair maintenance was impeccable. I never saw his hair without extensions.

He lived in Los Angeles on and off, and either rented a swanky house or stayed in one of the famed apartment-size bungalows in the Sunset Marquis Hotel or the Chateau Marmont in Hollywood. Both were bastions of legendary rock 'n' roll lore and a haven for celebrated artists, wild partying, drug and alcohol binges, and pure debauchery. They also had bars and restaurants that were frequented by the in-crowd and were hot late-night spots to hang, be seen, or just appear like you were part of the scene. When he wasn't holding court wherever he stayed, he cruised around town in a yellow Rolls Royce convertible with a camel top.

Rick was also a studio rat and spent hours upon hours recording, usually in the wee hours of the morning. It was common for him to record until dawn. I heard rumors that he once recorded for thirty-six hours straight without taking a break at the legendary Record Plant recording studios in Sausalito, California. The few times I visited him in the studios in LA, he created a party atmosphere. He worked diligently but liked to have a crew of onlookers and insider fans, and an array of drugs was always at arm's reach.

FALLING DREADS

Rick preferred that I set up interviews for him at his hotel. During this period, I had set up a late morning interview with Aldore Collier, who was the West Coast editor for *Jet*. Rick was intellectually bright, but I don't think he even knew how to spell *morning*. It was usually his bedtime, so 11 a.m. was the earliest possible. Aldore was a curmudgeon, a serious journalist who didn't seem happy covering self-obsessed artists of Rick's ilk, nor was he enamored of dealing with publicists like me, or just me.

Regardless, he was important, and I felt the need to cover the interview to make sure Rick was on his best behavior. He wasn't. I always arrived a little early to ward off any circumstances that required damage control. I called Rick's bungalow, and his bodyguard answered. He explained that Rick was running late and needed another fifteen to twenty minutes.

Aldore arrived in timely fashion, and I immediately apologized and told him Rick was running late. I asked him if he wanted a cup of coffee or something to drink. We shared some idle chit-chat, but I could tell it irritated him having to wait and he wasn't interested in being placated by me. After twenty minutes, I called again and was told to come up. The bungalows were behind the hotel, so they weren't visible from the street. You had to walk along curvy paths surrounded by the lush landscaping of bushes and trees.

Rick's favorite bungalow usually had one or two bedrooms, with a living room, dining area, patio area, and pool. We had to wait another five minutes for Rick to make a grand entrance. Finally, he comes strolling out wearing the hotel's full-length terrycloth robe and slippers, after making us wait for forty-five minutes. He wanted to do the interview outside on the patio adjacent to the pool. Aldore was recording it on a cassette recorder.

Rick sat in front of a table with a long, full-length white tablecloth over it. I seated Aldore across from him. Rick had a habit of running his fingers through his dreads, as if they had suspiciously moved themselves and obstructed his vision. On this day, as he was running his hands through them, several of his extensions fell out. I sat next to Rick, just close enough to extend my leg to slide the fallen dreads under the table.

Fortunately, Aldore was looking at his cassette player to make sure it was recording. He didn't see them fall out. It happened three times, and each time, I slid them under the table. Rick's bodyguard saw it happen. We were silently cracking up. Rick remained oblivious and apparently couldn't feel them falling out.

On my way out I momentarily reflected on how pathetic and silly I felt gingerly pushing Rick's dreads under the table to avoid an embarrassing optic for him. It was one of those absurd—albeit funny and introspective— moments when I asked myself, "So it has come to this—what in the hell are you doing with your life?" I never bothered to confront Rick, and preferred to forget it happened.

SUPER FREAKY SUCCESS

The response to Rick's album was even better than expected, and it kicked into another gear when they released the anthemic, sexually explicit single, "Super Freak," on July 10. It was an afterthought, the last song Rick recorded. Rick wanted to come up with a funky, new-wave-sounding, fun, cheeky song that embodied his playful and incorrigible persona. Like "Give It to Me Baby," it was cowritten and coproduced with his collaborator Alonzo Miller. It also featured background vocals by the Temptations and step-outs by Melvin Franklin, his uncle, whose signature bass was a staple on all the group's classic hits.

"Super Freak" reached #3 on *Billboard*'s R & B Singles chart and #16 on the Top 100 Pop charts. In a flash it became a summer smash. The third single from the album, "Ghetto Life," became a favorite and in November peaked on the R & B chart at #38. Another song that become a popular centerpiece of his live performances was the fiery romantic ballad, "Fire and Desire," which was over seven minutes long.

Street Songs was Rick's highest-charting pop album, peaking at #3. It stayed at #1 on the R & B Albums chart for twenty consecutive weeks and stayed on the chart for seventy-eight straight weeks. It sold three million copies in the US and eventually four million worldwide. He won an American Music Award for Best R & B Male, and two Grammy Award nominations in 1982, including Best Male Rhythm and Blues Vocal Performance. He was the first African American man nominated for Best Male Rock Vocal Performance (for "Super Freak").

Rick and his "punk funk" hits had ascended to the role of a frontrunner and crossover phenom in the R & B and funk movement, along with other prominent Black stars like Marvin Gaye, Lionel Richie, Stevie Wonder, Luther Vandross, Ray Parker Jr., and funksters George Clinton, Parliament, the Gap Band, the Brothers Johnson, and Cameo.

Although he didn't win either award, "Super Freak" became an even bigger hit eight years later when rapper MC Hammer sampled the melody and wrote new lyrics for his massive hit, "U Can't Touch This" (1990), without seeking Rick's approval. Rick's attorneys sued Hammer for copyright infringement and won. The case was settled out of court, but Rick and his collaborator Alonzo Miller were given songwriting credits, royalty rights, and a monetary settlement that was supposedly in seven figures.

At the 1991 Grammy Awards, "U Can't Touch This" was nominated for Record of the Year (the first rap song ever) and won for Best R & B Song and Best Rap Solo Performance. It also won for Best Rap Video and Best Dance Video at the 1990 MTV Video Music Awards and was a #1 record on *Billboard*'s R & B Singles chart. It was Rick's most successful cover. Since YouTube was launched, the "Super Freak" and "U Can't Touch This" videos have netted over 694 million cumulative views.

RICK TAKES ON MTV

A few months after *Street Songs* went platinum, a new rock 'n' roll music network emerged, MTV (Music Television). It officially launched on August 21, 1981. MTV announced its programming format would be AOR (album-oriented rock), and would include hard rock, new wave, and heavy metal videos (Paul McCartney, Adam Ant, Phil Collins, Bryan Adams, the Pretenders, Blondie, Eurythmics, Tom Petty and the Heartbreakers, Culture Club, Duran Duran, Van Halen, Bon Jovi, Def Leppard, Metallica) running

24/7 with five rotating VJs, including one Black VJ, J. J. Jackson. He was the only visible Black person on the network. A Black woman, Carolyn Baker, who became a longtime friend, was part of the founding group of executives and served as the original head of Talent and Acquisition.

Rick was one of the first Black artists from Motown to fight for the right to shoot videos. His brother LeRoi, who had taken over his management, convinced Motown to allocate a six-figure video budget in his recording contract that the label had previously refused to make available to him. Due to the success of *Street Songs* Motown finally agreed to fund videos for "Give It to Me Baby" and "Super Freak." Rick wanted MTV to air both videos, even though at the time they weren't airing any videos by Black artists.

He conceptualized his video concepts and collaborated with veteran director Nick Saxton to bring them to life. Saxton directed "Give It to Me Baby" and "Super Freak." He had also directed Michael Jackson's "Can't Stop 'Til You Get Enough" and Pat Benatar's "You Better Run." He was white and MTV-friendly, which Rick hoped would be assets to getting MTV to play his videos. Rick later used him direct videos for two of the Mary Jane Girls hits, "Candy Man" and "Boys." Nancy Leiviska headed up video at Motown and was instrumental in bringing his videos to fruition as well.

I found out there was a Billboard Music Video Conference being held in New York. A panel would discuss the influence of video in the music biz, and Gail Sparrow, a vice president of MTV, was on the panel. I called to see if there was an artist slot available and proposed that Rick fill it, and they agreed to add him. The plan was simple. I suggested Rick just pose a couple of questions that would hopefully spark a dialogue. Does MTV have a mandated policy against broadcasting videos featuring Black artists? And do they have any plans to air them in the future?

I wanted to position Rick as an ambassador and concerned Black artist and creator of Black music—and put a little pressure on MTV to publicly address their stand on playing Black videos. Not to Rick directly, but to all Black artists, record executives, and creatives who supported the broader commercial exploitation of Black music. Rick would get credit for opening a constructive dialogue within the industry and ultimately with the public, which might cause MTV to reconsider their programming format.

I stressed that he could not pontificate, advocate, mention his videos, or attack MTV. I consulted with LeRoi and Rick simultaneously to go over all the potential fallout and liabilities if Rick turned this into a personal vendetta against MTV. We didn't want to give them any added ammunition not to play Rick's videos or to make Rick a martyr. If handled correctly, it would generate some positive and meaningful mainstream media coverage. Crossing-over Rick into mainstream media was our shared goal. Rick said he was up to the task, understood the potential collateral plusses and damages, and promised to stay on script. We agreed to take the risk.

THE BATTLE WITH MTV BEGINS

The panel discussion was well attended. The moderator introduced everyone and handled the sequencing of when each panelist would speak. When it came time for Rick to speak, he started out on point, but within a few minutes went off script and pointedly attacked MTV's programming format for being discriminatory and racially biased. He took the exact stance we had told him to avoid, and his comments created a media firestorm contrary to my vision.

However, Rick knew he had touched a nerve and was reveling in the attention he was getting. In an interview with the *Los Angeles Times* shortly after the conference, he further accused MTV of being racist. By this time MTV had officially passed on playing his "Super Freak" video. In the same article, Bob Pittman, the founder of MTV, explained, "Rick James is great. So is Parliament Funkadelic, but we turned down Rick James because the consumer didn't define him as rock." He added, "But we do play black artists, Joan Armatrading, Gary US Bonds, and Jimi Hendrix, because they fit in with rock 'n' roll. So, it has nothing to do with race, but with sound."

The *New York Times Sunday Magazine* interviewed Rick along with a consortium of industry representatives for a piece they devoted to the issue.

Rick was also part of a group interview on ABC-TV's *Nightline with Ted Koppel*. But the more he talked about it, the more it became a personal vendetta for him against MTV. Behind the scenes he tried to rally support from other Black artists, but no one wanted to jeopardize their chances of getting their videos played on the network. He later made incendiary statements condemning Michael Jackson and Prince for not endorsing his efforts.

At one point, Gail Sparrow, MTV's VP in Talent and Acquisition, called to tell me that if Rick continued his public onslaught against them, they wouldn't consider programming any of his videos or airing the videos they had already passed on. Once he stopped, they would revisit airing Rick's videos in the future. As much as I wanted to silence Rick, I couldn't endorse her veiled threat. It was too late, and it made no sense to silence him and get nothing guaranteed in return.

The deeper concern for Rick and other Black artists was that the industry felt MTV had the power to revolutionize how music was being consumed. Being on MTV, as Rick pointed out, might generate thousands more record sales for him. By 1982, BET (Black Entertainment Television) was the only other option for Black artists, but it had only two million subscribers, just 20 percent of MTV's. And according to the RIAA (Record Industry of America Association), which maintains statistical data on the record industry, Black music (or urban contemporary music) only accounted for 2 percent of all record and cassette sales in the US.

Rick had sparked a controversy that spread throughout the industry and ensued for several years. MTV continued to hold its position and refused to play videos by "urban contemporary" Black artists in heavy rotation.

In 1983, the iconic rocker David Bowie was the first major Black or white artist to support Rick's views (without endorsing Rick), in an MTV on-air interview with VJ Mark Goodman. Bowie noted, "It occurred to me that, having watched MTV over the last few months, that it's a solid enterprise and it's got a lot going for it. I'm just floored by the fact that there are . . . so few Black artists featured on it. Why is that?" Then he pressed, "There seem to be a lot of Black artists making very good videos that I'm surprised aren't being used on MTV." Bowie used the same tone and sentiments I had scripted for Rick and was commended for speaking up.

Rob Tannenbaum and Craig Marks, in *I Want My MTV: The Uncensored Story of the Music Video Revolution*, chronicled the Goodman-Bowie interview. They also revealed that MTV's lone Black executive, Carolyn Baker, took credit for rejecting Rick's "Super Freak" video. She pointedly said, "It wasn't MTV that turned down 'Super Freak.' It was me, I turned it down. You know why? Because there were half-naked women in it, and it was a piece of crap. As a black woman, I did not want that representing my people as the first black video on MTV." Carolyn and I were friends, but at the time, I had no idea she had fought vigorously to block Rick's access to the channel.

Rick served as a sacrificial lamb in the fray, but his voice brought attention to the elephant in the room. Finally, it took Walter Yetnikoff, president of CBS Records, who was infuriated by MTV's rejections, to program Michael Jackson's videos, including one of his biggest hits "Beat It" (released in 1982). So, when CBS released Michael's #1 hit, "Billie Jean" he threatened to pull all CBS artists off the channel if they didn't change their policy and add "Billie Jean." He further declared, "I'm going to go public and fucking tell them about the fact you don't want to play music by a black guy." On March 10, MTV played the "Billie Jean" video and put it in heavy rotation.

Ironically, Michael's megastardom and worldwide fame as a Black artist revolutionized MTV's power and influence on contemporary music and culture. Other Black superstars, particularly the emergence of Black hip-hop superstars, helped to keep them relevant. In the years that followed, it remained challenging for R & B artists who weren't superstars to get their videos played on MTV.

$350 MILLION LAWSUIT

Rick kept me busy, and there was always some unforeseen crisis arising. Just four days after MTV launched, I got an urgent call from Rick. He was on tour and livid about a syndicated article published by UPI (United Press International) that had accused him of being bald. UPI was one of the biggest syndicated news wire services in the US. It had news bureaus in ninety-two countries and over six thousand media subscribers. A story syndicated on its wire service could break nationally in print, radio, and television.

On August 25, 1981, UPI ran a story titled "Bald Disguise" by Joan Hanauer: "Punk rock star Rick James disguised himself by taking off a wig instead of putting one on. With a bald head instead of his trademark shoulder-length braided wig, James eluded constables Sunday who were trying to tag him as he left a Dallas rock concert. James is being sued for $250,000 by a Denver production firm. The constables settled for seizing $50,000 worth of musical equipment. James is scheduled to appear Thursday in St. Petersburg, Fla."

Rick was beside himself; he wanted retribution and to clear his name. I felt the best way to disprove UPI's claims was to set up a press conference to show Rick wasn't bald and sue them for their erroneous reporting and the damage it had done to Rick's artist persona. I stressed that we had to get his lawyer involved and act as expeditiously as possible. We had to file the suit prior to the press conference, so it would show up in the public records. It was essential to show the media that the lawsuit was legitimate. His lawyer, Irv Shuman, lived in Buffalo, and I thought we could get the best media coverage if we held the press conference in New York. We agreed, and I put the press conference in motion.

I needed to get the legal jargon for what I could release to the press. Shelly Berger, a longtime friend of Berry Gordy's who served in several executive capacities at Motown, represented the label and was part of our brain trust. We arrived in New York in the evening and scheduled a meeting to complete our strategy. The biggest issue was to determine the monetary value of punitive damages to Rick's reputation and image suffered because of UPI's article. It needed to be significant enough to attract media attention and show Rick was serious.

Irv started off lowballing the figure, suggesting $15K, which Shelly and I both felt wasn't enough for anyone to care. At minimum, we thought it needed to be six figures, so we arbitrarily started throwing out numbers— $100K, $250K, $500K—and finally settled on $350,000. Irv started hyperventilating; he was nervous about protecting his reputation. He didn't feel Rick or his firm had the financial resources to mount a lawsuit of the magnitude we were proposing, especially against a highly funded corporation like UPI.

We gently encouraged Irv to relax. I stressed that we just wanted him to file the lawsuit. After we'd officially announced the lawsuit in a public forum and proved that Rick wasn't bald and was not the person the journalist claimed she saw leaving the venue, we would have achieved our primary mission. We wanted to see how the media and UPI responded to the suit, and then weigh our legal options to litigate. I had allowed one day to give us time to send out the photo news alert the next morning; I planned to hold the press conference the following day. It had to be close to 3 a.m. when we ended the meeting. I had written up the approved media release to distribute at the press conference. Irv would file the suit in the morning. I planned to make copies of the final media release to distribute at the press conference. We were all set.

The press conference went smoothly. Rick's demeanor was on point. He played the role of a relaxed victim, joked about the accusations of being bald, and began tugging on some of his dreads. He pulled them away from his head, on both sides, on the top, and a few from the back of his head. Then he asked everyone, "Do I look fucking bald to you?" He also addressed the Denver sound company's attempt to seize his music equipment in Dallas after he had defaulted on his required payments to them, which triggered the fracas. He explained there had been an accounting error and that he had settled with the company.

The latter was important to address, because we needed to reinforce to all his tour promoters and venues that he would deliver a technically sound first-class performance so they wouldn't pull any of his dates. We had about forty media personnel in attendance. UPI didn't bother countersuing or releasing a statement defending the information they had reported, which made it highly unlikely other music or entertainment journalists would contest the accuracy of Rick not being bald. They didn't cover the press conference either. The story had a short media cycle and vanished quickly, as we had hoped it would.

When Rick wasn't recording and touring, he loved to party. Hollywood was his playground, and he enjoyed hosting and curating his own experiential outings and parties. One of his favorite spots was the private El Privado Club, which was a stairway above Carlos and Charlie's, a popular Mexican restaurant for which manager Shep Gordon was one of the founding partners.

Both were magnets for celebrities and the in-crowd. El Privado was intimate, dark, had great DJs, and had a cut-loose, feel-free party atmosphere. Monday nights were always festive, and that was when Rick liked to hang. For a while, he and Eddie Murphy made it their spot. Several times right before closing (around 1:40 in the morning, to be out by 2 a.m.) Rick would invite twenty or more people from the remaining crowd to continue partying at his bungalow at the Sunset Marquis.

He extended personal invites to attractive ladies he swooned over. Those afterparties could last until four in the morning or until the hotel shut them down. I did my share of hanging with him but usually left between 2:30 and 3:00 a.m., so I missed experiencing how the marathon nights ended. I would get postmortem highlights from him or his bodyguards.

Le Dome, a French restaurant and haven for the music industry west of El Privado on Sunset Boulevard, had a great late bar scene. It was another spot that Rick liked and I frequented regularly on my own. A little east and a block off Sunset was Roy's, another cool restaurant. Roy's Restaurant was owned by Roy Silver, who managed Bill Cosby during his *I Spy* days. He served his version of American/Chinese fusion cuisine, but music executives and artists came for the friendly party atmosphere. Frances Davis, Miles Davis's first wife and a top model, dancer, and Broadway star in her own right, was the hostess. She knew everyone, and if she didn't like you, it was tough getting seated.

PARTYING WITH RICK AND MARVIN GAYE

For a while, Rick rented a lovely house not too far up the hill on Coldwater Canyon Road in Beverly Hills. He hosted a few parties there. He could be very gracious when he wanted to be. I brought a date with me to one of his parties. When we entered his house, he was standing in the foyer greeting his guests. I introduced her to him, and then she asked for directions to the restroom.

As soon as she walked away, Rick asked me if she was my girlfriend. I said, "No she's not, we're just dating." He responded, "Then give her to me!" I just laughed and told him he was crazy, adding, "I don't own her and she's not mine to give to you or anybody else. If you want to take a shot, don't do it in front of me." We had many playful exchanges like that, but I knew he was dead serious. Rick had nicknamed me Herpes, which I despised. As I was walking away, he said, "Come on, Herpes." When he looked back, I said, "Fuck you." I caught up with my date and warned her to be leery of Rick cornering her in the event we got separated. The highlight of the party for me was sharing a long conversation with Marvin Gaye. I had met him several times, albeit briefly, while I worked at Motown. I began to introduce myself, but he said he remembered me, which was a pleasant surprise.

We started talking about music and what he was up to, and I was dying to ask him about the dark theme of his double album *Here, My Dear*, which was his most recent album release. The songs focused on his divorce and subsequent relationship with Anna Gordy, Berry Gordy's sister. He was very transparent and explained that writing those songs was a cathartic process for him, and that he needed to exorcise those feelings. And he emphasized that it didn't matter to him whether people liked the record or if it was commercially successful. He had two albums left on his contract with Motown, so he stretched *Here, My Dear* into two albums, hoping to fulfill his legal commitment so he could exit the label.

Because of his divorce, he wouldn't get to keep any of the money, and he didn't want Motown to reap any further financial benefits from his music. It touched me that he took the time to be so transparent. Talking to him was the highlight of the party for me. Most critics panned the album, but eventually it was certified platinum. But he wasn't able to leave Motown at that point. His final album for the label was *In My Lifetime*.

THE DOWNSIDE OF FAME

Rick could never repeat the four million sales of *Street Songs*, and his ascension to fame as a solo artist had peaked in just three years, from 1978 to 1981. He was thirty-three. However, in subsequent years he expanded his superstar reputation as a hit-making songwriter and producer and continued to sustain his credibility as a top headlining live attraction.

Rick was also one of my most loyal clients, and although we butted heads from time to time, he never stiffed me on my retainer fee. He involved me with all the artists that he developed and used his platform to launch them in the same way he had done for Teena Marie. Rick and Teena continued to collaborate and perform together, but Teena kept her recording deals separate.

The year after *Street Songs* came out was one of his busiest. The Temptations, who sang backgrounds on "Super Freak," had reunited and were releasing their new album, *Reunion*. Their new configuration comprised seven members led by three of the group's most notable lead singers, David Ruffin, Eddie Kendricks, and Dennis Edwards. Rick wrote and produced the album's debut single, "Standing on the Top," and coproduced the album with Berry Gordy and Smokey Robinson. It ignited their comeback, reached #6 on *Billboard*'s R & B Singles chart, and peaked at #55 on the Pop charts.

Rick also followed up with his own album, *Throwin' Down*. The album's second and top single, "Dance wit' Me" (released April 22, 1982), featured a vibes solo intro by the legendary Roy Ayers. It peaked at #3 on the *Billboard* R&B Singles chart, and #64 on the Pop charts. It also reached #7 on *Billboard*'s Dance chart.

Besides Roy Ayers, *Throwin' Down* featured guest appearances by the Temptations, Teena Marie and Jefferson Airplane/Starship lead vocalist Grace Slick, Jean Carn, Lawrence Hilton-Jacobs, and Patti Brooks, among others. Motown released Rick's sixth album on May 13. The album was certified gold and received an American Music Award nomination for Favorite Soul/R&B Album. Rick supported the album with a thirty-six-city national concert tour titled "Rick James and the Stone City Band."

Rick was reaping some residual mainstream media interest from his success with *Street Songs* and the added attention from his flap with MTV, but he was becoming more irresponsible. I secured interest from CBS-TV national news and invested considerable time in trying to schedule a crew to interview him prior to one of his concert engagements. We decided to schedule it in Chicago during the first week of his tour, a perfect time to promote the rest of his tour.

On the day of the interview, I went back and forth on the phone with the *CBS News* segment producer because Rick kept pushing back the time of the interview. The segment required an interview and footage from his concert performance. Rick kept the crew waiting for eight hours. The producer was extremely patient, but with each delay he became more furious—and rightfully so. The interview had moved from late afternoon until after the show. Finally, the producer gave up and left, so we had blown the opportunity.

I sent Rick a curt letter detailing sixty tour interviews that my office had set up, including the CBS-TV interview, all of which he had canceled. I requested a follow-up call. Our calls could be light, candid, and humorous or intensely heated and laced with dueling *motherfuckers* and *nigger this or that* rants. Rick had a penchant for trying to bully and intimidate people, and if you didn't stand up for yourself, you were giving him the license to continue a pattern of verbal abuse. He didn't intimidate me, nor was I afraid of him. I spoke bluntly and as "street" as required to get my message across. In fact, he tapped into a level of street and Blackness I didn't know I had. I used to shock myself. In a thirty-minute combative rant with him, I said *motherfucker* enough to last for a year. And he used it twice as much as I did.

Rick started our follow-up call by whining and complaining about me not getting him enough crossover media. This was days after he was a no-show for the CBS interview. Of the sixty interviews he didn't do, roughly half were major-market mainstream newspapers. I was seething and adamantly said, "If you want to reach white people, then stop canceling the fucking interviews. You're paying me to get you media coverage. I'm delivering. And you have the gall to accuse me of not doing right by you—that's fucking bullshit. If that's how you feel, fire me." And I continued, "You're being irresponsible, unprofessional, and burning bridges you need to cross—and you may not get a second chance to do. Either we both win or we both lose."

Different iterations of this same kind of conversation happened all the time. I didn't look forward to them, but we gave each other the latitude to express our uncensored views. We usually reached an accord and always ended on a positive note. Sometimes that positive note ended with Rick trying to get the last word, "Hey Hervey, fuck you." And I would say, "Hey Rick, fuck you back." Next time we saw or talked to each other, we started fresh.

THE MARY JANE GIRLS

Rick stayed in constant motion musically and was intent on developing an R & B, soul, funk female vocal group. He originally planned to launch a solo career for Joanne "JoJo" McDuffie, an incredibly gifted singer who performed in the Stone City Band. But it morphed into a group concept, the Mary Jane Girls, which he signed to Motown. He got the inspiration for their name from his early hit single "Mary Jane."

He wrote, produced, arranged, and styled the group's image to comprise a Black street-savvy girl (JoJo McDuffie), a Black supermodel (Candice Ghant), a Latin valley girl (Cheri Wells, later replaced by Yvette "Corvette" Marin), and a white dominatrix (Kimberly Wuletich). He asked me to do their PR. I already knew JoJo and liked her a lot. The other girls were amiable enough, and Rick played a major role in introducing them to the public. Their eponymous debut album was released by Gordy/Motown on April 13, 1983.

It yielded three hits on *Billboard*'s R & B Singles charts—"Candy Man" (#23), "All Night Long" (#11), and "Boys" (#29)—and they packaged all three on one disco single that went to #7 on *Billboard*'s Dance chart. "All Night Long" became their biggest hit and helped get them on *Soul Train* and *American Bandstand*, and they got a lot of urban media coverage.

The album made it into the Top 10 on *Billboard*'s R & B Albums chart, reaching #6, and made some inroads on *Billboard*'s Top 200 Albums chart, peaking at #56. Rick recorded the entire album using JoJo and two other veteran singers, the Water Sisters: Julia Tillman Waters and Maxine Willard Waters, who sang background vocals on several of Rick's albums. The other three singers Rick picked for the look and brand image he wanted for the group.

Rick was touring annually, and on August 5, 1983, Gordy/Motown released his seventh album, *Cold Blooded*. He was dating actress Linda Blair, who had become famous with her head-turning performance in the hit film *The Exorcist*. She inspired the album title, which was also the album's first single. Other standout singles were "U Bring the Freak Out," "Ebony Eyes" (featuring Smokey Robinson), "P.I.M.P. the S.I.M.P." (featuring Grandmaster Flash), and "Tell Me (What You Want)," featuring Billy Dee Williams.

"Ebony Eyes" was an alluring and smooth ballad featuring Smokey and Rick sharing lead vocals throughout the song. It was another favorite of mine and became one of his most notable hits, reaching #22 on the *Bill-*

board R & B Singles chart and #46 on their Hot 100 Pop chart. The album sold five hundred thousand copies.

PRINCE'S COLD-BLOODED PRANK

Rick's "Cold Blooded" tour also featured Teena Marie and the Mary Jane Girls. A few weeks into the summer leg of the tour, Rick had an engagement at the Universal Amphitheater on August 21, 1983. It was one of the top concert venues in Los Angeles and they regularly booked the industry's superstar headlining artists. The concert sold out, and there was an electric energy in the crowd, which was anxiously waiting for Rick. The Stone City Band opened all the shows, so Rick could make a star entrance and warm up the audience.

I was standing in the center of the venue in the aisle above the orchestra seated sections. Suddenly, I looked toward the far side of theater and saw Prince being carried, cradled in his arms like a baby, by Big Chick, his famous blond, white, muscular, 6'8", nearly four-hundred-pound bodyguard. Prince had been making grand entries cradled by Big Chick at several major events. Some of the crowd noticed him and began roaring and jumping out of their seats. They were approaching where I was standing, headed toward the front of the theater.

Prince had meticulously planned his arrival to upstage Rick and ruin the opening of his performance. By the time Prince got to the front row, the whole theater knew it. Rick was walking on the stage and had presumed the crowd was roaring for him. Before Rick got to the center of the stage, Prince's bodyguard lowered him to his seat, and Rick figured out what all the extra hoopla was about.

He continued to work through his opening song. A few minutes later, Prince's bodyguard stood up, picked Prince up out of his seat, cradled him in his arms, and walked out of the theater the same way he came in. The crowd went crazy. Rick saw him leave but never addressed it with the crowd. I knew he was fuming, but he didn't bring it up after the show. It would have gone viral in seconds today, but the media never reported on it. It was one of those rare unbelievable experiences you had to witness to appreciate. Prince duped him and got the last laugh.

In the next two years, Rick's relevancy took an extreme nosedive. In 1984, Motown released his first greatest hits album, titled *Reflections*. It comprised ten of the biggest hits he recorded from 1977 to 1984, as well as three unreleased tracks, "17," "Oh What a Night," and "You Turn Me On." The album attracted little fanfare.

The bright spot of the year came in October, when Gordy Records released "In My House" as the lead single for the Mary Jane Girls' second album, *Only for You*. Rick wrote and produced the entire album. "In My House" became their biggest hit and only Top 40 hit. It reached #3 on *Billboard*'s R&B Singles chart and peaked at #7 on the Hot 100 Singles chart, spending weeks in the Top 40. It also went to #1 on *Billboard*'s Dance chart.

On Valentine's Day 1985, Gordy/Motown released the Mary Jane Girls' *Only for You*. The momentum of the first single carried over and set up the release of album's second single, "Wild and Crazy Love." It rose to #10 on *Billboard*'s R & B Singles chart and #3 on the Dance charts. It was their last album release. They recorded one more album, but Motown never released it.

Around the same time, Rick launched two other artists that he developed, as well as writing and producing their albums. Process and the Doo Rags was a young, male, '50s inspired doo-wop group that he signed to Columbia Records. Their debut album was titled *Too Sharp*. He also discovered singer Val Young ("Lady V"), whom he branded as a "Black Marilyn Monroe." Her debut album, *Seduction*, was released by Motown.

On May 21, 1985, Gordy/Motown released Rick's *Glow*, which peaked at #50 on the *Billboard* Top 200 Albums chart. The "Glow" single received more traction. It became Rick's tenth single to reach the Top 10 on *Bill-*

board's R & B Singles chart and reached #5. He also scored his second #1 on *Billboard*'s Dance chart. It would be his last.

RICK GETS ON MTV

Rick and Eddie Murphy had become good friends, and they partied and hung out together. Eddie was already a television megastar after his four-year run as a cast member on *Saturday Night Live* (1980–84). He was also becoming a major film and box office attraction after debuting with three major film successes, *48 Hours*, costarring Nick Nolte (1982), *Trading Places* (1983), and *Beverly Hills Cop* (1984).

Eddie wanted to test the waters as a recording artist and win a $100,000 bet Richard Pryor had made that he couldn't sing. He enlisted Rick to write and produce his first album, *How Could It Be*, which Columbia Records released in September 1985. Rick wrote, produced, arranged, and was a featured vocalist on the song. He also appeared in the video.

On September 4, 1985, MTV premiered the video for the song, which marked the first time Rick finally appeared on the channel. On September 15, Eddie hosted the MTV Video Awards. Rick attended the MTV afterparty, and he was featured in their post-party news segment covering all the celebrities who attended. The single peaked on *Billboard*'s Top 100 (#2), R & B (#8), and Dance/Electronic (#7) charts. It was also an international success in several European countries and Australia, selling one million copies and going platinum. The album was certified gold.

Rick was entering an inactive phase of his career and didn't have another album looming on the horizon. I had started shifting my attention toward management. We had worked together for six years, but since there was nothing to publicize or promote, we decided to end our business relationship. We stayed friendly, running into each other occasionally and taking the time to catch up and talk briefly from time to time.

He continued to record and perform, but his drug use and lifestyle began generating more headlines than his music. Then out of the blue, like a gift from heaven, in 1990 Rapper MC Hammer released his smash single, "U Can't Touch This." It indirectly put Rick back in the limelight, at least from a media perspective. He was paid handsomely due to MC Hammer's copyright infringement of Rick's "Super Freak."

In 1993, I read a sordid story about Rick and his girlfriend being arrested for kidnapping a young woman and torturing her for three days while on a crack binge in his bungalow at the Chateau Marmont. As crazy as Rick could be, I never fathomed that his life would spiral out of control to that extent. I was aware of him being incarcerated and having a stroke, and I heard he supposedly stopped using cocaine.

In 1996, after he was released from prison, I ran into him a few times in Los Angeles. He invited me to attend a performance he was doing with Billy Preston at the Red Parrot nightclub in Beverly Hills. Billy was a phenomenal talent I had known for years. Rick said they were collaborating on writing new material and putting a band together. He also worked with Andraé Crouch, who was a mentor to him. He was an amazing musician who suffered from drug addiction as well.

I went to see their show, and it was depressing. They were just a shell of who they had once been, and it was hard to watch. Another time I ran into him at Le Dome. He told me I should manage him, and we should talk, but he was high as a kite. We hugged briefly; I gave him my number and told him I'd meet with him. He never called, and I was happy because in my heart I knew I wouldn't be able to represent him.

In 2004, during the second season of the *Chappelle's Show*, I cracked up when I saw the "Charlie Murphy True Hollywood Stories" sketch on his show. The sketches and depictions of Rick were gut-wrenchingly hilarious. I applauded Chappelle for reviving his musical legacy, but seeing Rick on camera was disheartening. He looked noticeably unhealthy—worse than the last time I saw him. I feared the momentum jolt and fresh swig of fame from Chappelle would make him believe he could time-travel and recapture all the superstar trappings of his halcyon days. Unfortunately for Rick, fame and drugs were inseparable.

THE FUNERAL

Six months later, on the morning of August 6, 2004, Rick died at age fifty-six in his Oakwood apartment in Toluca Lake, California. Like everybody else, I saw and read about it on the news as soon as it was announced. I presumed drugs must have contributed, but it wasn't until an autopsy was done over a month later that it came out he had nine different drugs in his system at the time of death, but not enough of any one drug to cause his death, according to the coroner's report.

I attended his funeral service at Forest Lawn Memorial Park in Los Angeles. It was a massive production attended by tons of celebrities: Stevie Wonder, Louis Farrakhan, Berry Gordy, Teena Marie, the Mary Jane Girls, Chaka Khan, and Jermaine Jackson, to name a few. There were many video tributes from family and friends, as well as personal testimonies. After about two hours sitting at the funeral, I pushed my flight back, thinking it would allow enough time for me to stay until the end. I was wrong. After three hours, I had to leave.

Sitting there reflecting on our time together, I felt culpable for fueling his obsession with fame. I remembered thinking that maybe if he reached a comfortable level of fame, he'd experience enough personal happiness and comfort to bury his demons. I'm not sure Rick got his fifteen minutes, but he did make it to the big time. He earned enough fame to abuse it. And he experienced what happens when you let it control you instead of vice versa.

I later heard that his funeral lasted for five hours. Even in death, that was so Rick. I imagined he'd flash one of his patented braggadocious smirks and proclaim, "So what if it's too long? I'm Rick James, bitch!"

7

DREAM BEYOND
THE GLASS CEILING

As a publicist, I was peripherally involved in my clients' potential revenues and expenses, such as performance fees, television appearances, photographer and glam squad fees, and travel and accommodations, including airfares, hotels, and ground transportation. Once I became a manager, I assembled teams—usually a business manager, accountant, lawyer, talent agent, publicist, and marketing, promotion, and social media services, which played an integral role in managing and sustaining the financial livelihood of the artist or brand. Some artists also rely on their manager to oversee their finances. They may even give them power of attorney to collect fees and disburse and distribute funds to professional and personal service companies.

When you've served in both roles, you understand the drastic difference in responsibilities. In the late 1970s, I represented Andraé Crouch, an artist revered as the "father of contemporary gospel music." Andraé was the first and only contemporary gospel artist I represented as both publicist and manager. We sustained our business relationship for over two decades, which stands as the longest client relationship of my career.

In that span, he also became a cherished friend. We traveled the world together for his performances throughout Europe, Japan, Africa, Indonesia, and across the US. He flew to New York to attend my wedding. When

I got hit by a drunk driver while visiting a friend in Geneva, Switzerland, (November 2006) and was laid up in the hospital for four days, he and his sister Sandra called to check up on me. We weren't working together at the time, so the gesture reflected a bond we had built that superseded our professional relationship.

When I met Andraé, he was thirty-seven years old and had captured at least ten minutes of fame as one of the most famous Black contemporary gospel artists in the world. White Christians accounted for 70–80 percent of his core fan base, which was an anomaly for a Black gospel artist in the mid-1960s and '70s. That didn't make him a mainstream superstar, but he was deservedly acknowledged as a trailblazer who broke down many systemic racial barriers for artists of color in the gospel genre.

Andraé began his professional career when he was in his late teens, and over the next two decades he overshot his humble beginnings to become a seminal music figure. Like most artists, he started off as a struggling songwriter and singer, jumping from one group to another to find his artistry. Things changed rapidly after he formed Andraé Crouch and the Disciples with fellow musicians Perry Morgan, Reuben Fernandez, and Bili Thedford—his career took off.

Audrey Mieir, a popular Southern California Christian minister, composer, and sponsor of up-and-coming Christian artists, introduced Andraé to Tim and Hal Spencer. They founded Manna Music, a Christian publishing company, and secured the rights to "The Blood Will Never Lose Its Power." They also brokered an introduction to Ralph Carmichael, a noted Christian songwriter who had founded Light Records. Carmichael signed the group to Light Records, a division of Lexicon Music, distributed by Word Music. Word was the industry's leading distributor of contemporary Christian music. Andraé's relationships with Manna and Light played a significant role in his rise to stardom.

In 1968, Light released the Disciples' debut album, *Take the Message Everywhere*. They began touring extensively throughout the southern Bible Belt states and later across the country for over a year. They recorded six albums—*Keep on Singin'* (1971), *Soulfully* (1972), *Live at Carnegie Hall* (1973), *Take Me Back* (1975), *This Is Another Day* (1976), and *Live in London* (1978)—and won three Grammy Awards for Best Contemporary Gospel Album (1975–79). Andraé's biggest hits, "The Blood Will Never Lose Its Power," "Through It All," "Bless His Holy Name," "Soon and Very Soon," "Jesus Is the Answer," and "My Tribute," resonated with his predominantly white contemporary audience and fueled the group's global popularity.

Andraé was carrying the torch ignited by Thomas A. Dorsey and Mahalia Jackson, the preeminent and most influential gospel artists in the twentieth century. Dorsey was a singer, pianist, and composer recognized as an influential figure in the development of early blues and twentieth-century gospel music. He established a voice for the African American community in modern music and moved gospel music beyond the church and into the streets.

In addition, Dorsey brought Mahalia Jackson to the forefront of gospel music. Jackson is one of the most respected female vocalists of modern time and is affectionately referred to as the "queen of gospel." She was also a prominent and tireless activist during the civil rights movement. During her forty-year career she performed worldwide for integrated and secular audiences. She sold more than twenty-two million recordings and illuminated gospel music in Black churches throughout the country.

In 1972, Andraé made history as the first Black gospel artist to appear on the *Tonight Show Starring Johnny Carson*. In June, the Disciples performed at the inaugural "Explo '72," an evangelistic conference referred to by media as the "Christian Woodstock" and the most celebrated concert event of the 1970s Jesus movement. It was held at the Cotton Bowl in Dallas, Texas, and attracted 180,000 white Christians. The Disciples were the only Black artists on a bill that featured Billy Graham, Johnny Cash, and Kris Kristofferson.

In 1973, Andraé and the Disciples became the first gospel group to perform for sold-out crowds at New York City's Carnegie Hall. His performance was recorded and became his first live album, *Live at Carnegie Hall*.

It led to a second sold-out engagement six years later. In 1975, the Disciples joined evangelist Billy Graham's weeklong Crusade at the seventeen-thousand-seat Pit Arena in Albuquerque, New Mexico. Graham was the most influential live Christian attraction in the world.

In 1979, President Jimmy Carter and First Lady Rosalynn Carter hosted the Black Music Association's inaugural concert event at the White House. Andraé was among a celebrated list of headlining performers that included Chuck Berry, Billy Eckstine, Evelyn "Champagne" King, and Sara Jordan Powell. That same year, Andraé became the first gospel artist to have an album released by secular and gospel record labels, when Elektra Records and Light Records released his second solo album, *I'll Be Thinking of You*. A year after Andraé and the Disciples ended their relationship, Andraé became the first gospel artist to appear on the fifth season of NBC's hit show *Saturday Night Live* (1980). The following year he appeared in a cameo role as himself on the eighth season of *The Jeffersons* (1981-82) in the episode "Men of Cloth."

Andraé was thrilled about Elektra distributing his album to the secular marketplace. He reached out, hoping I could develop a PR strategy to help him cross over and reach a more mainstream audience—without alienating or giving up his core base. Andraé felt restricted and believed his style and approach to gospel music had universal appeal beyond his core gospel fans. He sought the freedom and financial support to prove it.

Cross over is standard record industry jargon; it is not genre-specific, it's simply crossing over from one genre to another. It's usually associated with niche artists who are seeking mainstream audience acceptance and a bigger piece of the revenue pie. No matter how you cut it, going mainstream usually equates to appealing to white audiences, which account for most of the US population, and every R & B and jazz artist I represented aspired to cross over.

I wasn't familiar with Andraé's music and wasn't knowledgeable about the infrastructure of the gospel music industry, but I knew that crossing over could be a costly endeavor. Andraé felt it wasn't part of Light's business strategy. Although he was a gospel superstar, his record sales never flourished enough for him to have leverage with Light. In fact, Light used Andraé's lack of sales against him to justify spending less money marketing and promoting his albums. Regardless of the genre, there's a never-ending love-and-hate relationship between record labels and artists about money. Sales revenue is the currency that fuels an artist's power and creative freedom.

After listening to Andraé share his plight, it was evident that even with all his exposure and success with white Christian audiences as a live performer, he had limited to access to the prominent contemporary-Christian radio stations. These stations had the most impact on record sales, and without registering a string of hit singles on Christian radio, his sales would remain tepid.

I thought Andraé was a bit past his prime to cross over. And while his artist- and business-related challenges were daunting and out of my control, they weren't drastically different from other Black R & B and jazz artists that I'd represented. The number of hit records and the sales threshold an artist has are necessary media bait—the media won't bite if the numbers for either are paltry. But as a publicist I was always looking for a backstory, whether it was human interest, rags to riches, a major rehab, against all odds, or an angle that just pulls your heartstrings.

Andraé's backstory was emotionally moving and touched me. Andraé and his twin sister, Sandra, were born in San Francisco. They were the second and third children of Benjamin and Catherine Crouch, who married in 1939. The first child, Benjamin Jr., had been born two years earlier. His parents were young entrepreneurs who founded a Christian street ministry while working at the Macedonia Church of God in Christ in Val Verde, California. They preached at local jails, hospitals, and drug rehabilitation programs. They also owned and operated two Crouch Cleaners locations and a restaurant in Los Angeles. In 1951, they founded Christ Memorial Church in a garage with a small group of parishioners and later moved it to a church in Pacoima, in the San Fernando Valley. His father was the pastor, and his mother managed Andraé and Sandra early in their careers.

When Andraé was eleven, he accompanied his father to a neighboring church, which had invited him to deliver a sermon as a guest pastor. After he began the sermon and had stirred up the congregation, it was time for some music, but the piano player had not shown up. Andraé was sitting attentively in the front row when his father peered at him and asked, "If God gave you the power to play piano, would you serve and be loyal to him?" He responded, "Yes, Dad, I would." Andraé had dyslexia as a child and had never played the piano. Encouraged by his father and the congregation singing, he sat down and instantly began playing. Miraculously, God anointed him. From that day on, without any formal musical training, he learned to play and write songs by ear. He shared that experience hundreds of times, and it never ceased to amaze me.

At fourteen, he wrote his first song, but he didn't like it. He crinkled it up and tossed it into a trash can. Luckily, his sister Sandra witnessed the incident, reached in, and retrieved it. Sandra read the lyrics and encouraged him to play the song. He titled it "The Blood Will Never Lose Its Power." It later became his first hit record and the most covered song in his career.

He had a great human-interest angle, was already a star and a gospel legend, and was attempting to make history by becoming a mainstream star as well. Andraé was a natural and engaging storyteller. I figured if I was going to take a shot on a gospel artist, I might as well roll the dice and bet my chips on the father of gospel music. Andraé acknowledged he wasn't expecting to become a crossover star overnight, which was key. He promised to mentor me in the nuances and pitfalls of the gospel industry. We hashed out an agreement, and I started working on his album *Don't Give Up*.

Musically it sounded phenomenal, but I wasn't convinced that it had the breakout singles needed to secure airplay on urban radio stations. The supportive cast of guest artists was impressive: bassist Louis Johnson (from the Brothers Johnson), the Winans, the McCrarys, bassist Hadley Hockensmith (formerly a Disciple), Greg Phillinganes, Steve Porcaro, David Paich, and Paulinho Da Costa, among the thirty musicians and singers that contributed to the album.

Lyrically the songs dealt with abortion, a young man who seeks fame in Hollywood and becomes a prostitute, and inspirational and prophetic songs—daring and progressive real-life pathos that most gospel artists wouldn't touch for fear of recrimination by the church. Andraé asked me to attend a few meetings with him before the record came out. One was with Lenny Waronker, the president of Warner Bros. He expressed enthusiasm about Andraé being on the label and pledged to support his album.

Andraé had a full professional support team behind him, and I was the only Black, except for Sandra. She was his partner in crime and protector, who wielded considerable influence over how he maneuvered. Bill Maxwell (formerly a Disciple) was his coproducer; David Del Sesto, the road manager; Will Leopold, the manager; Tony Tosti, the business manager; Marshall Resnick, his talent agent at William Morris; Gary Greenberg, his lawyer; and Marcia Piserchio, his longtime personal assistant. They were all seasoned and respected veterans in their areas of expertise, and I felt comfortable with them. Marcia was my primary contact to access Andraé.

Don't Give Up received moderate media coverage, mostly in Black media and contemporary Christian publications. There were gospel purists who felt he had sold out. Others felt his decision to do a secular record was courageous and an artistic triumph. It wasn't a commercial success, but ironically it won a Grammy Award for Best Contemporary Soul Gospel Album.

Andraé was rarely idle. When he wasn't writing and recording for himself, he collaborated with many other talented gospel artists, including BeBe and CeCe Winans, Walter and Tramaine Hawkins, Jessy Dixon (whom he brought to Light Records), the Clark Sisters, Wintley Phipps, Anointed, Israel Houghton, Donnie McClurkin, the Johnson Sisters, the Katina Brothers, Táta Vega, Reba Rambo, and Take 6. Andraé also contributed as a songwriter-producer on Sandra's solo albums.

He signed the Winans to his production company, and coproduced (with Bill Maxwell) *Introducing the Winans*, their debut album on Light Records. Their business relationship was short-lived, but they built a lifelong friendship. Andraé followed up *Don't Give Up* with *Finally*, which showcased more spiritual-rooted worship songs, including "My Tribute (To God Be the Glory)," which became one of his standards.

Amid everything that was going on, Andraé asked me to manage him. I viewed it as another risk but an opportunity to expand my brand identity and skill set. I had barely settled into the role when we butted heads over him accepting a booking at the Sun City Resort South Africa, a luxury destination that South Africa business and real estate tycoon Sol Kerzner founded in 1979. He didn't consult with me, and his timing was horrible. The struggle against apartheid had become a watershed issue internationally. The United Nations and the Organization of African Unity (OAU) had launched a cultural boycott barring any artistic collaboration with the racist apartheid state and had imposed sanctions intended to isolate the inhumane regime.

The OAU blacklisted and denounced all artists who performed in South Africa (which, of course, included Sun City) during the boycott. It aggressively publicized the artists' names with the intention of generating negative media coverage in an attempt to make the artists unattractive to venues that didn't want to risk the threat of potential financial and media fallout for booking them.

I gave Andraé a thorough account of all the liabilities he'd face and argued that whatever he was getting paid wasn't worth getting blacklisted and tarnishing his reputation. He insisted he was making the trip as a missionary, and it was a calling from God. Ignoring my advice, he did the date. They blacklisted him, and the negative backlash occurred immediately.

It took me several months of painstakingly stretching the truth to explain that Andraé had naively misunderstood his dual role as an artist and missionary and didn't realize he wasn't exempt from honoring the boycott. I had to submit an official letter of apology from him to the OAU, which was made available to the media. Upon acceptance of his apology, the OAU removed his name from the list.

BUSTED

Later that year, a couple of weeks before Thanksgiving, I arrived at my office on a Friday morning. My partner, Bob Gibson, had a spacious home, above Sunset off Doheny Drive, hidden away in the West Hollywood Hills, which doubled as our office. It was just Bob, his longtime associate Patti Mitsui, and me. Patti was much more than an assistant; she was the glue, handling the company's finances and managing the day-to-day operation of the company. And she served as a publicist on all of Bob's accounts.

Bob, planted on the living room couch, welcomed me by saying, "You'll never guess which one of our clients got busted last night." It wasn't our intent, but for a stretch of time it felt like we were a rehab publicity firm for superstar artists beleaguered with drug addictions and problems. I quickly ran off our most infamous artists with drug problems: Rick James, Natalie Cole, David Crosby, and Stephen Stills. He said nope to all of them.

So I surrendered: "Who?" He said, "It's Andraé, and the story is all over the news. Possession of a controlled substance, probably cocaine." I was speechless, and even more dismayed that neither Andraé nor Sandra had forewarned me. I immediately called him. Andraé never answered his home phone, so his assistant put him on. He confirmed that the police had pulled him over while he was driving back to his apartment on the Marina Freeway. They said he was driving erratically, which he denied, and asked if he had been drinking. One of the cops was peering into the car with a flashlight and saw sprinkles of white powder on the backseat of his Mercedes. Andraé said it was just residue from a box of Cambridge diet powder cannisters he had been given. The cops were suspicious and presumed it was cocaine. They told him to get out of his vehicle and minutes later arrested him.

I prodded him for more clarity: "Are you saying the police falsely arrested you?" He said, "Yes." They jailed him after 2 a.m., kept him for three or four hours, and then released him on bail. He didn't seem to know what they had charged him with. I asked him if he had spoken to an attorney yet, and he said no. I suggested he get some rest and told him I'd try to find a criminal attorney who specialized in DUI cases to represent him.

I shared the gist of the call with Bob, and he suggested I try Bob Shapiro, a high-profile attorney who had a reputation for representing big-name celebrities charged for DUIs and drug possession. He had handled drunk driving cases for Johnny Carson, Christian Brando, and several others. And he was part of the "dream team" of lawyers that represented O. J. Simpson in his murder case. I called and left a message with a brief explanation about why I was reaching out.

In the interim, I read the UPI wire story, which noted, "The singer was stopped by sheriff's deputies on the Marina Freeway at 2:40 a.m. for driving erratically, and officers who searched his car found the drugs inside. He was arrested and was released after paying a $2,500 bail several hours later." Within an hour Shapiro called me. I gave him the information Andraé had shared with me. He agreed to investigate the case and would call to get specific details from the police report. He promised to get back to me shortly.

A few hours passed. I called to find out if he planned to get back to me that day, so I could decide when to release an official statement. When we connected, he immediately asked, "What were you planning to announce in the statement?" I said, "Hopefully, Andraé's innocence and that he was falsely arrested." He stated succinctly, "The police report states they arrested him after one of officers did a body search, reached into the front pocket of his pants, and found a vial with cocaine in it."

Luckily for Andraé, it only contained 0.2 grams. That's the minimum amount California state law requires to prosecute a person for possession of a controlled substance, such as cocaine. He noted that the court had the option to prosecute, but many judges would be reluctant to do so. The consensus view was they felt convictions were tougher to get based on the minimum, especially for first-time offenders—like Andraé.

He also advised me that a few local ministers, community leaders, and Jesse Jackson had reached out to the LA district attorney's office to give character references for Andraé. As a result, they had dropped the charges and closed his case. He informed me that the courts normally release a brief media statement announcing their ruling when they drop charges. He noted that there was nothing else he could do. I thanked him profusely for his help and advice.

I felt a sense of relief for Andraé, but thought it was unconscionable that he had blatantly lied to me about what happened. When we spoke, I openly expressed my ire regarding his cavalier breach of trust. He didn't offer any apology or explanation as to why he lied. I wasn't feeling empathetic, but I was concerned about his bust spiraling into a sensational global media story.

The initial damage was irreversible. Unlike the fallout most pop or R & B artists would face, his arrest as a gospel artist could have monumental and disastrous long-term repercussions on his career. I knew the court's statement about the charges being dropped would pale compared to the sensational and visceral headlines his arrest had garnered. I called Andraé again to hopefully get the truth. I told him I felt the best way to keep the story from escalating was to issue a public statement and apology. But I couldn't decide if that was a viable option until he gave me an accurate and transparent account of what had transpired. I reminded him that whatever statement he made would live in perpetuity. And if he lied to the media, it would be irreparable and would make matters worse.

Andraé began his story by saying that he had never used cocaine. He had let a musician friend stay in his apartment in Marina Del Rey while he was on the road performing. When he returned home, he found the vial of cocaine on his bathroom counter. Shocked and angry, he intended to confront his friend, reveal the evidence, and scold him for his egregious behavior. Later that evening, he left his apartment with the vial in his pocket. He met some friends for dinner, had a glass of wine, time slipped by, and it was too late for him to visit his friend. On his way home, he forgot he had the vial in his pocket. "So, that's the whole truth?" He affirmed it was.

I recommended that we release a statement saying that he had never used cocaine with a brief explanation of why it was in his possession. He would accept culpability for making a grave error in judgment and offer a contrite and empathetic apology to his family, friends, and fans, along with a pledge to make better decisions in the future. He agreed to the content. I advised him I wouldn't issue the statement before seeing the court's notice about the charges being dropped.

Looking objectively at his story as a publicist, Andraé's explanation didn't sound irrefutable—but it was his truth. Although he initially lied to me, I didn't have any reason to question his honesty. I never witnessed him using drugs or saw him tipsy or drunk, though he liked to drink wine occasionally. Whenever we traveled or were out, he would ask me to order his drinks, usually wine, for him because he didn't want people to know he drank.

My advice to famous people who endure self-inflicted setbacks and falls from grace is to tell the truth—it's crucial. Lying is a precursor, usually followed by a trail of more lies. When you tell the truth, it's not necessary to craft or spin the story. When you make a statement, don't jump the gun. Make sure you have all the facts and it's timely. Be authentic, use your own voice, be brief, accept culpability, stick to the facts, and avoid editorializing or making excuses. If you're sorry and contrite, mean it, and say it with conviction.

To reinforce Andraé's transparency and honesty, I recommended he do a handful of in-person interviews with the major white Christian television networks and programs and Black media that had been fervent supporters of his for years, such as the *700 Club*, *PTL Club* (Jim and Tammy Faye Bakker), Bill Gaither, TBN, and Bobby Jones (BET).

Understandably, Andraé didn't embrace the idea of talking about the incident with media. I reiterated that the media's and the public's interest in the incident would eventually wane, but we had to get through this first wave. The media strategy was effective, but even though the issue's relevancy faded, it was never forgotten, particularly in the white Christian market. They almost unilaterally canceled him. They didn't trust him, and over time performance offers for the major Christian venues and festivals vanished.

There was a camp of Black pastors and churches who were also miffed by Andraé's run-in with the law, but the larger Black gospel community rallied in support of him. They became his mainstay and core base for the rest of his career. The fallout had an enormous impact on Andraé personally. He took a self-imposed hiatus from recording solo albums for what felt like an interminable period.

During 1983, Andraé began focusing on his next album, *No Time to Lose*, his first since his infamous incident. Leading up to the release, he performed for the second time on *Saturday Night Live* at the behest of Jesse Jackson, who was the guest host. *No Time to Lose* (released in 1984) was one of his strongest albums, featured several of his most popular tunes, including the title track, "Living This Kind of Life," and "Always Remember." The album earned Grammy Awards for Best Soul Gospel Performance, Male, and Best Contemporary Gospel Album. It was also Andraé's first #1 on *Billboard*'s Contemporary Albums chart, his last album on Light Records, and his last solo record for the next ten years.

During his recording hiatus, he didn't totally shut down creatively, but as an artist, he sank into a deep hole. Whenever I asked if he had written any new songs, he told me he was writing all the time—but wasn't ready to share them yet. Occasionally, after persistent pleading, he caved in and invited me to a listening session at his house. It was the only way I could gauge where he was musically. There were boxes full of cassette tapes of songs in varying stages of development—but all unfinished. He rummaged through his stash and played bits of songs for a couple of hours.

Some of the tracks had just a melody and piano, others had more instrumentation. He'd play keyboards with the track and talk me through the song, giving cues for when the lead sang or the choir came in. I usually felt a rush and a motivational high when I left those sessions.

The following year Andraé had the good fortune of being asked by Quincy Jones to write choir arrangements and have his choir perform for the motion picture and soundtrack *The Color Purple*, based on the Pulitzer Prize–winning book by Alice Walker. Menno Meyjes and Steven Spielberg wrote the screenplay and directed. It starred Danny Glover, Whoopi Goldberg, Desreta Jackson, Margaret Avery, Oprah Winfrey, Rae Dawn Chong, Willard Pugh, and noted actor Adolph Caesar in one of his final film roles before he passed away in 1986.

Quincy served as one of the film's producers in addition to producing the music. He used Andraé's choir in the soundtrack, and Táta Vega, one of Andraé's singers, sang the songs performed by actor Margaret Avery in her role as Shug Avery. The film was a monumental box office hit, grossing $142 million. It received eleven Academy Award nominations including Best Picture. Andraé was one of twelve contributors to the music score who shared a nomination for Best Music, Original Score. It didn't win a single award, which was especially unfortunate since it was an African American story, and all the actors nominated were Black. Steven Spielberg, one of Hollywood's most successful directors, was overlooked in the Best Director category.

The mainstream success of the film helped expose Andraé's patented arrangements and choir sound to the film industry and major contemporary pop artists as well. It cemented a lasting relationship with Quincy, who became an advocate for Andraé and continued to retain his services on many high-profile projects.

On the heels of the film's success, Andraé made his second guest appearance on *Johnny Carson* in 1986, performing "Right Now" and "Got Me Some Angels" from *No Time to Lose*. That same year, his friend and coproducer, Bill Maxwell, brokered an introduction for him to Ed Weinberger, who was the executive producer for the long-running NBC-TV sitcom *Amen* starring the comedian and actor Sherman Hemsley. Bill was overseeing music for the show. Ed liked Andraé and hired him to write the show's theme song.

"MAN IN THE MIRROR"

In a five-year span the seminal musical collaboration between Michael Jackson and Quincy Jones on three albums (*Off the Wall*, *Thriller*, and *Bad*) monopolized and altered the direction of contemporary music, having an effect on par with or even greater than the impact of the Beatles or Elvis Presley on pop culture. Michael was simply the most famous and successful artist on the planet. Quincy asked Andraé to contribute to Michael's seventh album, *Bad*, which debuted as #1 on *Billboard*'s Top 200 Pop Albums chart.

Andraé arranged the vocals for a large choir that also featured guest artists the Winans on the song "Man in the Mirror." Siedah Garrett and Glen Ballard wrote the song, and Michael and Quincy served as producers. Released in February 1988, "Man in the Mirror" became the fourth of five #1 singles from his album and Michael's tenth #1 single to be certified triple-platinum.

The highlight of the release was witnessing one of the most exhilarating and historic performances in the history of the Grammy Awards—live in person. Andraé and Sandra put together a twenty-five-member choir that was featured as part of a medley of songs capped off with a seven-minute-long extended version of "Man in the Mirror." The whole segment lasted over ten minutes, which only the self-proclaimed king of pop had the power to command on the Grammy broadcast. Michael also featured Andraé prominently upstage, close to where Michael was performing. The performance received a resounding and lengthy standing ovation.

Bad was Michael's last album produced by Quincy. "Man in the Mirror" ranks as one of his most famous songs. Josh Tyrangiel of *TIME* named it among his Top 10 and "one of Jackson's most powerful vocals and accessible social statements, not to mention the best-ever use of a gospel choir in a pop song."

"LIKE A PRAYER"

The following year, contemporary pop music's most celebrated and controversial female artist, Madonna, featured Andraé's patented choir sound and arrangements in her song "Like a Prayer," which she cowrote and coproduced with Patrick Leonard. She added Andraé's choir after they completed the initial recording of the song. I wasn't the initial contact on getting Andraé involved. Andraé used a friend, singer and arranger Roberto Noriega, who contracted the choir. Roberto also did the contracting for Andraé's choir with Michael Jackson, Thomas Dolby, and Julio Iglesias.

After they finished the definitive version with the choir, Madonna's office called to invite Andraé and his choir to perform in the video. I thought Andraé performing in a Madonna video could be a fantastic opportunity. I told them we were interested and that I looked forward to reading the treatment and sharing it with Andraé.

The video treatment graphically depicted a young southern white girl who falls in love with a Black saint (played by actor Leon Robinson). She is obsessed with him, and they become entangled in an interracial love affair. The subplot deals with racism, bigotry, a homicide, sexual and religious ecstasy, the Ku Klux Klan shooting a mixed-race couple, and burning crosses. Madonna's character also suffers bleeding wounds in the palm of her hands, eerily like Christ's crucifixion. She didn't censor any aspect of the visuals to make them less controversial or offensive to the religious Right. The most controversial scenes were all filmed in a church.

After reading the first two paragraphs, it was clear Andraé couldn't risk being within a mile of the set. The potential collateral damage would be epic. We chatted briefly, and he shared my sentiments. I called Madonna's office to advise them that Andraé had to pass. They seemed genuinely disappointed but were empathetic and understood his decision.

The video was released the day after Madonna appeared on the Grammy Awards, and Pepsi featured the song in a new commercial premiered during the Grammy broadcast. Condemnation and controversy about the video happened instantly. The Vatican and Pope John Paul II called the video blasphemous and decreed that Madonna be boycotted. Several other organizations threatened boycotts a few weeks later.

Andraé went unscathed but could never avoid antagonists who felt he was a rogue Christian. However, he never strayed musically, compromised, or diluted his integrity as a gospel artist to placate the pop and R & B artists he collaborated with. It was the pureness and authenticity of his choir sound and arrangements they wanted to replicate in their songs—including Madonna.

In addition to Madonna and Michael Jackson, Andraé contributed his patented choir sound to Barbara Mandell, Billy Preston, Melissa Manchester, Quincy Jones, Julio Iglesias, Deniece Williams, Nancy Wilson, Curtis Stigers, Diana Ross, Rick Astley, Elton John, Paul Simon, Donnie McClurkin, Prefab Sprout, the Oslo Gospel Choir, Pat Boone, David Foster, El Debarge, Take 6, Elvis Presley, and Bob Dylan—over forty albums by major artists from 1968 to 2008. The longer I managed him, the more frustrated I became with the veiled hypocrisy that existed in the gospel/Christian music industry.

A PASSAGE

On April 11, 1992, Andraé's mother, Catherine Hodnett, died of heart failure at age seventy-four. She and Andraé's father had wed in 1939, and at the time of her death they had been together for fifty-three years. She was a petite, quiet-spoken, elegant, and warm person. I had the pleasure of being in her company a few times, and though we didn't engage directly, I could feel her checking me out. She spoke with her protective eyes.

It was a monumental loss and a devastating blow to the family—especially to their father. Andraé always spoke glowingly of her, and I know she meant the world to him. She was a calming voice in his life and kept them anchored as a close-knit family unit. Andraé needed some time and space to grieve, which I respected.

Fortunately, once again Quincy had made a timely intervention. He invited Andraé to headline the first ever Gospel Music Night at the Montreux Jazz Festival in Montreux, a small municipality about an hour from Geneva, Switzerland. Montreux was the second largest music festival in the world. Quincy had partnered with the festival's venerable founder, Claude Nobs, to produce nineteen nights of shows during the festival's run throughout July.

It had only been three months since they lost their mother, and Andraé and Sandra's father was still reeling from her death, so they asked him to join them on the trip. He rarely traveled or attended any of their performances, which made the trip even more special for them. Andraé's performance would also feature the forty-member Atlanta Super Choir. The day after our arrival, a soundcheck and rehearsal were scheduled so everyone could meet and run through the songs for the show.

Quincy, the choir, and Andraé's performing entourage were all set to rehearse when Pastor Crouch stepped out and expressed his desire to bless the event with a prayer. The room went silent. We bowed our heads, and most held hands as he began reciting the prayer. He was charismatic and captured everyone's attention. At one point, he acknowledged his wife and noted that he knew her spirit was present. Then in midsentence he choked up and broke down in tears. He tried to continue but couldn't stop crying.

The entire room teared up or cried, including Quincy. Andraé and Sandra were crying but gave him the space to collect himself. They moved closer and stood by him so he could feel their loving energy. He wiped away his tears, gathered himself, and finished the prayer on solid ground. It was one of those beautiful, rare shared moments when a collective of people bond and experience a touching moment as a family. It set the tone for their phenomenal performance, which they capped by bringing their father on

THE FAME GAME

stage to perform with them. Later, they said it was the first time they had performed live together as adults. I've always gotten inspired when I fondly reminisce about that day.

Unfortunately, two years later Andraé's father passed away from liver cancer, just before Christmas, on December 23, 1993. When he died, Andraé's older brother, Benjamin Jr., took over as pastor of Christ Memorial. I couldn't imagine the inner emotional struggle he was dealing with, losing both his parents in such a short time.

Careerwise, Andraé had hit a wall. When artists are virtually out of sight and out of mind for ten years, they potentially lose twenty years of relevancy—especially aging stars. And unlike in love, absence doesn't make the heart grow fonder. At fifty-one, Andraé's fame and star power was in continual descent, and I wasn't sure I could help resuscitate it. I started questioning whether there was any mutual value in continuing our business relationship.

When we finally connected, I expressed my dissatisfaction and my doubts about continuing my role as his manager. He responded by saying that God had sent me to him, that we were supposed to work together, to be patient and things would work out—that's the abbreviated version. A soliloquy by Andraé lasted much longer than I talked. When you manage a gospel artist who dedicates his music and life to serving God, you realize you're representing a duo—they're inseparable. Andraé professed that he never made major decisions without consulting God first. If we reached an impasse in a contested debate, or he needed supportive evidence to accentuate his stance, he cleverly played the God card. It was always two against one.

When he referenced the words of God, he scripted it as a phone conversation they had that he was playing back verbatim. He was ultrapersuasive and fluid. I sarcastically poked fun at him and asked, "So, when did he call?" He retorted, "When did who call?" I responded, "God! It's uncanny how you remembered everything he said. Can you give me his number? Since he seems to know so much about me, I'd like to give him a little more insight about you."

He chuckled, "You're just not a believer, but I'm going to convert you." I rebutted, "Not true—I'm Catholic and don't need to be converted. I just don't seem to have the same access as you do." Andraé told me more than once, "You know, I love and appreciate you, Ramon." I responded gratefully, "I love you too, but could you please finish writing some songs?" It was tough to say no to Andraé and God. They were undefeated and victorious again. I accepted the challenge to funnel more optimism into my psyche and persevere.

We kept meandering along, and then I received an urgent call from Sandra advising me that Andraé was in the hospital. His diabetes had flared up, and he had had a heart-related incident. Sandra said the doctors told them he was lucky. It was a legitimate scare, but they expected him to fully recuperate. The next day Quincy called. He had heard Andraé was in the hospital and wanted to know the severity of his condition. I gave him a status update.

Our conversation continued, and we got a chance to catch up on what we were doing. Quincy could talk for twenty minutes just sharing highlights. His business plate eclipsed mine by miles. He was running a marathon every day, and I was clocking in a mile or two. Then he asked what Andraé was doing recording-wise. In a frank tone, I told him Andraé was struggling creatively to finish songs and was unsigned. We had interest from a few labels, but they wanted to hear music to get a feel for his musical direction. Andraé didn't want to audition. He responded, "Let's bring him to Qwest, I'd love to have him."

Quincy was like a guardian angel for Andraé. He had impeccable timing for reaching out whenever Andraé was down and needed an uplifting hand. He suggested I discuss his offer with Andraé, and if he was game, he'd connect me to the label executive who would handle negotiating the deal. The idea of Quincy signing Andraé elated me no end. Andraé had enormous respect for and valued his friendship with Quincy, so I was confident he'd want the deal to happen.

Thankfully, I didn't need to convince Andraé to consider Quincy's interest. I emphasized that he had brought up the idea (not me) and stressed that we didn't discuss any deal points. But with Quincy championing it, I was confident it would be a respectable offer. Andraé gave me his blessing to pursue the deal. When I got back to Quincy, he responded enthusiastically. A few days later I connected with his contact, and we began negotiating the recording agreement.

It was Andraé's third association with the Warner Bros. family but his first time on a multigenre record label like Qwest. Warner Alliance distributed all the label's gospel products, and both were part of the Warner Music Group. Quincy had built an eclectic artist roster comprising young burgeoning R & B acts Tevin Campbell, Keith Washington, and Tamia; R & B and pop acts Siedah Garrett and James Ingram; classic artists Lena Horne and Frank Sinatra; jazz artists Patti Austin, Hiroshima, and Robert Stewart; and gospel artists the Winans and later Táta Vega.

Signing to Qwest with Quincy's ringing endorsement was a lightning rod for motivating Andraé musically and creatively. Andraé gathered several gifted guest lead vocalists for his debut album, *Mercy* (1994), including El DeBarge, Kristle Murden, and Táta Vega. He coproduced with Scott Smith. *Mercy* became Andraé's first #1 gospel album, and it peaked at #16 on the Contemporary Christian Albums chart. He earned his seventh Grammy Award for Best Pop/Contemporary Gospel Album.

The highlight of the *Mercy* marketing campaign was securing an appearance on the *Arsenio Hall Show*. Arsenio was a godsend for Black artists, with the only nationally syndicated late-night talk show that regularly featured performances by top Black artists from different genres of music like R & B, gospel, jazz, rap, and hip-hop. The timing was optimum because two months later, on May 7, 1994, Arsenio's five-year run ended.

Mercy was an auspicious and well-received comeback. It didn't blow the roof off—but he was back in the game. It led to him contributing to the monstrous success of Disney's original animated film and motion picture soundtrack *The Lion King*. Elton John and Tim Rice penned the songs for the film, and Hans Zimmer composed the score. Andraé contributed choir arrangements on several songs. The album reached #1 on the *Billboard* Top 200 Albums chart and was certified platinum 10X, becoming a global success and the best-selling animated film soundtrack ever.

A little over a year after Qwest released *Mercy*, Andraé and Sandra's older brother, Benjamin Jr., who was pastor of Christ Memorial Church, died on February 7, 1995. He had only served in the role for four months. As a rite of passage or by default, Andraé begrudgingly ascended to pastor—a role he had never aspired to fulfill. He immediately asked Sandra to be co-pastor. She stepped up and took over the daily management and administration duties of running the church. Andraé adjusted, assuming many of the traditional responsibilities of being a pastor. He delivered sermons on Sunday, met with parishioners, visited hospitals, and gained a deeper respect and reverence for his father's years of devotion and perseverance as a pastor.

I remember asking him how it felt being a pastor, and he commented that it was exhausting. It troubled him that so many parishioners needed financial aid over spiritual guidance, and he wished he could do more to help them. He sarcastically noted, "Sometimes I want to tell them the sign says Christ Memorial Church, not Christ Memorial Bank," and we both broke into laughter. He could catch you off guard with his sense of humor.

It was an active time for Andraé; he was also recording and occasionally doing performance dates when they were financially practical. Michael Jackson featured Andraé, Sandra, and the Andraé Crouch Choir on the inspirational track "Earth Song," from his album *HIStory: Past, Present and Future, Book 1*.

Behind the scenes, Andraé found himself embroiled in a bitter battle with the Church of God in Christ congregation, which prohibited women from being pastors. He fought vehemently to get the rule changed, and at one point threatened to leave the congregation. After the organization officially named him pastor of Christ Memorial in 1996, he continued to advocate for Sandra to become copastor. Two years later, after the *Los Angeles Times* and other media outlets reported on the controversy, Sandra was ordained as copastor.

From 1996 to 1998, Andraé released three critically acclaimed albums in consecutive years for the first time in his career. Some of his most noteworthy songs were featured on the album *Tribute: The Songs of Andraé Crouch* (released on Warner Bros. Records). An ensemble cast of stars, such as Michael W. Smith, Take 6, CeCe Winans, the Winans, and the Brooklyn Tabernacle Choir, performed the songs. The album won a Grammy Award for Best Pop/Contemporary Gospel Album.

In 1997, Qwest released his second solo album, *Pray*. I scrounged up enough money from Qwest to shoot a low-budget concept video, the first of his career. I served as executive producer and collaborated with director Marc Bennett, a close friend who pulled tons of favors to get it shot. The record peaked at #39 on the Gospel charts and won a Grammy Award for Contemporary Gospel Album of the Year.

In 1999, Andraé recorded his first Christmas album, *The Gift of Christmas*, with guest appearances by Yolanda Adams, Chaka Khan, Patti Austin, and a classic medley of holiday songs performed by Kristle Murden and Andraé. The album reached #17 on the Gospel charts. That same year, the Berklee College of Music awarded him their Honorary Doctor of Music Degree.

After three moderately successful albums with Quincy, Andraé had cemented a comeback, but unfortunately Qwest suddenly closed its doors, releasing Andraé along with most of its roster. Andraé became a free agent again.

While I was trying to shop another label deal for him, I called Andraé about unrelated business matters. During our conversation he nonchalantly mentioned that he and his coproducer, Scott, had signed a deal to launch a production company and record label. Scott had identified an angel investor named Renae, who committed six figures to launch the label. They did this without consulting me or having his business manager or attorney review the contract.

I didn't have any personal issues with Scott and respected his musical talents as a producer. He had been a loyal friend, supporter, and collaborator with Andraé for years. But I didn't feel either had the business acumen or executive experience to run a record label and manage the funds they raised. Their relationship was often virulent, and they called me individually to arbitrate settlements in their tiffs. I was fully transparent and advised them separately that they were in over their heads, and that their proposed partnership was a disaster waiting to happen.

I wasn't willing to nurse them though the venture, nor did I want to mop up the mess when it failed. I advised Andraé that I was moving on. I didn't harbor any resentment against him or Scott. We said goodbye, and I wished them the best of luck.

Between 2001 and 2002, Andraé's business manager, Bruce Kolbrenner (a longtime friend that I set Andraé up with), called to tell me that Andraé wanted me to help him. He was struggling financially, his relationship with Scott had reached an impasse, and they had ceased recording. He painted an even bleaker catastrophe than I had predicted. I felt bad for Andraé, and though I wasn't enthusiastic, I agreed to talk to him.

When we spoke, he was surprisingly repentant and apologized for not listening and taking my advice. Andraé was "I'm sorry"—challenged, so just hearing him say it was refreshing. He levied a barrage of complaints at Scott, which included creative differences and budget issues. There wasn't enough money left to finish recording the album. They had reached a stalemate and weren't talking to each other, and Andraé wanted to pull the project from him and finish the album with another producer.

It was a convoluted mess, like a broken marriage gushing with irreconcilable acrimony. At the minimum, I told Andraé I'd at least speak to Scott to try to navigate a fair compromise. Scott's attacks on Andraé were as potent as the ones leveled against him. Neither accepted culpability, and both were willing to discard their twenty-plus years of friendship. From my vantage point they were both culpable (as was Renae, the investor). It was an ill-fated deal for everyone from the outset.

I agreed to help Andraé in the short term. I pulled in a young attorney friend of mine, Darryl Thompson, and we were able to convince Renae to end her existing contract with Scott and Andraé. She had to pay Scott a buy-out fee for him to relinquish the masters. In turn, he would agree to give up all his rights and have no further involvement with the project. Renae's rights as an investor would remain intact. I committed to find a label or distributor that might consider licensing the album and cover the costs of finishing it. It was the only viable way Renae stood any chance of recouping her investment.

By happenstance, I discovered that Andraé's fortieth anniversary in the recording industry was coming up. It was a bonus marketing hook I could dangle to hopefully tip the scales in securing a deal for the project. I mentally mapped out a blueprint for a yearlong marketing campaign starting with a major launch event, national and international concert tours, a television special, the launch of a Worship Music Conference hosted by Andraé and Sandra, development of a musical based on their life story and Andraé's redemption and comeback, corporate sponsorship, and a book deal. One phenomenal year—a grand finale to punctuate and set up the final leg of his legacy.

I decided to approach Max Siegel, a bright young Black attorney turned record executive who was president of Verity Records, vice president of Zomba Music Group USA, and helmed Zomba Gospel and Tommy Boy Gospel. Max had the foresight to collaborate with GospoCentric Records, an indie label based in Inglewood, California, founded by two young Black entrepreneurs, Vicki Mack-Lataillade and Claude Lataillade (whom I later represented briefly). They discovered Kirk Franklin, who quickly became the biggest-selling Black gospel superstar in history. Verity's artist roster also included Fred Hammond, Yolanda Adams, Hezekiah Walker, John P. Kee, Vanessa Bell Armstrong, and Vickie Winans.

He was extremely receptive and agreed to sign Andraé to Verity. In addition to making the deal with Verity, I secured a major copublishing deal with Universal Music Publishing for Andraé's new publishing entity, Vaughn Street Music (named after the street his church was on), which I proposed he form. The deal was worth a quarter million dollars. Once I closed the Verity deal, I began pursuing avenues to market and publicize his fortieth anniversary.

In 2004, Andraé was inducted into the Gospel Music Association Hall of Fame. That same year, I arranged for him to become the third contemporary gospel artist honored on the Hollywood Walk of Fame. Reverend James Cleveland was the first gospel artist to be honored, in September 1981, and Mahalia Jackson was next, in September 1988. Andraé's late morning ceremony was well attended.

One of his close friends, Fred Webo, a real estate developer, hosted a lavish afternoon brunch and garden party at his palatial mansion in Beverly Hills to celebrate Andraé's milestone achievement. It was an intimate gathering attended by Andraé's closest friends, along with some singers, musicians, and business associates. It was a typically gorgeous, sunny, and hot early summer day in Los Angeles. Guests vividly showed their appreciation for the five-star catered spread by the generous portions of food they piled on their plates. The mood was celebratory—one big family rejoicing, paying homage to Andraé's incredible legacy and career.

The following year, Andraé received a Lifetime Achievement Award at the Inaugural Salute to Gospel Music event held by the National Association of Recording Arts and Sciences (NARAS) in Los Angeles. It was prestigious for Andraé to be the first gospel pioneer and recipient of the award—a true testament to his resiliency and staying power.

In November, Verity released *Mighty Wind*, which Andraé and Mano Hanes produced. The album included fourteen tracks and featured several guest artist appearances, including Marvin Winans ("All Because of Jesus"), Karen Clark Sheard ("Jesus Is Lord"), Fred Hammond ("Oh Give Thanks"), and Crystal Lewis ("We Give You Glory").

A review by *Contemporary Christian Music Magazine* noted, "Andraé Crouch proves yet again why he is such a seminal figure in the history of contemporary Christian music—and why, forty years down the line, he's still making an impact." It was a triumphant feeling to see his long-awaited album come to life after nearly losing it forever.

After a desperate search to secure a broadcast partner for a television special to commemorate Andraé's fortieth anniversary, it finally happened. The negotiations were lengthy, but I made a deal with the Feed the Children Organization to produce *Andraé Crouch and Friends*, a one-hour television special bolstered with special guests Natalie Cole, Walter Hawkins, and Yolanda Adams. It was later broadcast nationally via major cable television affiliates throughout the US. Funds raised from the broadcast supported Feed the Children's worldwide hunger and famine relief efforts.

MICHAEL JACKSON'S MEMORIAL SERVICE

On June 25, 2009, I was in Montego Bay, Jamaica, attending a celebrity event with a friend, the comedian Tommy Davidson, a trip that I booked as a favor to him. I wasn't his manager, but we collaborated on projects occasionally. The afternoon after we arrived, I popped into the business center at the hotel to catch up on emails. Comedian and friend Bill Bellamy, who was also performing, was sitting a couple of computer stations away checking his emails as well.

He caught a news flash from the *TMZ* tabloid show announcing that Michael Jackson had died. I nonchalantly remarked, "*TMZ*? I don't trust that show. Sounds like one of those hoax deaths!" I searched quickly, and all the major networks were reporting that he had been pronounced dead at 2:21 p.m. I felt overwhelmed by sadness for his family and young children. I represented Michael and his brothers for *Destiny*, their debut album as the Jacksons after leaving Motown. As the day progressed, the finality and magnitude of his death felt more surreal and unimaginable.

Upon my return to Los Angeles, I got a call from Tisha Fein, who was an associate producer with the noted veteran TV producer Ken Ehrlich. Ken was producing the memorial service for Michael at the Staples Center, and Kenny Ortega was directing. Ken wanted Andraé and his choir to back up a few of the featured artists scheduled to perform at the service, including Stevie Wonder, Mariah Carey, Lionel Richie, Jennifer Hudson, Usher, Jermaine Jackson, and Jon Mayer. He needed Andraé and the choir for two days of rehearsal.

It was eerie being on the same stage where Michael had been rehearsing for his forthcoming fifty-concert comeback tour. Besides knowing Michael, I knew several of his musicians. Michael Bearden, his musical director and keyboardist, told me that he and Michael had stayed after rehearsals to go over music bits the night before he died. The tour was scheduled to start in three weeks, so his sudden death reverberated and was a devastating blow to all his musicians, singers, dancers, and staff who were employed for the duration of his world tour.

The memorial was extravagant—a massive parade of Hollywood glitz, fame, and celebrity, fused with an aura of discernible solemness, authentic sadness, teary eyes, spontaneous crying, lingering shock, and dismay. Andraé and his choir were well received and added an emotional and special spiritual touch to the artist performances they supported. After feeling shrouded by unfeigned sadness while being sequestered in that arena for three straight days, I felt an enormous sense of relief once it was finally over.

THE FINALE

Andraé was approaching another five years without releasing any new music, and the demand for him as a live concert attraction in the US and abroad was negligible. To keep his relevancy from further declining, I started fielding offers for him to perform at Black churches. We had to streamline his show and do live-to-track performances with just a keyboardist and musical director and four singers. It was humbling for him and disconcerting for his singers and music director, who had to take pay cuts to do the dates.

Most churches could barely afford to pay Andraé or market the performances. They just assumed Andraé would sell out. Not all the churches made money on his dates. There were instances when bishops and pastors failed to honor their contractual obligations and stiffed Andraé by refusing to pay the final balance of his fee. To his credit, Andraé was a trooper and preferred to be active and perform for less rather than become stagnant.

Internationally, the financial dynamics had changed as well. Promoters couldn't afford to pay for his regular entourage to join him, so they hired local musicians once he got to his destination. His revenues from performances and publishing royalties were dwindling, and he relied on both for his financial security.

More disconcerting, Andraé was approaching seventy and had developed some undesirable behavioral patterns that made him less desirable to book. He had become obstinate, irresponsible, and perpetually and unapologetically late for everything: interviews, promotions, lobby departure call times, and starting and ending shows. The latter two had adverse financial ramifications that were levied against promoters, who threatened to deduct the penalties the venue charged them out of the back end of his performance fee.

On stage, his sense of timing began slipping. He started overtalking and preaching too much, and dragged out songs with too many reprises, leaving the band and singers exhausted and befuddled about when the song would end. He had become a shadow of the magnetic performer he once was. Later, I found out he was dealing with health issues that exacerbated the problems.

For the next year, we kept plodding on, and I oversaw several international bookings for him. In Accra, Ghana, he headlined Harvest Praise, an annual worship and praise concert that featured top African gospel artists and attracted over five thousand fans (he exceeded the length of the show by more than thirty minutes). When he headlined a Christian festival in Amsterdam, he was an hour late—and the theater was in our hotel. It was inexcusable behavior. He was unapologetic and scoffed at me for pointing it out after the show. He later eked out performances in Ireland, Japan, and the Jakarta Jazz Festival in Indonesia.

In June 2010, I booked him to headline "A Father's Day Concert— A Blessing for Fathers" at the King's House in Kingston, Jamaica. It was the most telling show, and the first time I thought he should retire from performing live. He wasn't fully lucid, looked frail, and was severely late again. His debilitating state was depressing to witness—I felt guilty and didn't feel I could justify continuing to watch him labor and embarrass himself on stage.

My final business interaction with Andraé occurred after learning that Mano Hanes, his musical director, had offered him an artist deal with Riverphlo, a new record label. I sensed another debacle brewing, similar to what occurred with Scott and Renae, but this time Andraé asked me to look at the contract before he signed it. After reviewing the contract, I told him it wasn't artist-friendly, but I'd try to negotiate to get it balanced more in his favor. Mano wanted to launch his label with Andraé's project.

I met with Mano and tried following up with him several times. His lack of responsiveness was inexcusable, and it wore out my patience. When we finally connected to discuss the key points in the contract, it was apparent we lacked compatibility or the desire to work together.

Regardless, I felt a responsibility to Andraé to close the deal, which never hinged on whether I was involved. Once they executed the contract, I reminded Andraé about the payment we had agreed upon. He resisted and said that since I didn't bring the deal to him, he shouldn't have to pay me. Without my input, he would have become entangled in another horrendous deal. That was the final straw. It wasn't the money; it was his absurd position. I resigned in January 2011. As a last token, he eventually decided to pay me. Riverphlo released his album, *The Journey*, in September.

"A CELEBRATION OF LIFE"

In 2015, I was covering a show for a client, the songwriter and singer Kellylee Evans, at Sculler's Jazz Club, Boston's premier jazz venue. It was her debut headlining performance there. I was watching the show from the bar, sipping a glass of wine, and occasionally checking my phone. A post popped up announcing that Andraé had died. I immediately went numb and starting quivering. I went backstage to the dressing room for privacy and called Sandra.

She didn't mask feeling devastated by his loss but said he had made a peaceful transition. I offered to assist her in any way I could. After the show, when I was finally alone, sitting on the edge of my bed at the hotel, I became overwhelmed with sadness. I bent over, cupped my face in my hands, and burst into a monsoon of tears.

Sandra organized "A Celebration of Life," a two-day memorial extravaganza held at Christ Memorial Church and West Angeles Church of God in Christ. I opted not to go and preferred to grieve privately. It attracted four thousand people, including family, friends, and dozens of prominent music stars and celebrities. Six hundred thousand people from around the globe viewed a live simulcast broadcast on BET.com. I only watched a portion of the four-hour telecast.

Whenever I reflect on my long friendship and business association with Andraé, it's with fondness and love. We forged a bond that weathered a few pernicious storms, endured fractured and bruised egos, overcame untenable breaches of trust, and shared enough mutual love and appreciation to sustain a lasting friendship.

Andraé was one of the most naturally gifted artists I've represented. Although he left an indelible imprint as the father of gospel, I never felt he reaped the monetary rewards or level of fame he deserved. His ascension to superstardom came during the post–civil rights movement, when white America repressed and marginalized Black people, enacting laws designed to prevent Black people from becoming successful in the entertainment business and other professions.

I never felt Andraé was obsessed with fame but did feel he struggled to find a balance between his devotion to God and his human fallibility as a person and artist. And I thought he desperately sought the freedom to explore and experience life outside the parameters of the person people expected him to be as a gospel artist and pastor.

Although I played an integral role in extending and sustaining his career, I felt personally disappointed that I couldn't help him make the quantum leap to a higher plateau, which had eluded him throughout his career. He may not have broken through the glass ceiling long enough to appreciate his lofty climb, but he cracked it open wide enough for other artists to get through. Andraé was a beloved messenger who unselfishly spread the gospel worldwide through his music and songs. Maybe that was God's plan all along.

8

ATTAINING FAME REQUIRES
THE MEDIA'S ENDORSEMENT

During my embryonic days as a publicist in the 1970s, I cut my teeth handling public relations and publicity for mostly Black artists, a few superstars and several who were talented but weren't considered famous—at least not to mainstream audiences. I quickly learned there was a discernible difference between Black fame and white fame, for artists, actors, brands, and companies across all mediums in the entertainment business. Securing major press coverage in mainstream media outlets was an ominous challenge, especially for Blacks on television.

An early case study which reinforced that media inequities were deeply rooted and rampant in the television industry came when I started representing Don Cornelius, the star, creator, producer, and visionary who launched the legendary *Soul Train* brand. He realized there was a dearth of television programs created by Black talent that also aptly reflected and captured the richness and importance of Black culture. He understood the power of television and strategically positioned himself to become the face of the *Soul Train* brand as its host and executive producer, but he tactically sublimated his own celebrity cachet to make the brand famous.

During the late '60s, television had become the major medium of mass communication in the US. Ninety-five percent of Americans had a TV set—more than bathtubs or telephones. In 1969, television sets were predicted to outnumber passenger cars. In 1970, the year Don launched *Soul Train*, the average American with a television set watched it five and a half hours a day. Americans spent more time watching TV than any single activity other than sleeping and eating. But they were only seeing a smidgeon of Black faces on their sets.

Although I never served as an official publicist for the *Soul Train* series, Don sought my advice and input on occasion. I knew he struggled with the complexity and liabilities of becoming famous and creating an equitable balance between charting his own fame and *Soul Train*'s fame. He felt achieving more personal fame could jeopardize and undermine *Soul Train*'s brand identity. He didn't aspire to be a celebrity per se but wanted to be respected as an innovative television producer, entrepreneur, and entertainment business luminary. These weren't my subjective assumptions; he divulged his theories and approach and gave me a forum to openly share my views.

My formidable and tricky challenge was to convince him that personal fame can infringe on brand identity, but one drives the other. If strategically balanced and handled properly, there is a way for both types of fame to coexist. It fueled a vigorous and endless debate throughout our association, and it was a challenge to convince him that he needed healthy doses of media coverage to successfully grow his persona and brand identity.

GETTING TO KNOW THE MAN BEHIND *SOUL TRAIN*

I don't remember the exact circumstances of when I met Don Cornelius, but I know it was at the KTTV studios, where *Soul Train* taped for many years. Don was an imposing figure, tall (6'4"), lanky, lean, with broad shoulders. In those days, like so many of us, he wore a substantial Afro. Don created his own star aura, which included being nattily dressed in fashionable outfits not only for *Soul Train* but as a lifestyle choice.

He usually wore stylish wide-lapel suits, wide-collared shirts with an array of bright printed full Windsor knotted ties, and thin-rimmed glasses (usually round). He moved around deliberately and with a strident cadence—never rushing. He had a deep voice, spoke eloquently, and until I got to know him well, spoke minimally. As soon as he walked on the set, he commanded attention. He was very businesslike and ran a tight ship. When he spoke, he commanded respect and silence.

And although he was a moderately serious man, he had a dry sense of humor, a beaming smile, and an infectious laugh. *Soul Train* was a historic and unprecedented achievement by any standard. It was more than a television show and became a cultural phenomenon. He spurred radical changes in the way the public viewed Black culture, music, fashion, dance, and artists. Most importantly, he built and solely owned *Soul Train*, which gave him the right to leverage licensing and distribution deals to syndicate it.

His legacy had intrinsic cultural and human interest and drama, as well as being a rags-to-riches minority business success story. When Don hired me to publicize the Soul Train Music Awards, I lobbied Don to let me pitch lifestyle pieces to magazines like *Ebony*, *Essence*, *People*, *US Weekly*, and *Entertainment Weekly*. It would require giving them personal access to his home and intel about his personal life. He had no interest in sharing that side of his life. We discussed business publications such as the *Wall Street Journal*, *Business Week*, and *Forbes*, but he didn't want to share his financials, which was essential for business stories.

He was only open to doing stories about *Soul Train* or later the Soul Train Music Awards, mostly telephone interviews or a few quotes in press releases. Don was obstinate and stubborn and was most concerned about sustaining *Soul Train*'s ratings and keeping his sponsors happy. Our opinions and strategies for accomplishing those goals weren't fully aligned. He instinctively took a "Don against the world" posture. Ultimately, we found common ground on defusing that mindset (especially if a crisis surfaced), and he agreed to do media that centered specifically on the series—and not him. It wasn't an optimum strategy, but it was better than him having no voice or media presence at all.

THE EARLY YEARS IN CHICAGO

His path to fame defied what one would presumably expect for someone who became a contemporary pop culture icon. After graduating from Jean Baptiste Point DuSable High School, a public high school in the Bronzeville neighborhood on the South Side of Chicago (other notable graduates were John H. Johnson, Chicago mayor Harold Washington, and jazz artists Eddie Harris and Dorothy Donegan), he joined the Marines and served for eighteen months in Korea. When he returned home to Chicago, he held several odd jobs selling tires, automobiles, and insurance. He also did a stint serving as an officer with the Chicago Police Department. In 1966, he quit his day job to take a three-month broadcasting course.

By that time, he was thirty years old, married with two adolescent sons, and reputedly only had $400 in his bank account. After completing his broadcasting course, he was hired as a backup DJ, on-air announcer, and news reporter for WVON Radio. A year later he landed a gig with Chicago's local television station WCIU-TV and hosted a news program called *A Black's View of the News*. Simultaneously, he was hustling on the side, hosting and promoting a concert touring series of "record hops" that he presented throughout high schools in the Chicago area. He titled his touring shows "The Soul Train."

THE BIRTH OF *SOUL TRAIN*

WCIU-TV caught wind of his success and offered him a deal to present it locally. *Soul Train* attracted sponsorship from one of Chicago's and the nation's top retail chains, Sears, Roebuck and Co. Founded by Richard Warren Sears and Alvah Curtis Roebuck (who was Black), the future conglomerate opened in 1893. Once Sears Roebuck committed a portion of funds to sponsorship, *Soul Train* debuted locally on WCIU-TV in August 1970.

Don and the show's syndicator initially targeted twenty-five markets beyond Chicago to air the show but were only able to get seven regional markets and stations to purchase the program: Atlanta (WQGA-TV), Birmingham (WBRC-TV), Cleveland (WJW-TV), Detroit (WJBK-TV), Houston (KIAH-TV), Los Angeles (KTTV), and Philadelphia (WKBS). *Soul Train* began airing on a weekly basis on October 2, 1971. By the end of the first season, eleven additional stations had been added throughout the country. Don's ability to attract sponsors contributed significantly to the growth of *Soul Train*. In addition to Sears, he later garnered sponsorship from Johnson Hair Products (Afro Sheen), Coca-Cola, and Sprite.

HIS NEMESIS

When Don embarked on his television journey with *Soul Train*, he faced considerable odds. Although his concept was unique, he had an enviable white competitor and nemesis who had already been successful for fourteen years with a contemporary pop music and dance series titled *American Bandstand*. It had become the most influential show targeted at American white teenagers. The twenty-six-year-old Philadelphia DJ Dick Clark took over hosting duties of the show in 1956. Five years later, the Clark-hosted series was launched nationally on sixty-seven ABC affiliate stations, which aired it five days a week in the midafternoon until 1963.

The program's identifiable conceptual elements included high school gym–like bleachers on the set and a segment dedicated to the teenage studio guests rating the newest records on a scale from 25 to 98. Their responses and assessments were purposely light, such as "It's got a good beat" or "You can dance to it." Clark's signature formula was fusing performances by music's most celebrated pop stars with an everyday, all-American-looking, white teenage audience of "regulars" dancing and wearing the latest fashions and hairstyles.

Occasionally, Clark would feature Black artists who had achieved some pop crossover success and appeal with mainstream audiences. Most of the Black artists that appeared on the show were making their debut performance on national TV, and they were also being paid. Clark booked popular

R & B acts such as the Coasters, the Shirelles, the Impressions, Smokey Robinson and the Miracles, James Brown and the Famous Flames, Marvin Gaye, and Aretha Franklin.

While he wanted to feature the top Black artists, he refused to allow Black teenagers to be part of the regular studio audience. There were published reports that Black teenagers would show up and wait in line indefinitely, but they were never selected. Clark's audience policy for Blacks eased up when the show moved to Los Angeles. In February 1964, *American Bandstand* debuted nationally on ABC from Los Angeles with Clark as the host and ran for twenty-five years, through 1989. Clark's and Cornelius's paths rarely crossed, but over the years they became behind-the-scenes rivals and endured a few fierce business battles.

Don was well aware of the influence and clout that Clark and *American Bandstand* possessed, yet he was undeterred. He felt his concept of creating a kaleidoscope of Black hipness, coolness, urban fashion, and attractive dancers with choreographed and free-style acrobatic dance moves would outclass *American Bandstand* by leaps and bounds.

Don developed *Soul Train* into "the hippest trip in America" (which later became the title for a book by my longtime friend, noted pop music journalist and filmmaker Nelson George, released by HarperCollins in 2014). The *Soul Train* set was modern, slick, and designed to feel like a nightclub. All featured guest artists performed on risers and lip synced or sang live-to-track. Because of prohibitive American Federation of Television and Radio Artists (AFTRA) performance rates, Don couldn't afford to pay bands to perform live.

Don was very selective about his guest artists. He regularly studied the music charts, primarily *Billboard* and *Radio and Records*, and he knew which artists were relevant and making waves on the R & B charts. He would do a brief interview with the artists after their performance.

Soul Train showcased a who's who of the most famous Black artists in modern contemporary music: Stevie Wonder, Diana Ross, Earth, Wind & Fire, Michael Jackson, Al Green, James Brown, Dionne Warwick, the

O'Jays, Mariah Carey, Aretha Franklin, Whitney Houston, Mary J. Blige, D'Angelo, Tina Turner, Barry White, B. B. King, Prince, Patti LaBelle, Bill Withers, Jill Scott, Lionel Richie, Donna Summer, Donny Hathaway, and Destiny's Child, to name just a few. The show also featured some of pop music's most revered white stars, such as Elton John, David Bowie, Justin Timberlake, Hall and Oates, Herb Alpert, Sting, the Beastie Boys, Michael Bolton, Duran Duran, and Sheena Easton.

The *Soul Train* dancers were just as important as the guest artists. Don and his righthand man, the dancer and choreographer Clinton Ghent, recruited the best dancers in Chicago to audition and become regulars on the local show. They installed the same system when the show moved to Los Angeles. He prominently featured close-ups of hand-picked talented dancers such as Jody Watley and Jeffrey Daniels, dance partners who later formed the R & B group Shalamar with Howard Hewett, and Damita Jo Freeman, who along with her dance partner, Don Campbell, made "pop locking" famous. Campbell and Fred "Rerun" Berry were in the original Lockers street dance group that was birthed from exposure on *Soul Train*. Rosie Perez, Cheryl Song (the first Asian dancer featured on the show), Adolfo "Shabba-Doo" Quiñones (from the *Breakin'* movies), and Nieci Payne were also core regulars on the show. The dancers weren't paid, but they benefited from the national television exposure.

One of the show's patented elements was the "Soul Train line," which became a highlight of the show. This began with one line of male dancers and one line of female dancers. A couple breaks off at the beginning of the line and then freelances and has dance-offs down to the end of the line, followed by the next couple. It allowed dancers to improvise and showcase their own interpretation of the latest dances, use props, or make acrobatic flips.

He also created the popular "Scrabble board" segment (sponsored by Johnson Hair Products), which featured two dancers who were given one minute to decode a famous person's name from jumbled scrabble-like tiles spread out on a blackboard. Don picked a prominent figure in African

American history, like Thurgood Marshall or Harriet Tubman, so the game had an educational component. What most people didn't realize was that he told the dancers in advance who the person was, so they wouldn't fail or look stupid on national television. Occasionally, he featured leading Black activists and leaders as guests, including Jesse Jackson and Al Sharpton. Don closed every show with his patented sign-off, "As always, we wish you love, peace, and soul!"

Clark was a shrewd businessman and felt *Soul Train* threatened its success. He sensed it could siphon off viewers and dilute his ratings dominance in the marketplace. So in 1973, he launched a new dance show, *Soul Unlimited*, to compete with and try to undermine *Soul Train*. *Soul Unlimited*, hosted by Black Los Angeles DJ Buster Jones, would fill in for *American Bandstand* every fourth Saturday on ABC.

Pundits viewed the controversial move with skepticism and saw it as racially motivated. Don fought against Clark's covert action, which he felt was designed to push *Soul Train* off the air. He enlisted the help of the Reverend Jesse Jackson and Operation PUSH. They in turn leveraged their case directly with the vice president of ABC. For his part, Clark felt that *Soul Train* was encroaching on his turf. However, in an interview with *Rolling Stone* reporter Ben Fong-Torres (whom I had solicited for a job as a writer and later as a publicist), Clark stated it was ABC who wanted the show for the time slot, and he was just honoring their request. After ABC was confronted by Don and Jackson, they convinced Clark to suspend production of *Soul Unlimited*, and in late spring 1973 the network dropped it.

Soul Train and *American Bandstand* remained invariably competitive, at least in terms of booking the top Black artists. My strategy was to book Black clients on both shows, if possible. That was easier said than done, especially if the artist wasn't a superstar. Both shows were protective of their brand identity, and neither wanted to copy the other. Because *American Bandstand* had been around longer and had cultivated a mainstream audience base, many established Black artists who were trying to garner crossover appeal wanted to appear on the show.

American Bandstand didn't want to book Black acts scheduled to appear on *Soul Train*. And vice versa. Don resented when major Black crossover artists whom he had debuted on *Soul Train* opted to do *American Bandstand* rather than *Soul Train*. In truth, Black artists with the potential to cross over needed exposure on both shows. My only recourse was to prioritize when an appearance on one show or the other would best serve the record I was promoting. Since booking both rarely happened, I tried the other show on the next single release. The competitive dynamics to booking celebrities on other entertainment programs was prevalent throughout the industry and still exists today, regardless of whether the celebrity is Black or white.

The practice occurred on other music shows, like *The Midnight Special*, *Don Kirshner's Rock Concert*, and *Solid Gold*, the top-rated morning news/entertainment programs the *Today Show*, *Good Morning America*, and *CBS Good Morning*, and daytime and nighttime talk shows, like *Michael Douglas*, *Merv Griffin*, *Phil Donahue*, *Dick Cavett*, the *Tonight Show*, *Tom Snyder*, and the *Late Show with David Letterman*. They all sought exclusives on guests and would pass if a star was booked within the same time frame on a competitor's program. They didn't make their restrictive booking policies public—but if you were a publicist, you knew.

There were two prevailing booking conditions that you learned fast: one was that if you had a famous superstar, you could circumvent and manipulate their policies—which remains the same. They were automatically more receptive because they didn't want to miss the boat. Most superstars specify the talk shows they're willing to appear on. Sometimes, they try to dictate what topics are off-limits as well. The bigger the star, the more leverage you have.

Secondly, booking Black stars or superstars wasn't easy. You might as well drop on your knees, assume the prayer position, and hope they'd make an exception. They had to be A-level talent, and even that wasn't automatic. The uphill battle never changed—regardless of how professionally successful I became.

Over the first five years I knew Don, I felt like he developed a respect for me professionally and personally. He gave me access to speak to him directly, which wasn't guaranteed. And most of the time he would book the client I was pitching. He passed on several as well but would take the time to explain why. Don was very opinionated and wasn't the least bit shy about expressing his views. If he didn't like an artist or song, he let me know. His "can't happen" responses were emphatic nos—under no circumstances, with no room for negotiation or reconsideration.

DON CORNELIUS AND O'BRYAN

About a year after I left Rogers & Cowan to start my own company, Don invited me to lunch. We met at Le Dome, which was one of the entertainment industry's most revered eateries and hangouts—especially for the music industry. It was on Sunset Boulevard right in the middle of Sunset Plaza, a popular strip of European designer fashion boutiques and hip in-crowd restaurants and cafés with patio seating in the front.

Le Dome was built in the style of a French chateau. An impressive circular bar near the entry was its centerpiece. There were banquet rooms against the walls on each side; the main dining area was in the back. The owner, Eddie Kerkhof, had gotten seed money from Elton John and Rod Stewart to open it. It was a magnet for stars, execs, and musicians, and it was legendary for its party-life atmosphere and bar scene.

In those days, if you weren't breaking furniture or physically fighting, Eddie would allow you to let loose. In the evenings, the restrooms had lengthy lines of people waiting to freshen up with a bump. I can remember one time being in the restroom, and one stall had four guys in it, all standing, and you could hear extemporaneous sniffing. A guy walked in, glanced at the stall, and yelled, "Hey, I really must use the toilet!" I had a house account at Le Dome and have countless fun memories of hanging out with friends there until it closed at 2 a.m.

When I met with Don, he was still recovering from twenty-one-hour brain surgery he underwent in 1982 to correct a congenital deformity in his cerebral arteries. He was enduring seizures, a chronic condition that resulted from his operation. As we became closer over the years, he confided to me that the seizures never went away. They caused a severe imbalance and shift in his moods, and became a life-threatening detriment to his mental health. During our meeting, he told me he had agreed to manage O'Bryan, a young R & B act whom he had signed to Capitol Records. He believed O'Bryan could become a star. He wanted me to be his publicist.

Don didn't want to rest on his laurels and the fame he had achieved with *Soul Train*. He was savvy and understood the underpinnings of the record industry. In 1975, four years after launching *Soul Train*, he founded Soul Train Records with Dick Griffey, a prominent Black promoter and producer in Los Angeles. They signed an R & B vocal quartet they named the Soul Train Gang (Gerald Brown, Terry Brown, Judy Jones, Patricia Williamson, and later Denise Smith) as their first act.

The Soul Train Gang recorded *Soul Train*'s many theme songs, and their first album released on the label was titled *Don Cornelius Presents the Soul Train Gang*. They also formed the genesis of the group Shalamar with two former *Soul Train* dancers, Jody Watley and Jeffrey Daniels. They added another singer, later replaced by Howard Hewett. Shalamar (with Hewett, Watley, and Daniels) became one of the most celebrated R & B acts of the 1980s. In 1978, Don felt he was spreading himself too thin. Griffey bought his interest in the label. After Don exited, he renamed it Solar Records.

We had a great meeting, and I told him I was interested in working with him. I had never hung out with Don and didn't know much about his personal life. I waited with him to get his car from the valet and discovered he was driving a light-beige classic Rolls Royce convertible. It was a gorgeous car, and I joked about him rolling like a superstar. Months later he invited me to his house for a meeting. He lived on Mulholland Drive, up in the hills of West Hollywood. It was nicely appointed, not ostentatious, with an open, airy floor design. It was spacious but not palatial. There was a pool and patio area in the backyard with a picturesque view of the hills and the valley. He was living moderately large and had a lovely wife, Victoria, who was an attractive Russian. I was happy that he was enjoying some perks that his fame and *Soul Train* had afforded him.

O'Bryan was a young singer-songwriter and multi-instrumentalist (keyboards, piano, drums, and percussion) originally from Sneads Ferry, North Carolina, whose family had moved to Santa Ana when he was a teenager. Ron Kersey, a producer and former keyboardist with the noted Philly disco group the Trammps, introduced O'Bryan to Don. He was twenty-one, good looking, and a very competent singer with a killer falsetto. Don signed him to Capitol Records, invested in overhauling and styling him, and served as executive producer on his records.

His association helped make O'Bryan more media-friendly so I could get him placed out of the box. His first single, "The Gigolo," was a funky up-tempo track, released in January 1982, which became a hit. It set the tone for his debut album, *Doin' Alright*, which reached #10 on *Billboard*'s R & B Albums chart that spring. He also had another hit with his cover of the Four Tops' "Still Water (Love)" and two ballads, "Love Has Found Its Way" and "Can't Live Without Your Love," which became fan favorites.

It was a respectable debut for him, but his vibe didn't connect with any of the major East Coast R & B radio stations in New York, Philadelphia, DC, or Boston. New York's WBLS radio program director, Frankie Crocker, was perhaps the most influential R & B radio personality in the country. Along with WKSS radio, many other R & B stations mirrored its programming choices and playlists throughout the northeast corridor. Don was a former DJ, and he really understood the importance of Black radio.

O'BRYAN GOES UNDERGROUND IN NEW YORK

O'Bryan felt artistically safe singing ballads, which fared well on the West Coast, but he wasn't edgy enough for New York radio. But Don didn't want to risk cutting another record with the same vibe and said he was battling with O'Bryan over his musical direction as a singer-songwriter. He asked me to coordinate a trip for us to go to New York for a few days, so O'Bryan could check out the city and the club scene, and get a feel for the New York urban and underground music scene.

I had hung out in New York several times and had a few favorite haunts, but I didn't consider myself an expert in the New York club scene. Luckily, I knew people who were. I had a wonderful friend, John Brown, who was a seasoned Artist and Repertoire (A &R) veteran at A & M Records. He had a background in dance music and knew the club scene in New York very well. He lived in Los Angeles.

I contacted him and shared my mission, and he connected me with Judy Weinstein, who had started in the biz with David Mancuso, a legendary figure in the New York club scene who founded and curated the Loft, a legendary and coveted dance party concept that became the genesis and foundation of disco, as well as spurring subsequent DJ-driven dance-style music genres like house, techno, and electronic dance music (EDM). He cofounded the New York Record Pool with Weinstein, the first DJ collective in the nation.

Record pools became the conduit for getting records from labels to working DJs to help generate club plays and unit sales. Weinstein knew all the top DJs and helped guide the careers of some of the most notable DJs, including Frankie Knuckles, Satoshi Tomiie, and David Morales. She also knew all the top club owners. Judy was fabulous and immediately understood what I required. I cut a deal with her to set up a three-day itinerary for Don, O'Bryan, and me to come to New York. Judy had all-access wherever she took us. The first place was the Copacabana, one of New York's iconic night clubs. The night we went, an up-and-coming hip-hop group, Run DMC, was performing live.

Hip-hop music was a new genre and was becoming the rave throughout the Bronx, Queens, and Brooklyn. We were catching hip-hop in its embryonic stages. Judy felt it would soon become a dominant music genre—and she was right. Run DMC were wearing polyester jogging suits, Kangol hats, and what would become their signature Adidas without shoelaces. They exuded a hardcore street vibe and had abandoned shoelaces because they knew jail inmates were prohibited from having them (a safety precaution to prevent inmates from using them to hang themselves).

Run DMC was the first hip-hop group I had seen perform live, and they ended up being the most influential hip-hop group in the '80s. After witnessing their performance and seeing the crowd's reaction, it was clear they were special. Yet from that one performance, I did not envision that hip-hop music would become a preeminent musical genre that would revolutionize pop culture for the next forty years. Judy also took us to the Paradise Garage, arguably one of the wildest and most revered gay dance clubs ever. People would stand in line starting at 3 a.m. on Sunday morning to get in on what most club-goers considered after hours on Saturday night. It was a nonstop dance party that could last until noon the next day.

Everything you could imagine, or wouldn't believe possible, happened in there. It was all-inclusive: multicultural, gay, straight, and transgender. Every kind of fashion, hair style, jewelry, and piercings were worn—nothing was off limits. The inherent beauty of the atmosphere was that it was dimly lit, the music was thunderous, and everyone had the freedom to let loose, indulge, drink, ingest, snort, or smoke their favorite drug, dance their asses off, and party till dawn. When you walked out the door in the morning to make your "walk of shame" home, the sun was glaring, and people were walking to church. That night, it was a business trip, so we observed carefully and left at a reasonable time.

Judy also took us to Limelight, an old church converted into a club that was a staple in the New York club scene. The trip was fruitful. Don was pleased and O'Bryan felt enlightened by his up-close-and-personal experience of the underground club scene in New York—something the average New Yorker didn't know existed.

O'Bryan started recording his second album after returning to Los Angeles. He opted to do a cover of Stevie Wonder's classic hit "You and I," which was the second single and the title of the album. The first single, "I'm Freaky," was a funky up-tempo song that became a hit. The album, released in 1983, also included an upbeat track, "Soul Train's a Comin'," which became the theme song for *Soul Train* from 1983 to 1987. O'Bryan had used the tutelage he gained from the trip and scored another Top 20 chart album.

He released two other albums that charted in 1984 and 1986, but Don and O'Bryan were not seeing eye-to-eye about his overall career direction. Don could be obstinate, and since he was funding O'Bryan's career development, he wanted to protect his investment. O'Bryan was developing a viable fan base and wanted to control his artistic creative freedom. In the interim, their relationship had deteriorated considerably. After his fourth album release on Capitol, they severed their business relationship.

After the breakup, O'Bryan cut one more record that Atlantic Records had planned to release, but it was never released. After just five years, despite his promise of ascension, his career came to an abrupt and screeching halt. The music business is unforgiving; it has shuttered many more stars than it has birthed. Fame isn't fair or promised. I felt bad for O'Bryan—he got a taste, and I hoped he would get a second chance.

THE SOUL TRAIN MUSIC AWARDS

Working with Don as a manager was an educational experience. We developed a closer friendship and business relationship, and over the years he confided more in me. In retrospect, I think O'Bryan was an experiment for Don—but not a lark. Soon after, he turned his attention to creating other ways to further enhance and monetize the *Soul Train* brand. He was struggling with the series on several fronts. He was battling with AFTRA behind the scenes because they wanted to force Don to pay *Soul Train* performers comparable fees paid to performers who appeared on network shows.

Since *Soul Train* was a low-budget syndicated series, he didn't feel it should have to pay the higher network fees. The riff became public, and stories about the conflict appeared in *Hollywood Reporter* and *Variety*, the leading industry trade magazines. Don rarely shied away from confrontations and wasn't afraid to fight for what he believed. Winning most conflicts in a public forum isn't possible. Don could make incendiary remarks that would only further embroil the situation. I was empathetic but felt he had made his point. He got infuriated by some remarks and untruths a rep from AFTRA had made in an article and wanted to go on a tirade in a public rebuttal.

I convinced him not to be combative and to handle the matter privately. Simultaneously, he was also dealing with Tribune Entertainment, which was becoming less effective in maintaining his Saturday morning time slot for *Soul Train*. The show's ratings were dipping, and stations were looking to fill his slot with programming that would cater to younger demographics. Viewers also had more options with the emergence of cable television, music video channels, and video games.

Most of *Soul Train*'s audience counted on that time slot, and shifting it around was detrimental. Many stations started programming it at 1:00 or 2:00 a.m., which was a graveyard for a teenage music and dance series. Most local stations just weren't willing to invest the additional advertising funds necessary to build and sustain a prime-time audience base for any Black programs—not just *Soul Train*.

The switch justifiably irked and frustrated Don to no end. He had proven himself as a producer and had sustained quality content for over two decades, yet he was still not able to overcome the institutional restraints he faced. Other syndicated Black theme shows like *Essence*, *Ebony/Jet Showcase*, and the *Tom Joyner Show* also struggled to develop loyal audience bases and ratings because they couldn't secure prime-time slots for their programs. Black programs were used as filler to follow the highest-rated late-night program in that market: the late-night news or one of the late-night talk shows.

Privately, he dealt with dramatic mood shifts and was becoming very unpredictable and short-tempered. Sometimes he would light into me and make denigrating and accusatory comments that lasted longer than necessary. I would listen calmly, ask him if he was finished, and then try to get him to refocus on finding a solution for the issue he had raised. Days later, unsolicited, he would apologize and explain that he was having issues that he obviously could not control.

He also realized he needed to expand his production company so that he wasn't relying solely on *Soul Train*. There was a need in the marketplace for a contemporary awards program dedicated solely to Black music and artists. The two most popular award shows were the Grammy Awards and the American Music Awards.

Black artists rarely appeared on either program unless they had achieved major crossover success. The only other Black awards ceremony was the NAACP Image Awards, which honored Black entertainers from all entertainment mediums, not just music.

Don committed to launching the Soul Train Music Awards. He enlisted my services and allowed me to contribute to the creative development of the show. It thrilled me. I had represented Bette Midler when she cohosted the first MTV Video Awards with Dan Aykroyd. The MTV team included Bette and Dan in all the creative meetings, which Bette requested I attend. I had learned a lot from that experience and felt it made me more of an asset to Don.

Don and I met regularly, usually late afternoon. We discussed all aspects of the production, the look, the award trophy, who should host it, featured performers, and all the nuts and bolts. He also included me in meetings with Tribune executives to convince them to push their stations to commit to live telecasts of the show. Tribune already had a formula in place for selling Don's programs. Essentially, programs were sold to regional stations in blocks of time, which gave stations the autonomy to broadcast in the time slots they felt would deliver the most viewers in their market.

However, it was optimum to broadcast the show live during prime time for it to be competitive with the Grammys and the American Music Awards. Unfortunately, the major networks didn't believe Black-themed content, particularly music programs, could deliver high ratings to qualify for a prime time programming slot. So, Tribune offered the Soul Train Music Awards to stations for a multiple-day window. Most programmed it late night on the weekends. It wasn't an optimum situation, but Don had been dealing with this issue for years with *Soul Train*.

If there was a silver lining, it was that Don wholly owned *Soul Train* and had invested his own money building the brand. He realized that he needed a national broadcast partner to distribute the show, and syndication was his best option. He also had been successful in securing sponsorships and had enlisted Sprite, Coca-Cola's new soft drink, as a major sponsor for the Soul Train Awards.

Coca-Cola was actively marketing Sprite to the African American market and felt that partnering with Don on the first major music awards program honoring Black artists and music would help them accomplish that goal. Don was hoping Sprite would commit to a higher level of sponsorship, but at least he got his foot in the door. The Grammy Awards and American Music Awards were multimillion-dollar productions, and he aspired to the same for the Soul Train Awards. They had preexisting fan bases, longevity, were staunchly supported by the music industry, and received major marketing, promotion, and advertising budgets from the networks. Securing Sprite was a meaningful first step. Don's goal was to develop a reputable awards program that Black artists and record labels would embrace and respect as theirs—a family affair, with Black people being honored and celebrated by their peers. To make it media friendly, the most popular Black artists needed to perform and attend the awards ceremony. Just as important, record labels needed to include the show in their marketing budgets and cover some expenses for artists to participate (airfares, hotels, production costs for rehearsals, staging, etc.). Most important, we needed labels to advertise and promote the winners to validate the significance of receiving the award.

The voting body included active industry professionals, such as radio programmers, record retailers, artist management, and recording artists. The awards honored the top records and performances in R & B, hip-hop, and gospel music (and, in its earlier years, jazz music) that had charted in the most prominent music trade publications, such as *Billboard* and *Radio and Records*, in the year prior to the deadline set for nomination consideration. There were about twelve award categories plus two honorary awards, the Sammy Davis Jr. Entertainer of the Year Award and the Heritage Award. Noted artist and sculptor Artis Lane designed bronze trophies for each award. The Heritage Award was an African mask of an abstract seated human figure known as the Vanguard.

THE BIRTH OF THE SOUL TRAIN MUSIC AWARDS

On Friday, March 23, 1987, the first Soul Train Music Awards were held at the Santa Monica Civic Auditorium. I set up the press area and the red carpet arrival area. Things were hectic, but there was an aura of exhilaration and a great buzz. The audience was dressed to the nines, with most of the award nominees in attendance. The media turnout was better than I had anticipated. Many photographers showed up without getting clearance in advance, but I knew most of them, so I let them in.

Don came out to welcome everyone to the ceremony and explain the proceedings. Dionne Warwick and Luther Vandross served as cohosts, and the show's list of performers and presenters included George Benson, LL Cool J, Grace Jones, Isaac Hayes, Andraé Crouch, David Sanborn, Shirley Caesar, Al Jarreau, Little Richard, George Duke, and Vanessa Williams, many of them present or former clients. Stevie Wonder received the first Heritage Award for Career Achievement, and Janet Jackson received the Entertainer of the Year Award. Sprite hosted the afterparty at the downtown Sheraton Hotel. Considering that it was our first foray, it was a triumphant success.

Award shows are exhausting, whether you're working or just attending. You might invest eight to twelve hours of your day, depending on how long you party. It was a memorable evening, but I was relieved when it ended. It wasn't a flawless production—there were some technical glitches—but the reviews were mostly favorable. There were genuine feelings of affirmation and pride to have an award show that paid homage to Black artists and music. I continued to work with Don on several more shows. They were held at the Santa Monica Civic Auditorium until 1994, when he moved the show to the Shrine Auditorium.

Dionne and Luther cohosted three of the ceremonies, as did Patti La-Belle. I had represented Luther, and several other clients—Anita Baker, Natalie Cole, Babyface, and Vanessa Williams—also served as cohosts. During Don's welcoming segment for the second show, the audience was unruly and would not quiet down long enough for him to speak in a normal tone. He got perturbed and lit into the audience, calling them rude and disrespectful. He had made his point but kept ranting. Some audience members responded with unappreciative booing. Don was livid, but after the show he calmed down.

I convinced him that he shouldn't fulfill that role anymore and to use a comic who could warm up the audience and give them the rules. Probably the pinnacle of the Soul Train Awards was in 1989, when Michael Jackson received the inaugural Sammy Davis Jr. Award (originally the Entertainer of the Year Award) and the Heritage Award. Sammy Davis Jr. spoke via simulcast from Oslo, Norway, to express his thanks for having the award named in his honor and his elation at having Michael named the first recipient.

Eddie Murphy and Elizabeth Taylor presented the award to him live during the show. The segment also included a video that showcased Michael's many historic and record-setting worldwide accolades. The video, prepackaged by his management, was a mandatory element of his award presentation. The entire segment lasted for twelve minutes, which far exceeded the normal time allotted for award presentations. Michael endorsed the hyperbolic title "the king of pop," and whenever he had a national platform to reinforce his stature, he exploited it.

Jackson was a television ratings magnet at the time. When he appeared on an awards show, he spiked the ratings. He knew that and leveraged his clout whenever the opportunity presented itself. I thought his video was over-the-top and self-indulgent, but when the king demands twelve minutes, you give it to him. I had represented him and his brothers on their first album project after they exited Motown, so I understood him—a little. His appearance was a phenomenal boost to cementing the integrity of the show. Future recipients of the special awards included Whitney Houston, Arsenio Hall, Queen Latifah, and Gladys Knight & the Pips. Don continued to expand his production slate with the Soul Train Comedy Awards in 1993, which only survived one broadcast.

In 1995, he launched the Soul Train Lady of Soul Awards, which honored achievements by Black female performers. He duplicated the Soul Train Music Awards format by including two special awards, the Aretha Franklin Award for Entertainer of the Year and the Lena Horne Award for Outstanding Career Achievements. By then, the public had grown tired of the oversaturation of award shows. Many people felt the entertainment industry had become overly narcissistic and self-absorbed.

The Soul Train Music Awards proved to be resilient. However, it suffered an unfortunate negative hit when unknown assailants murdered legendary rapper Notorious Biggie Smalls while he was leaving a private *Vanity Fair* afterparty celebrating the Soul Train Music Awards.

I was transitioning into full-time management, and although I still maintained my PR company, I had turned over the day-to-day routine and upkeep of clients to my associates. I consulted with Don from time to time on an as-needed basis. Whenever he requested my input, I made myself available. One day he called and asked me to meet him at his office. We spent a few minutes catching up, then he said he wanted me to join his company and become his right-hand man. He intimated that he saw the end approaching and wanted to have someone he trusted in place, so he could slowly reduce his level of involvement. He didn't imply that he was planning to retire soon.

His offer flattered me. His son, Tony, had been working with him for several years, and I had presumed he would become the heir to Don's company. I had enormous respect for Don, but he could be unmanageable and very unpredictable. He was enduring recurring health issues and didn't seem to know if his symptoms might become more severe. I asked him once if he had been given any options to correct his condition, possibly undergoing a second operation. He felt the risk was too great. His doctors could not guarantee that the surgery would fully eradicate his symptoms, and there was a risk it might make matters worse. He was living precariously, enduring far more pain than I think he let people know.

I had enormous respect for Don and learned a lot from him. However, I felt the fact that I wasn't a full-time employee made our relationship more special and successful. I didn't want to risk possibly losing our business relationship and friendship, and felt I needed to continue following my own entrepreneurial path. I just needed time to attain my goals, so I instinctively wanted to pass. However, I didn't feel comfortable doing it in his presence. I knew Don would have a litany of reasons why I was making a mistake and would try to convince me otherwise. I thanked him, and a few days later, I called and told him I needed to stay focused on fulfilling my own goals. He understood and we occasionally spoke thereafter. I had given up my PR company, devoting all my energy to developing my management company, and I had moved to New York.

In 2008, it saddened me to hear about his arrest on a felony domestic violence charge. I had been in the presence of Don and his wife, Victoria, several times, and they seemed like a model couple. I felt even worse when I found out four years later that he had committed suicide. The combination of the spousal abuse charges and the suicide tarnished his legacy. I'm sure if he could produce a second take of his exit, he would have scripted it differently. In an article after his death, his son Tony reported that Don lived in constant pain and was under severe duress before he took his life.

It's difficult to truly appreciate Don Cornelius for his legacy as a true pioneer and a champion of Black lives and culture without examining what opportunities existed for Blacks hosting or starring in television shows prior to *Soul Train*. Historically, exposure for Black artists and content on television has been minimal at best. Don once argued that as Black people, we didn't have a talent deficit but an opportunity deficit. In a 2010 documentary about his show, he affirmed, "I had a burning desire to see Black people depicted on television in a positive light."

OTHER NOTABLE BLACK TELEVISION PIONEERS

There was no proven template for Don to follow, but here is a brief retrospective view of some talented Black pioneers who cracked open a door and created some access for others to follow.

The actress and singer Ethel Waters was the first Black performer, male or female, to host her own one-hour variety special, which ran on NBC on June 14, 1939. There is speculation she may have also been the first Black entertainer to appear on television.

Hazel Scott, a noted jazz singer and pianist, became the first person of African descent to host a US network television series. The series ran on the DuMont Television Network (now defunct) from July 3 to September 29, 1950. The shows were fifteen minutes long and featured Scott performances along with a few guest appearances by other artists.

Amos 'n' Andy began as one of the first radio comedy series and originated from station WMAQ in Chicago in 1928. It was originally created and written by Freeman Gosden and Charles Correll, white actors who starred and portrayed Black characters, Amos Jones (Gosden) and Andrew Hogg Brown (Correll), as well as some other bit characters. It moved to CBS in 1951 and became the first television comedy series featuring Black actors in the main roles, Alvin Childress (Amos), Spencer Williams (Andy), and their sidekick Tim Moore (Kingfish). The actors were instructed to keep their voices and speech patterns close to Gosden and Correll.

The sitcom was shot in Harlem as the first television series to be filmed with a multicamera setup, and was sponsored by the Blatz Brewing Company. Following the first broadcast the show was beset with protests from the NAACP, which felt the lead characters perpetuated demeaning Black stereotypes and ignored real-life problems facing Blacks. The NAACP initiated a boycott of Blatz Beer. In 1953, after filming fifty-two episodes,

CBS ended the series. It shifted to syndication and continued to run until 1966.

In 1956, the legendary jazz singer and pianist Nat King Cole became the first Black man to host a nationally broadcast program, the *Nat King Cole Show*. It debuted on NBC but only lasted for one year.

The *Ed Sullivan Show*, which premiered in 1948, was the gold standard, running for twenty-four years. Although Sullivan wasn't Black, he was singularly influential in showcasing top Black entertainers. Rock 'n' roll legend Bo Diddley was the first Black person to appear on the show. Over its run, the show featured performances by Stevie Wonder, B. B. King, the Supremes, the Temptations, the Jackson Five, Gladys Knight & the Pips, James Brown, Sam Cooke, Marvin Gaye, Smokey Robinson and the Miracles, Count Basie, Pearl Bailey, Louis Armstrong, Eartha Kitt, Duke Ellington, Ike and Tina Turner, comedians Flip Wilson and Richard Pryor, athletes Jackie Robinson and Muhammad Ali, and activist Coretta Scott King, among others.

In 1965, NBC's *I Spy* broke a racial barrier by casting Bill Cosby as a lead actor alongside Robert Culp—the first time a Black man had secured a lead role in a network prime-time action-adventure series. Cosby and Culp played American secret agents who traveled undercover as international tennis bums. Culp (as Kelly Robinson) posed as an amateur player, and Cosby (as Alexander Scott) was his trainer. They competed against wealthy opponents in return for food and lodging. Their work involved chasing villains, spies, and beautiful women. Over the series's three-year run, Cosby was instrumental in getting a number of notable Black actresses cast as guest stars on the show, including Eartha Kitt, Cicely Tyson, Barbara McNair, Nancy Wilson, Leslie Uggams, Janet MacLachlan, Diana Sands, and Gloria Foster.

In 1959, CBS signed Harry Belafonte to host a limited series, *The Revlon Revue Tonight with Belafonte*, directed by the future Oscar nominee Norman Jewison. The show was described as "a musical trip through black America with songs performed by respected black musicians, covering the wide spectrum of contemporary and historical black musical styles, including gospel, folk, blues, and jazz." Belafonte intended to exclusively feature Black guest entertainers. In the debut episode he featured jazz great Odetta, but Revlon and CBS pressured him integrate the show for the rest of the series. Before the second show, they reached an impasse, and the series was dropped. However, Belafonte became the first Black to win an Emmy when the first episode won an Emmy Award for Outstanding Performance in a Variety or Musical Program in 1960.

In 1968, three watershed breakthroughs for Black Americans occurred on national television. In February, at the pinnacle of the US Tet offensive in the Vietnam War, when the country was immersed in civil unrest, war protests, and racial disparity, Johnny Carson invited singer and activist Harry Belafonte (I served as a management consultant for the launch of his artist-driven social justice organization Sanfoka.org in 2013) to host the *Tonight Show* for the week of February 5–9.

Belafonte accepted, and during the week fifteen of his featured twenty-five guests were top Black talent. He opened doing poignant interviews with Robert F. Kennedy and Martin Luther King Jr., just months before both were assassinated (King on April 3, and Kennedy on June 5). Some of his other Black guests included Sidney Poitier, Bill Cosby, Lena Horne, Dionne Warwick, comedian Nipsey Russell, singer Leon Bibb (who was blacklisted), and Wilt Chamberlain. Other notable guest artists and activists were Paul Newman, Greek actress Melina Mercouri, Zero Mostel, Petula Clark, Buffy Sainte-Marie, Robert Goulet, comedians Tom and Dick Smothers, and American poet laureate Marianne Moore.

On the night of April 2, the day before Martin Luther King Jr.'s assassination, Belafonte appeared as a featured guest on the popular British pop star Petula Clark's debut one-hour NBC special. Plymouth Motors, a division of Chrysler, sponsored the special. Clark and Belafonte performed "On the Path of Glory," an antiwar song cowritten by Clark. During the performance she touched Belafonte's forearm, the first time a white woman had touched a Black man on national television. It caused shock waves throughout the country. Chrysler condemned the momentary clutch, along with many white Americans, who viewed it as racially offensive.

After King's assassination, tumultuous race riots broke out in 120 cities, most notably in Washington, DC, Baltimore, and Chicago. On April 11, 1968, President Lyndon Johnson signed the Civil Rights Act of 1968, a follow-up to the Civil Rights Act of 1964. A year later, the Voting Rights Act was passed.

The Fair Housing Act of 1968 prohibited discrimination in the sale, rental, and financing of housing based on race, religion, national origin, or sex. The Fair Housing Act stands as the final great legislative achievement of the civil rights era. Two months later, on June 5, Bobby Kennedy's assassination at the Ambassador Hotel was taped in real time (he died early on June 6) and broadcast on national television. I remember watching with dismay and shock as Sirhan Sirhan was able shoot him at almost point-blank range.

On August 26–29, anti–Vietnam War protests and riots broke out at the Democratic National Convention, and national television audiences witnessed flagrant police brutality vividly captured for three days. The way police brutalized protesters at the Democratic Convention was unnecessary and inhumane. They weren't quelling the riots; they were purposedly and violently attacking unarmed protestors.

On September 12, 1968, *Mr. Soul!* premiered on PBS and became the first African American–themed talk and variety series hosted by a Black man. The show's host and producer, Ellis Haizlip, was an openly gay, soft-spoken intellectual whose vision was to create an innovative variety program devoted to portraying the full expanse of the African American experience and bringing Black love, strength, and encouragement to American households. He aspired to feature Black poets, intellectuals, dancers, and musicians, both prominent and unknown. I met Haizlip's niece, Melissa Haizlip, who consulted with me in an unofficial capacity on her award-winning documentary *Mr. Soul* (2018), which she produced and directed with Sam Pollard. I had not seen the show during its initial run.

The first episode was taped at the studios of the New York PBS station, WNET, and featured Patti LaBelle and the Bluebelles. During the show's five-year run, Haizlip featured Muhammad Ali, Louis Farrakhan, James Baldwin, Amiri Baraka, Wilson Pickett, Marion Williams, the Last Poets, Max Roach, Toni Morrison, Stokely Carmichael, Ashford and Simpson, Nikki Giovanni, Stevie Wonder, and countless others. A 1968 Harris poll found that in its first few months alone, 65 percent of Black households in the United States watched the show regularly. In 1969, PBS started as a private, nonprofit corporation.

PBS picked up the show and syndicated it to their member stations. PBS gave Haizlip an ultimatum to integrate the show—and he refused to acquiesce. They maintained their stance that the show was "too Black" and canceled it.

In 1969, singer and actress Della Reese became the first Black woman to host her own nationally syndicated talk show in the US, *Della* (distributed by RKO). It ran for 197 episodes over one season. *Della* was a late-night talk show that featured her hosting and singing. She had many notable celebrity guests on the show, including George Burns, Tony Bennett, Gypsy Rose Lee, Ethel Waters, Little Richard, Steve Allen, Eric Burdon, and Ike and Tina Turner. She also had a sidekick comedian, Sandy Baron, and a regular comedy segment called "improvs" (akin to *Whose Line Is It Anyway?*). She later made history as the first woman ever to guest host the *Tonight Show Starring Johnny Carson*.

The following year NBC launched the *Flip Wilson Show*, a one-hour variety show that premiered on September 17, 1970, and starred the heralded comedian Flip Wilson. The show was the first American variety program hosted by a Black man to become successful with a white audience. During its first two seasons, the show was the nation's second-most-watched show according to Nielsen. In January 1972, *TIME* featured Wilson on its cover and named him "TV's first Black superstar." The show was canceled in 1974 amid declining interest in the variety-show format, which contributed to the show's lower ratings. Given that trend, along with the show consistently running over budget and Wilson seeking higher fees, the network opted to pull the plug.

On January 2, 1984, Chicago-based Oprah Winfrey launched the *Oprah Winfrey Show*, which later became known as *Oprah*. It was syndicated nationally as a daytime talk show and remains one of the most celebrated and highest-rated syndicated talk shows in modern American television history. The *Oprah Winfrey Show* aired for twenty-five seasons, from 1986 to May 25, 2011. In 2011, Winfrey launched her own TV network, the Oprah Winfrey Network (OWN). She was preceded by Bob Johnson, the founder of Black Entertainment Television, who became the first African American to launch and own a television network in 1980, and Cathy Hughes, whose company Urban One purchased TV One from the cable giant Comcast in 2004. OWN was initially structured as a mainstream television network, whereas BET and TV One were focused on programs targeting African American audiences.

On January 3, 1989, the *Arsenio Hall Show* debuted as the first syndicated late-night talk show with a Black host. Arsenio was a godsend, becoming a platform to showcase Black artists in a prime-time slot. The show lasted for five years, ending in 1994. I booked several music clients on the show, including Luther Vandross, Babyface, Vanessa Williams, and Andraé Crouch.

More recently, the *Wendy Williams Show* proved resilient for more than a dozen years (2008–2022) as one of the most popular syndicated daytime talk shows. The controversial Williams, who like Don was initially a popular radio DJ (at WBLS, one of New York's most popular urban music stations), serves as the show's host and executive producer.

The nationally syndicated *Tamron Hall Show* became an instant hit after it debuted in September 2019. Hall won the Daytime Emmy for Outstanding Informative Talk Show Host after just one season, and recently ABC announced they've renewed the show through the 2023–24 season.

For the past eleven years, radio and television personality Angela Lee has served as one of the anchors of the *Breakfast Club*, which has been broadcast on New York's 105.1 radio station since 2010 and simulcast on

Revolt TV since 2014. It reaches eight million listeners a month; in 2020 the show was inducted into the Radio Hall of Fame.

Since the first era of modern television, only a couple dozen Black talents and programs were given access and exposure on any of the major television networks. Television was almost impenetrable for Blacks, and short-lived for the ones who snagged a few minutes of fame. Very few strides were made compared to their white counterparts.

Don not only survived and thrived but he miraculously sustained the *Soul Train* brand for a thirty-five year run and 1,100 episodes. Soul Train is still the longest-running Black first-run nationally syndicated program in American television history. Until 2016, it also held the same distinction for all first-run, nationally syndicated programs. *Entertainment Tonight* overtook *Soul Train* in 2016. In 2018, *Wheel of Fortune* took over the top spot. *Soul Train* now ranks third overall on the all-time list.

When Don passed, he received an outpouring of adulation and appreciation from celebrities, artists, and people from all walks of life whom he had touched or influenced in some way. "He was able to provide the country a window into black youth culture and black music," said Lonnie G. Bunch III, director of the Smithsonian's National Museum of African American History and Culture. "For young black teenagers like myself, it gave a sense of pride and a sense that the culture we loved could be shared and appreciated nationally."

"Don was a visionary and giant in our business," producer and composer Quincy Jones said in a statement. "His contributions to television, music and our culture as a whole will never be matched."

Aretha Franklin said Cornelius "united the young adult community single-handedly and globally. He transcended barriers among young adults. With the inception of 'Soul Train,' a young, progressive brother set the pace and worldwide standard for young aspiring African American men and entrepreneurs in TV."

The show's "overall sense of blackness at this particular time was groundbreaking," Todd Boyd, professor of critical studies at the University of Southern California, noted, adding that "Cornelius effectively capitalized on the changes that took place in America socially and politically and culturally in the 1960s and in the next decade by giving national exposure to acts that previously were seen only in segregated settings."

Kenny Gamble, who, with his partner, Leon Huff, created the Philly soul sound and wrote the first theme song for *Soul Train*, said, "It was a tremendous export from America to the world, that showed African American life and the joy of music and dance, and it brought people together."

What I revered and admired most about Don was his love and respect for Black culture, and his commitment to being its ambassador. He never wavered from his mission, even when some Black artists and influential industry veterans refused to support him. He understood the lure of crossing over and how it altered the perception of some artists. Yet he wasn't willing to forfeit his integrity or marginalize his core audience to achieve it.

He believed in Black empowerment, entrepreneurship, sweat equity, and ownership. He realized that these tools could eradicate and disrupt systemic racism and the choke hold that kept Black talent and professionals from advancing in our industry. He consistently endorsed Blacks supporting Blacks and felt Black flight to white representatives circumvented our ability to build any measurable collective bargaining power. In his view, Blacks hiring white executives permeated the status quo and perception that Black executives weren't capable of rising to upper echelon positions in the industry.

Most important, I appreciated him giving me a chance to prove myself, along with his encouragement, trust (most of the time), camaraderie, brutal honesty, loyalty, and respect. I revered Don as an iconic figure, one of a kind, who educated, enlightened, and empowered me to become a better professional. I'm happy that I took the time to thank him personally several times throughout our friendship—when I knew he would be most receptive.

9

FAME IS NOT A DESTINATION— IT'S AN ACCOLADE

By the mid-1980s and early '90s I was brimming with confidence and had represented a wide range of notable clients who had snagged varying levels of fame. I had learned about and become attuned to the wide spectrum of perceptions about fame: how some artists viewed it, their obsession with manifesting it, or how it may have crippled them or created overwhelming anxiety and insecurity in their lives. Most of them were already famous, and a few had tasted small portions of fame for the first time.

When I initially met Kenneth "Babyface" Edmonds, he was twenty-eight years old. He wasn't famous but had achieved a moderate level of popularity with Black audiences. He was virtually invisible to mainstream audiences. I had signed Vanessa Williams to Wing Records (distributed by Mercury/Polygram) in late 1986 based on interest from the label's founder and president, and my friend, Ed Eckstine. We were in the early process of discussing potential songwriters and producers to collaborate in crafting material for her debut album.

Ed had seasoned Artist & Repertoire (A & R) tentacles and was aware of the buzz Kenny and Antonio "L.A." Reid were forging as a burgeoning songwriter/producer tandem. He thought they might be a good fit for Vanessa. We didn't have a big budget for her record, and he felt we could get them at a reasonable price—before they blew up and became pricey. We took Ed's lead and agreed to meet with them. Ed hosted an introductory meeting for everyone at his office in Los Angeles.

Kenny and L.A. came into the meeting in shiny suits and shoes that didn't look expensive, wearing black sunglasses with dark lenses. They had styled their artist image after the noted songwriting-producer team Jimmy Jam and Terry Lewis, who also wore suits, dark sunglasses, and fedoras. L.A. imitated Jimmy as spokesperson, and Kenny mimicked Terry as the silent one.

They played us a few songs they had written for name artists and four canned songs they had previously written. The canned songs were okay, but we wanted them to collaborate with Vanessa and tailor new songs to embody an identifiable artist direction for her. However, there was one song, "Girlfriend," a catchy, up-tempo urban pop song with a memorable hook, that grabbed our attention.

Ed proposed they cut a demo of "Girlfriend" featuring Vanessa as the lead vocalist—on spec. It would give them a chance to get to know each other and see if they jelled. They agreed to record the demo at a makeshift studio they had set up in their apartment. If the demo sounded great, Ed would contract them to write and produce a few songs for Vanessa's album.

Kenny was from Indianapolis, and L.A. was from Cincinnati. They were in Los Angeles shopping songs after exiting from the Deele, a seven-member R & B band L.A. had founded to focus on developing their songwriter-producer partnership. Kenny had launched his career as an artist, songwriter, and producer when he was eighteen years old, serving as a principal member of several other R & B bands from the Midwest, including Manchild ("Especially for You"), Crowd Pleasers, and Red Hott (produced by the funk music pioneer and producer George Kerr), before joining the Deele.

I wasn't familiar with any of the groups Kenny or L.A. were in, but I had heard a few of their hit songs on the radio: "Two Occasions," "Slow Jams," and "Rock Steady" (by the Whispers). I knew the Whispers, and "Rock Steady" was a #1 record and one of my favorite R & B songs.

Vanessa had started recording her vocals on "Girlfriend," and things were going well. As we were trying to schedule a couple more sessions to finish the demo, we suddenly couldn't get Kenny or L.A. on the phone. Ed tried, I tried several times, and Vanessa even called them. We left messages, but they completely ghosted us.

After several weeks with no response, Ed called to advise me that he had found out they had given the song to Pebbles. She was a new R & B singer signed by Jheryl Busby, MCA Records' president of Black music, whom I had known for years. Ed attacked them with a profane tirade that went on for several minutes. When Vanessa heard the news, she was close behind (minus the profanity) in echoing Ed's sentiments. They vowed never to work with the pair again. I was angry and thought it was a cowardly act to not notify us or return my calls. But I didn't see any benefit in wasting energy over spilled milk or hoarding resentment toward them.

The rumor mill was rampant with innuendo about how Pebbles had colluded with L.A. and Kenny to steal the song from Vanessa. It became fodder for the tabloids and Black press. There were multiple versions of what had transpired, but Vanessa's version is most accurate. She was in L.A.'s apartment when Pebbles showed up and heard the rough demo of "Girlfriend" with Vanessa's vocals and loved it. It was a simple snatch-and-grab scenario, and the song went to the highest bidder. Pebbles wasn't a villain, but she was certainly opportunistic.

She had the financial backing of Jheryl and MCA, who had offered Kenny and L.A. more money, which they needed. And her husband, George Smith, a successful contractor from Oakland, kicked in some bonus perks to help get the song for Pebbles. We only had a spec deal, which meant Kenny and L.A. had no contractual obligations to Wing Records or Vanessa. "Girlfriend" became the lead single for Pebbles's self-titled debut album on MCA Records in October 1987. It reached #5 on the Hot 100 chart.

EMERGENCE OF LAFACE RECORDS

After "Girlfriend" became an enormous hit, Kenny and L.A. soared, becoming one of the most sought-after songwriter-producer tandems in the industry. In the short span of a few years, they had written and produced hits for Karyn White, the Whispers, Johnny Gill, After 7, Sheena Easton, Paula Abdul, Bobby Brown, and Whitney Houston, among others. They founded LaFace Records in Atlanta in 1989 and signed a multimillion-dollar joint venture with Arista Records engineered by its president, Clive Davis. Their eclectic artist roster included Toni Braxton, Usher, TLC, Tony Rich, Outkast, and Pink. They had taken a gargantuan leap in their level of fame within the industry.

RUNNING INTO KENNY AND L.A. AGAIN

After not speaking to either Kenny or L.A. for almost two years, I was attending a Lakers game and hanging out in the Forum Club, a private VIP club and restaurant that Lakers owner Jerry Buss had set up in the arena to be enjoyed by VIPs, high rollers, celebrities, sponsors, friends, and avid Lakers supporters who were premium season ticket holders. I saw L.A. and Kenny talking on the other side of the club, so I walked over to say hey. It surprised them that I took the time to come over because they thought I hated them.

I congratulated them on their success and took a minute to bust their balls about not returning any of my messages. They both apologized and admitted they didn't handle the situation professionally. Then I said sarcastically, "Seriously, I don't hate you guys, but I can't speak for Ed or Vanessa—not sure where they stand these days."

A few seconds later, Ed, who was a huge Laker fan, appeared out of nowhere. He extended a warm smile and brother-to-brother head genuflection to me and a brief hello to Kenny. He turned his head slightly, and with leering eyes said, "Fuck you, L.A.!" Then he abruptly walked away. It was a cold-blooded move, so to lighten the mood, I remarked, "Well, that

confirms he still hates you guys. Or for sure he clearly hates you, L.A."
We shared a laugh and went our separate ways.

BECOMING KENNY'S MANAGER

Several months later I received a call from attorney Stephen Barnes.
Stephen was one of Hollywood's top Black attorneys. He represented
both Kenny and me. Much to my surprise, he said Kenny had reached out
to discuss the possibility of me managing him. My interest was piqued.
I thought, the worst-case scenario is we meet, we talk, and nothing happens.

We initially spoke on the phone. Kenny was affable and refreshingly not
self-absorbed or scattered. He was recording his next solo album and writing and producing material for several other projects, and he proposed we
meet in person. Our conversation was brief, but I felt that from a purely
selfish business perspective, signing him would be a phenomenal boost to
my company.

Kenny lived in a modern high-rise condo apartment building with a
concierge in Buckhead, the most affluent area of metropolitan Atlanta. It
was comfortably spacious and well decorated in muted earth tones. He had
an oversize couch that looked comfy and I imagined would swallow you up.
We started talking in broad strokes about our lives and how we got to where
we were. He was the second youngest of six boys, born and raised in Indianapolis, Indiana, to Marvin and Barbara Edmonds. His mother was a production operator at a pharmaceutical plant. When he was in eighth grade,
his father died of lung cancer, and his mother raised her sons alone from
that point forward.

He openly described himself as reserved and shy. He used music,
learning guitar and keyboards, and songwriting to channel his feelings,
thoughts, and emotions. I was surprised by his openness and his dozens
of hilarious band stories and anecdotal recollections about what inspired
his songs.

After listening to several songs from his album, there wasn't one I didn't like. Then he asked if I'd be cool with him playing a song he wrote but didn't demo as he wasn't sure it fit his artist image. He sat at the edge of the couch and pulled out an acoustic guitar. I didn't realize he even played guitar. The title of the song was "When Can I See You." His raw performance blew me away, and I instantly thought it was a smash. I suggested he keep the production bare bones, so the acoustic guitar would carry the melody the same way he had just performed it.

During my visit, he set up an informal lunch meeting with L.A. and introduced me to his longtime friend and collaborator Daryl Simmons, who lived nearby. While in the car he played "Give U My Heart," a duet song he had written and produced featuring him and Toni Braxton, a new R & B artist signed to LaFace Records. They had arranged for the song to be featured in the film *Boomerang* and planned to release it as a single to launch her debut album on LaFace. She didn't have a manager yet, and Kenny wanted to broker an introduction for me to manage to her.

He wasn't looking for an all-encompassing management relationship with me. He only wanted me to manage and further develop his artist brand (not his songwriter-producer career). We talked about making live performances and touring a priority, growing his brand globally, and illuminating and creating a more identifiable artist persona. I didn't feel Kenny exuded an "it" personality factor, at least not at first sight, but his songs did. His songs were superstars, and I felt we needed to raise his artist persona to the level of his songs. We negotiated an equitable monthly retainer fee and agreed to negotiate a flat fee on bigger deals such as a national concert tour, corporate endorsements, ancillary products, merchandise, television, and film.

I started managing Kenny around the same time his duet Toni became the second single released from the film soundtrack. *Boomerang*, a romantic comedy film, starred Eddie Murphy, Robin Givens, Halle Berry, David Alan Grier, Martin Lawrence, Grace Jones, Eartha Kitt, and Chris Rock. Reginald Hudlin directed, and Brian Grazer and Warrington Hudlin produced the film. It was a joint venture between Eddie Murphy Productions and Imagine Entertainment (Grazer's production company). Paramount Pictures released it on July 1, 1992. It grossed $131 million. Kenny, L.A., and Daryl produced the soundtrack album, which was released by LaFace/Arista in June 1992.

KENNY AND TRACEY

It didn't take long for me to figure out that Kenny had a zillion other things going on besides his involvement with LaFace and his artistic career. While he was on the verge of severing his songwriter-producer partnership with L.A., he was about to start a new life partnership with Tracey McQuarn, whom he had been dating for a while. They had fallen hard for each other, were a happy couple, and outwardly expressed affection toward each other. Tracey is a stunner—bright and not demure. She rarely filtered her opinions and had considerable influence on Kenny's career decisions.

He shepherded a deal for her to head up her own record label, Yab Yum Records, with Polly Anthony's new label, 550/Sony. Polly was a highly touted record promotion veteran and one of the few women to head up a label at one of the major record distributors. She had previously been VP of promotion at Sony/Epic, and I had worked directly with her on Kenny and Luther Vandross, who was his label mate on Epic. She also broke Celine Dion.

Tracey was ambitious and wasn't interested in riding Kenny's coattails. She aspired to earn and establish her own brand persona and fame, and Kenny seemed happy to oblige. Yab Yum's debut artist was Jon B, a talented white R & B and soul songwriter, singer, producer, and musician. His vocal phrasing and artistic vibe were influenced and inspired by Kenny. Kenny recorded a duet with him, "Someone to Love," which became his first hit single from his debut album, *Bonafide*. It received a Grammy Award nomination for Best Pop Collaboration with Vocals in 1995 and helped his album go platinum, selling a million copies. I had no official role with anything related to Yab Yum or Tracey individually.

Kenny's fame and brand identity were morphing and running parallel in three distinct arenas: his core business as a prolific songwriter and producer, his artist brand, and his business ventures with Tracey. After Yab Yum, they set up Edmonds Entertainment, a film and television production division, publishing entity, and record label. Sometimes I would just shake my head in amazement because I felt he was spreading himself too thin. He consistently exuded calm optimism and never got frazzled. Our personalities were similar in that way, which allowed us to stay balanced and focused.

Kenny and I were forging a meaningful friendship beyond our business association—and he sought my input in some personal matters as well. The afternoon before their wedding I got a distress call from them asking if I could help put together the guest list and seating chart for their wedding reception. They had to be at their rehearsal dinner and wanted to drop off all the documentation on their way to the dinner. Tracey said Kenny's assistant, Solombra Ingram, had agreed to stop by to assist after she finished her normal workday.

They came to my office looking noticeably flustered, rushed in, and dropped a couple of bags filled with bits of paper and a partial list of names. I had underestimated the level of disarray I was inheriting, and my office staff had left for the day. Solombra and I had a marathon night, working until 3 a.m. piecing together a master guest list and seating chart for over three hundred people. Solombra was a life saver. Desperate times call for desperate measures. Their wedding and reception were a blur for me, but they were glitch free.

KENNY AND L.A. SEVER THEIR SONGWRITER-PRODUCER PARTNERSHIP

Kenny's estrangement from L.A. had mushroomed, and they stopped communicating. The heart of their conflict involved core issues over the division of their writing and publishing rights. The last week of July 1993, the *Los Angeles Times* announced that Kenny and L.A. were severing their songwriter-producer relationship. However, their business partnership, their shared ownership of LaFace, and its contractual obligations to Arista stayed intact.

FOR THE COOL IN YOU

Amid everything else that was going on, Kenny was finishing up his next solo album, *For the Cool in You*. He put together a collection of gripping and radio-friendly songs. There were a handful of solid options for singles, but I felt "When Can I See You" had all the intangible components to make it a smash when it was released. There was a detectable buzz about *For the Cool in You* within the label. Tommy Mottola, the president of Sony, liked the album and loved the song. He requested Kenny to perform at Sony's International Music Convention in Miami, and felt performing "When Can I See You" could help launch the album and break him internationally.

The convention assembled all of Sony's major international label heads and marketing executives to go over strategic plans for the year and to showcase artists they needed to prioritize to reach their annual sales and revenues goals. Performing in front of that audience is a game-changer for any artist, because only a handful of artists are prioritized globally every year. Getting more international recognition from his records would open doors for him to expand his brand, perform outside the US, and generate additional revenue streams.

The performance slot they offered to Kenny was at 9:30 a.m., which we didn't view as optimum. Tommy wanted Kenny to perform the song solo, with no band, which I thought was a fantastic idea. Kenny was initially reluctant to do so, but understood the leverage he'd gain and agreed to fulfill Tommy's request.

They staged his performance on a proscenium stage in a theater with a capacity of about a thousand seats. His one-song breakfast gig received a gracious standing ovation. Tommy and Sony delivered by making Kenny and his album an international priority. Soon after, I began engaging with their international division to develop a European promotional tour.

KENNY SCORES WITH HIT SINGLES

Though there were several choices for singles, everyone felt the title song for the album, "For the Cool in You," which Kenny cowrote and coproduced with Daryl Simmons, should be released as the lead single. Epic Records released the single on August 10, 1993. The video was directed by Andy Morahan, a top British video and film director who had directed videos for many superstar pop artists, including George Michael (with Aretha Franklin), Billy Joel, Michael Jackson, Mariah Carey, and Elton John.

The song peaked at #81 on the *Billboard* Hot 100 and reached #10 on the R & B charts. It earned a Grammy Award nomination for Best R & B Vocal Performance, Male (1994). In addition, it was featured in ABC-TV's hit show *Family Matters*, in the episode titled "Dr. Urkel and Mr. Cool," which featured actor Jaleel White as the show's popular character Urkel.

While "For the Cool in You" built momentum, we were gearing up for the next two single releases, "Rock Bottom" and "Never Keeping Secrets." We came up with a strategy to shoot both videos in Paris, France. The goal was to have them in the can and ready to go when necessary. In the interim, Kenny could schedule a few production projects without worrying about being interrupted.

We hired noted entertainment photographer and director Randee St. Nicholas to direct both videos. Kenny and I both liked Randee a lot. She was innately collaborative, organized, had a great visual range, and was acutely sensitive to the vibe and feel of the music. She and Kenny clicked on every level. We shot in the fall, and it was rainy and cold throughout our stay in Paris.

For "Never Keeping Secrets," we shot scenes in several arrondissements throughout the city, during the day and at night, from the famous Gare du Nord train station in central Paris, near the Champs-Élysées, and along the banks of the Seine River. We shot "Rock Bottom," an up-tempo song, in an old jazz club as a live performance video and hired a mixed band of French musicians to perform with Kenny.

The success of the lead single positioned the album the way we hoped it would. When Epic released it on August 24, there was significant anticipation, and radio stations started playing several songs with no prompting from the label. We had determined that "Rock Bottom" should be the second single, but radio's powerful reaction to a ballad, "Never Keeping Secrets," foiled our strategy. We couldn't ignore the unsolicited airplay it was generating. And it made little sense to force radio to play a track they had not gravitated toward on their own.

In January 1994, Epic released "Never Keeping Secrets," which Kenny wrote and coproduced with Daryl and L.A. Luckily, our strategy to shoot two videos simultaneously paid off. It peaked at #15 on the US Hot 100 chart and at #3 on the US R & B chart.

"And Our Feelings," the third single, was released in April 1994. The video featured Tracey as Kenny's love interest, and it was the third video shot by Randee. We had developed a wonderful creative rapport and friendship with her team and were following the adage "If it's not broken, don't fix it." She was delivering high-quality and cost-effective videos within our budget, and Kenny felt safe in her hands.

The videos were conceived to play a pivotal role in raising Kenny's visual persona, connecting his face to the songs, raising his artist persona to the level of superstardom he had achieved as a top R & B and pop songwriter and producer, and attracting more media attention and coverage.

We filmed the "And Our Feelings" video in late afternoon in the desert a couple of hours north of Los Angeles to avoid the scorching heat. But after sunset, the temperature dipped significantly. Kenny and Tracey's wardrobe wasn't designed to accommodate the near-freezing temperatures. They were shivering and between takes were being wrapped up in blankets until the shots were set up.

It was one video where I couldn't wait to hear, "That's a wrap!" Kenny,

Tracy, and I drove back to L.A. in a limousine. They immediately turned the heat on high, which they did habitually. This time, I was all for it. But after about thirty minutes the chill had subsided. I was feeling faint and short of breath, while they were all cuddled up sleeping. Out of sheer courtesy, I didn't want to wake them to ask to turn down the heat. So I cracked the window a sliver or two and let the air and wind hit my face—much like the average dog does in cars. When they awoke, I candidly shared how I had been gasping for air, and they happily obliged in turning down the heat. The song became the third hit single from the album, peaking at #21 on the Hot 100 charts and #8 on the R & B Singles charts.

The most popular single and video from the album became "When Can I See You," which remains the most successful single release for Kenny as a solo artist. Randee directed and shot a performance video of Kenny singing and playing acoustic guitar at the Living Room, a hip and popular coffeehouse on La Brea Avenue in Los Angeles. We used a few extras to create a chill ambiance.

The song and video's mainstream success led to securing guest appearances for Kenny on major network television morning and evening television shows from the *Today Show* to the *Tonight Show*. He performed the song with a trio for several shows, and we added a cellist for a few as well. Released during the last week of May 1994, "When Can I See You" became Kenny's highest charting single on the *Billboard* Hot 100, peaking at #4. The song also peaked at #6 on the R & B Singles chart. It earned him his first Grammy Award for Best Male R & B Vocal Performance at the 36th Annual Grammy Awards.

That same year he also captured the Grammy Award for Producer of the Year, Non-Classical. The album was certified triple-platinum, making it the biggest-selling solo album in his career to date. And as we hoped, it opened the floodgates for Kenny internationally. The record performed well in the UK, Japan, and other European markets, including Holland and France. It later propelled his first major national concert tour as a coheadliner with Boyz II Men.

KENNY AND CLIVE'S IMPASSE

Kenny had stopped communicating with L.A., and not long afterward he and Clive Davis became estranged as well. After he and L.A. broke up, several songwriters, producers, and artists were questioning who was more influential in writing and producing their songs. Kenny was disgruntled and felt his integrity and credibility were being questioned. So he was on a mission to flood the market with a slew of hit records to legitimize his solo imprint as a songwriter and producer—and silence any doubters who questioned his skill set.

The crux of the impasse with Clive was a clause in LaFace's deal with Arista that put a cap on the number of songs Kenny and L.A. could write, produce, and release for artists distributed by other major record labels. Kenny knew about it but objected to Clive controlling whom he could write and produce for independently. He refused to abide by the contract. In turn, Clive was taking a strong-arm approach to remind Kenny that he had the contractual rights and power to shut him down—if he desired to do so.

I became an unofficial mediator and mitigator throughout their standoff. My hunch was that Clive understood Kenny's reasoning, even though he wasn't fully embracing his method. The truth was that Clive would be the beneficiary of Kenny's increased fame by writing and producing more hit records, regardless of whether they were released by Arista and its subsidiary labels.

MADONNA'S "TAKE A BOW"

During Kenny's sprint to self-proclaimed artistic freedom, he wrote and produced hit songs for El DeBarge, Jon B, Tevin Campbell, Boyz II Men, and Karyn White. His most acclaimed exploit outside of his Arista deal was cowriting, coproducing, and performing the #1 hit "Take a Bow" with Madonna. This midtempo ballad about unrequited love was the second single released from her sixth studio album, *Bedtime Stories* (Maverick Records, 1994).

Madonna didn't want the vocal arrangement crafted as a traditional duet but opted to feature Kenny prominently as a guest vocalist. They backed the track with a full orchestra, which marked the first time Kenny recorded and produced a track with live strings. To support the single release, she had strategically committed to premiere the song on the American Music Awards and the Sanremo Music Festival in Sanremo, Italy, on February 22, 1995, which was televised by the Italian television station Rai 1 TV. The broadcast reached a cumulative audience of over twenty million people throughout Europe.

I had worked peripherally with Madonna and her management team when my client Andraé Crouch wrote the choir arrangements for her hit "Like a Prayer" but never met her personally. Her manager, Freddie De-Mann, and I were friendly and had worked together on the Jacksons. I liked him and her longtime Warner Bros. Records publicist, Liz Rosenberg.

Madonna impressed me. I respected the way she strategically crafted her brand persona and always stayed ahead of the curve musically. She understood the power of fame and how to effectively leverage it, and she set trends instead of following them. She continually took risks, challenged the status quo, and remains a seminal figure in the evolution of contemporary pop music.

I don't know what I expected, but she was friendly, thoughtful, professional, and a welcoming and giving collaborator. Her goal was to make their performance complementary, so it aptly reflected their collaboration as cowriters and coproducers. She didn't want it to appear as a gratuitous and self-serving gesture and sought our input on everything.

She set up several days of rehearsals in Los Angeles, took the time to videotape them, and invited all the principals to view the rehearsal footage each day when we finished to give input and feedback. Initially, she staged her and Kenny on round platforms. They placed his several feet behind hers, so it jutted out about a foot or so on one side. After reviewing the taped rehearsal, she felt Kenny's riser was too far away, so she had it moved up the next day. She later used higher platforms and positioned them side by side for the American Music Awards appearance.

For the performance at the Sanremo Music Festival we stayed in Monte Carlo, which was my first time staying there. They booked us at Hotel de Paris, one of Monaco's most famous hotels. The Sanremo Festival was one of the biggest in Europe, and it was being broadcast live. It had a rich legacy hosting dozens of major international artists who had debuted their songs on the broadcast, including Louis Armstrong, Stevie Wonder, José Feliciano, Roberto Carlos, Paul Anka, the Yardbirds, Marianne Faithfull, Shirley Bassey, Kiss, and Italian stars like Andrea Bocelli, Laura Pausini, and Giorgia.

Madonna assembled an incredible band, which included Omar Hakim on drums, Victor Bailey on bass, and Michael Reardon on keyboards. The performance was staged with a full orchestra stacked on risers behind the band. They had set up a caravan of six or seven Mercedes to drive us across the border to San Remo, which was just an hour's drive from Monaco. Kenny and I had our own car.

As we arrived in the city and turned onto the road that led down to the theater, crowds of people had overrun both sides of the street and stood packed in rows surrounding our caravan. More people filled balcony terraces and porches, screaming, "Madonna! Madonna!" It was sheer bedlam.

We were moving at a snail's pace, and people were peering into the cars, hoping to see Madonna. The disappointment on people's faces when they saw two unidentifiable Black guys sitting in the car was significant. Kenny was becoming a little disconcerted. He looked at me and said, "I never want to become this famous. I wouldn't be able to handle it." It was a once-in-a-lifetime experience, and their performance received a rousing response.

"Take a Bow" was the only #1 pop hit on the Hot 100 that he cowrote, coproduced, and performed on as an artist. It became Madonna's eleventh #1 single on the *Billboard* Hot 100 and her twenty-third top five hit—both records for a female artist. However, she didn't use Kenny in the video and never performed it live on her concert tours. Had either occurred, Kenny would have gained immeasurably more fame for collaborating with her on the song.

KENNY, CLIVE, AND LISA STANSFIELD

Meanwhile, Kenny and Clive still weren't talking, and the multiple-award-winning songwriter Diane Warren was calling me incessantly to try to get Kenny to do a duet on a song she had written for the English pop and R & B singer Lisa Stansfield, whom Clive signed to Arista. She burst on the scene with the massive hit "All Around the World" (inspired by Barry White and including a short intro from him). Diane said David Foster was slated to produce and that Clive was enthusiastic about Kenny doing the duet with Lisa. But Kenny was lukewarm about the song and felt that if Clive really wanted him to record it, he should make the request directly.

I was a fan of Lisa as an artist. She performed at my club R & B Live in Los Angeles when she was breaking in the US. I wasn't trying to block the idea, but there weren't signs that Kenny and Clive's impasse would end soon. Diana kept calling, so instead of trying to chase her off, I felt if I could get Kenny to extend an olive branch and do it as a favor, it might lead to a détente between him and Clive.

Kenny and Lisa cut the song. David Foster produced it, and we got Randee St. Nicholas to direct the video. Arista released the single in November 1994. Unfortunately, it only reached #109 on the pop charts and #80 on the R & B charts. The animated film *Pagemaster* included the song on its soundtrack, and it appeared on Lisa's album *Natural*. Despite its failed commercial success, it rekindled Kenny and Clive's relationship and put their beef to rest.

THE FIRST JAPAN TOUR

This was probably the most hellacious time of my managerial term with Kenny. The commercial success of *For the Cool in You* opened the door for Kenny to do his first major national concert tour as a solo artist, and we were being approached by several top booking agencies to represent him. The album was doing well in Japan, and I received a call from Yuji Fukushima, a young Tokyo-based promoter who wanted to book Kenny to do a minitour in Japan (the second-biggest global market for music, especially urban and R & B music). I thought it would be a good preliminary step to work out kinks in the show without media scrutiny before launching a major tour in the US.

Concert tours in Japan need to be booked four to six months in advance, sometimes longer. I put together the tour without meeting Yuji. We scheduled the minitour for December 7–13, 1994, with concert dates in Sapporo (12/7), Tokyo (12/10), Kobe (12/12), and Nagoya (12/13). I was able to get Yuji to add taping a concert special for Japan's largest national public television network, NHK-TV, to the overall deal. It would become Kenny's first music special. We talked regularly on the phone and sent emails back and forth for a couple of hours, usually starting around 2–3 a.m., for several months.

Kenny wanted a set designed for his show, a full band, backup singers, and dancers for the tour. So we put together a seven-piece band, three background singers, and four dancers. He dedicated eight weeks of staggered rehearsals at Center Stage Studios in the San Fernando Valley for the band, with a smaller dance studio not too far away for the dancers. We often shuttled together from one rehearsal to the other.

The *For the Cool in You* music special was taped at his performance at Tokyo Bay NK Hall, a five-thousand-seat theater about an hour from Tokyo and close to Tokyo Disneyland. NHK-TV broadcast the special in May 1995. The tour presented many challenges, none more than dealing with the language barrier and using translators, but it was also a commercial success, and Yuji and I have remained close friends ever since.

In the interim, and well before the Japanese tour happened, I was exploring opportunities to book a tour in the US to follow up on the Japan tour. Several of my longtime talent agent friends asked about representing Kenny, principally Jeff Frasco, whom I had known for years. He was one of the top veteran music agents at Creative Artists Agency (CAA) and handled superstar acts from the Spice Girls to Kanye West. I trusted Jeff and felt he could champion Kenny internally to the agency's other divisions, film, television, and corporate sponsorships, which might elevate Kenny's artist brand on the heels of a successful concert tour.

But Kenny didn't want to meet with him, and it made no sense to push the issue further. When I told Jeff that Kenny was passing, he got intensely irritated and took it personally. It put a strain on our business relationship for a while. The bottom line was Kenny didn't want an agent and felt we could put the tour together ourselves.

Soon afterward we received a timely call from Al Haymon. He had a tour package he wanted to present to Kenny. We both knew and had worked with Al. He was the most prominent Black promoter in the country for over a decade, handling concert tours for superstars such as MC Hammer, New Edition, Whitney Houston, Janet Jackson, Mary J. Blige, Rick James, and the historic national Budweiser Superfest—thirty-city annual tours sponsored by Anheuser-Busch. Superfest featured the crème de la crème of R & B acts, including Michael Jackson, Stevie Wonder, Luther Vandross, Aretha Franklin, Smokey Robinson, Teddy Pendergrass, the Bar-Kays, Mary J. Blige, Ashford & Simpson, and TLC.

Al invited us to lunch in West Hollywood to discuss his touring concept. He was lithe and tall, wore stylish business suits, had a trimmed beard, and had a low-key demeanor. He never flaunted his success, was intelligent and shrewd, and didn't waste time engaging in idle chatter. I respected and appreciated his minimalistic way of cutting to the chase. He wanted to package a coheadlining national concert tour featuring Kenny and Boyz II Men. Kenny had cowritten and produced two of their biggest hit songs, "End of the Road" and "I'll Make Love to You," which were #1 hits on the Hot 100 Singles chart and combined to stay at #1 for twenty-seven weeks.

Their album was nearing twelve million in sales, and Kenny's was around two million in sales. They had a young mainstream fan base, which was attractive, and the strategical timing couldn't be better. We knew the band and were enthusiastically receptive to the idea. The tour he proposed would comprise twenty-four arena-capacity concert performances in major markets across the US, including New York; Los Angeles; Philadelphia; Boston; Washington, DC; Hartford, Connecticut; Charlotte; Dallas; Houston; Las Vegas; Cleveland; Detroit; and Cincinnati.

The tour would start late in the year and continue through the first quarter of 1995. Al committed to paying Kenny a total performance fee that was close to $1 million and suggested rotating the headliner slot every other date. Each artist's set would be the same length (a max of ninety minutes). In some markets we added a third act to the bill, either Brandy or Tevin Campbell (Kenny had written and produced hit songs for both of them as well). We gave Al a verbal commitment to do the tour during our meeting, but it took more than a month to pull everything together, get the contracts signed, and have firm dates locked in.

The difference between using Haymon Enterprises to book a tour and signing with a booking agency like CAA is that Al packaged and offered all-inclusive deals. His company had an infrastructure that enabled them to package, book, and produce the concerts. He handled transportation for all the production components, sets, staging, lighting, equipment rental (back line and sound), venue contracts, marketing, advertising, publicity, and routing the tour. He paid 50 percent of the total guarantee upfront and the balance at the end of the tour.

The response to Kenny's performances was phenomenal. We created one show-stopping moment in his show that created pandemonium and brought the house down in every city. While performing one of his most popular songs, "As Soon as I Get Home," Kenny would surprise a female from the audience and bring her on stage, sit her in a chair and sing to her.

He sings about giving his lady love, buying her clothes, cooking her dinner as soon as he gets home. Then just as he says "I'll pay your rent," he moved closer, grabbed her hand, and slapped $500 into her palm, one $100 bill at a time, with passionate accentuation. Audiences screamed and gave the gesture a thunderous response.

Most of the women acted like it was a million dollars and either cried profusely, went limp, or almost fainted. One girl had to be helped off stage and immediately treated by paramedics with oxygen. The response to Kenny's performances was phenomenal, and most of his reviews were favorable.

It was a win-win for Kenny, Boyz II Men, and Al. Almost all the dates sold out, including a New Year's Eve show at Madison Square Garden. It created a national buzz, triggering interest from other major venues. Al presented a formal offer to add six more shows to the tour, which would have triggered $500K in touring support from Epic Records (for a minimum of thirty shows). I felt it would extend his momentum, enhance his persona as a viable live performer, and potentially raise his performance fee on his next to tour. He listened but to my dismay he passed on the offer.

WAITING TO EXHALE

Along with adding successful tours in Japan and the US to Kenny's résumé, Clive engaged him to write and produce the music for the *Waiting to Exhale* motion picture soundtrack, which would be the most adventurous and commercially successful album of his career. Clive had secured the rights for Arista to do the soundtrack, which was Whitney Houston's follow-up to her motion picture debut in the box office hit film *The Bodyguard* (1992). It yielded the smash hit, "I Will Always Love You," the greatest-selling single by a woman in history.

The film was based on Terry McMillan's novel. Forest Whitaker directed, and along with Houston, the film costarred Angela Bassett, Loretta Devine, Lela Rochon, and an all-Black ensemble cast including Wesley Snipes,

Gregory Hines, Wendell Pierce, Giancarlo Esposito, Leon, Dennis Hays-
bert, and Donald Adeosun Faison. The soundtrack featured original songs
that Kenny wrote and produced for Whitney Houston, Toni Braxton, TLC,
Brandy, Aretha Franklin, Chaka Khan, Faith Evans, Patti LaBelle, SWV, and
Mary J. Blige.

The album comprised sixteen tracks all produced by Kenny. He wrote
twelve songs and cowrote three others. The only cover song was the classic
hit "My Funny Valentine," performed impeccably by Chaka Khan. Arista
released the soundtrack five weeks before the film, on November 14, 1995,
along with seven singles (from November 1995 to July 1996). Three more
songs from the album garnered unsolicited airplay and charted.

The *Waiting to Exhale* soundtrack became one of the top commercial
successes of 1995. It yielded two #1 hits on the US *Billboard* Hot 100 chart—
"Exhale (Shoop Shoop)," performed by Whitney Houston, and "Let It
Flow," performed by Toni Braxton—and three top-ten hits, "Sittin' Up in
My Room" (Brandy), "Not Gon' Cry" (Mary J. Blige), and "Count on Me"
(Whitney Houston and CeCe Winans). "Exhale (Shoop Shoop)," "Let It
Flow," and "Not Gon' Cry" were #1 R & B Singles hits. The album sold over
twelve million copies worldwide and received eleven Grammy nomina-
tions in 1997, including Album of the Year and Song of the Year for "Exhale
(Shoop Shoop)," which won the Grammy for Best R & B Song.

The album also won two American Music Awards, four NAACP Image
Awards, several Soul Train Awards, sixteen Recording Industry Association of America (RIAA) Awards, and *Billboard* Awards, among others. It was
rated in the Top 100 albums recorded in the 1990s, and *New York Times*
music critic Steve Holden described Kenny as "the most creative pop-soul
musician since the prime of Stevie Wonder."

The film grossed $82 million and was the twenty-sixth-highest-grossing
film of 1995. Noted film critic Roger Ebert gave the film a thumbs-up, and the
Los Angeles Times called it a "social phenomenon." Yet even with all accolades
given to the film and the soundtrack, the Golden Globes and the Academy
Awards flagrantly snubbed both—neither received a single nomination.

I'M FIRED

It had been a banner year, and Kenny was heading into the 1995 music award season riding a wave of momentum. He received four Grammy nominations for songs he wrote for other artists and a nomination for Producer of the Year, which he won. I routinely attended all the major award shows with Kenny, though he normally sat with Tracey. I ushered them in and out of the ceremony, helped them through the press area, and served as a troubleshooter.

It was gratifying to see Kenny win the Producer of the Year award. I sensed he felt fulfilled and vindicated for all the doubts that had been swirling around about his credentials as a songwriter-producer. Normally, we'd attend an afterparty, but while we were waiting for the limo to arrive, he barely spoke or acknowledged me. It was awkward and out of character, especially on such a celebratory night. I helped them into the car, and neither said a departing word.

In the ensuing week we didn't speak, and then Stephen, his attorney, called to tell me Kenny was terminating my services. He didn't give me any specific reasons. It miffed me that Kenny didn't tell me directly, especially since I felt I had done a spectacular job on his behalf. They say the true test of one's character isn't when you're successful—it's when you fail. It wasn't cool, but it was out of my control. So I lamented briefly and rechanneled my focus on things I could control.

We had a flat deal, and he still owed money for the tour, so in the short term, I was more concerned about him honoring my payment, which was in the six figures, than questioning his motives. We negotiated a settlement payment, and our parting of the ways ended without any significant up-heavals.

Not long after our split, I heard that Kenny had signed with Benny Medina's management company, Handprint. Benny and I had known each other for years and had worked together a few times. We weren't close, but I didn't view him as an adversary. He guided Kenny on his fourth solo album, *The Day*, which yielded the hit single "Every Time I Close My Eyes" and became a big pop success. During the same time Kenny produced Eric Clapton's big pop hit "Change the World" and starred in an *MTV Unplugged* music special that was recorded and released as his first live album (released in 1997). Benny managed him for a little over a year.

KENNY REHIRES ME

Out of the blue, Kenny called to tell me he was coming to New York and wanted to talk to me about managing him again. We didn't discuss details, but I agreed to take the meeting. We met for lunch at the Four Seasons Hotel on East 57th Street, which was his favorite place to stay. When we started talking about his relationship with Benny, I commented that I felt he was doing a great job. He didn't offer any specific details about their split, but I could tell they were no longer on the same page. Before accepting Kenny's offer to manage him again, I wanted him to come clean about why he fired me. He said, "I just felt I needed to make a change."

Kenny was rarely fully transparent about sharing pressing issues in his life. He only revealed what he felt was necessary for me to know. He had started recording his next studio album and was investing a lot of time in developing Edmonds Entertainment with Tracey. They had purchased the building on Cahuenga Boulevard that Dick Griffey bought when he launched Solar Records—the same label that signed Kenny's group, the Deele. It was a major renovation that would house their further expansions into music, film, television, and publishing.

Their company picked up the rights to the Black indie film *Hav Plenty* (1997), a romantic comedy released by Miramax Films, and they served as executive producers. They were also among the producers (with Robert Teitel) for the film *Soul Food* (1997), a comedy-drama written and directed by George Tillman Jr. It featured an ensemble cast that included Vivica A. Fox, Nia Long, Vanessa Williams, Michael Beach, and Mekhi Phifer. They later developed it as a TV series for Showtime that ran for five years and seventy-four episodes (2000–2005).

Kenny made his debut as an actor in the *Soul Food* TV series, which was filmed in Vancouver. It earned him an NAACP Image Award nomination for Best Supporting Actor in a TV Drama. He also earned an Emmy Award nomination for Outstanding Main Title Theme Music for "That's the Way Love Goes," the series title song, which he cowrote, produced, and performed with Al Green. After reuniting, I joined him in Vancouver for his shoot days. He was nervous about his lack of acting chops but stepped up and won over the cast and producers.

Kenny's level of stardom was still ascending based on the back-to-back success of his three previous solo albums, *Tender Lover*, *For the Cool in You*, and *The Day*. His *MTV Live Unplugged NYC* 1997 album (November) and his *Christmas with Babyface* album (October 1998) performed moderately well but didn't reach the multiplatinum status of his studio albums.

He was busy recording his next studio record, but his relationship with Epic had become more tenuous than it was when I exited. Tommy Mottola and the rest of Epic's A & R staff gave his new project a lukewarm response. They didn't feel it had any breakout singles, which essentially meant they didn't feel confident in releasing it as is.

It was an unusual predicament for him to have one of his albums rejected—especially at that point in his career. He became perturbed after discovering that the director of Urban A & R had licensed a remix of one of his tracks without getting his permission. The incident became a catalyst for him to secure an artist release from Epic.

I consulted with his attorney, Peter Lopez, and he suggested I call Tommy and make a personal plea for the release on behalf of Kenny—more of a divorce due to irreconcilable differences regarding Kenny's musical direction. If Tommy agreed to let him go, he would negotiate the termination agreement and both parties would bypass a lengthy litigation battle.

I sent Tommy a letter explaining Kenny's desire to terminate his contract with the label. He expressed disappointment about him wanting to leave, but didn't want to pressure him to stay if he wasn't happy. However, he said Kenny would have to pay a fee to leave. Kenny had a hefty unrecouped eight-digit balance owed on his artist account. So Tommy proposed two possible scenarios. If Kenny planned to retire and not sign with another label, he could walk away scot-free. If he planned to sign with another label, they would negotiate a buy-out fee for his artist's rights in good faith. He didn't specify a number, but I knew it would be in the millions.

Kenny and L.A. Reid had rebounded from their estrangement and were on good terms personally and professionally. He discussed his dilemma with L.A., who had just replaced Clive Davis as the head of Arista Records. L.A. stepped up to the plate and agreed to pay the multimillion-dollar buyout fee to Epic/Sony to sign Kenny to Arista. The fee was totally recoupable, which put Kenny in a steep financial hole with Arista out of the box. In essence, both labels charged Kenny to move from one to the other. So he paid for his freedom—but had a new lease on his artistic life.

Almost simultaneously, Kenny advised me that he had partnered with Andre Harrell to launch his own record label, Nu America Records. Andre and I had been friends for a long time and got along well. He had hired me as his publicist a couple of times. However, at times I felt Andre's own sense of fame and celebrity undermined his effectiveness as an executive. We didn't share the same views on what was best for Kenny, but we found a way to collaborate effectively on his behalf.

L.A. had graciously agreed to release Kenny's first solo album for Arista using his Nu America imprint. Andre had convinced Kenny to dramatically overhaul his visual presentation, from head to toe. He also convinced him to collaborate with a list of younger, hot hip-hop, R & B, and urban/pop songwriters and producers who had more mainstream appeal (Pharrell/ the Neptunes, Heavy D, Mike City, Jimmy Jam and Terry Lewis, Timbaland, Tim & Bob, Buckwild, Brion James, and Anthony Nance).

Kenny was forty, which isn't an optimum age to suddenly reinvent your artist image. There's a risk of it appearing overtly contrived as an attempt to look younger—which could possibly alienate your core fans. His new look was quasi-inspired by Lenny Kravitz, with a shorter, twisted dread-style Afro, light-lens sunglasses, and less glamorous, grunge-looking attire. He wore torn or weathered jeans, Timberland-style boots, and a two- to three-day stubble. He also invested time with a trainer to look more fit and muscular.

It was a precarious time for Kenny. His fame and relevance as an artist were waning a bit. His new image was pushing the envelope to the edge, but we were gambling he wouldn't fall off the cliff. I encouraged him to follow his instincts: "If you're confident you can it pull off and make people believe these image changes are authentic to who you are now, go for it."

He was juggling a lot, and for the first time he became more open to socializing and using his voice to support causes and issues he believed in. As a couple, Kenny and Tracey were becoming media darlings, thanks to their publicist, Raymone Bain. She was influential in arranging for them to host a major fundraiser in support of then–vice president Al Gore's run for the presidency in 2000. They held the event at their $14 million estate in Holmby Hills, and President Bill Clinton served as the special guest speaker.

It wasn't my first time dealing with the White House or meeting a president, but it was the first time dealing with the Secret Service on an event the president planned to attend. We had to provide personal ID verification for every single guest in advance of the event. A large detail was sent out to screen and scan every part of the house and the surrounding neighborhood. As I recall, the event was for about five hundred people, all seated in the backyard. We had a stage set up for an all-star band to perform.

Kenny performed a short set and coerced President Clinton (with little resistance) to join the band on saxophone. The president didn't embarrass himself, but I didn't sense he was ready for prime time or to make being a musician his second career. The turnout for the event was exceptional. President Clinton took one-on-one photos and remarkably chatted with each guest. I was seated next to supermodel Naomi Campbell, which was a delightful surprise and the highlight of my evening.

While Kenny finished up his next record, Sony released *A Collection of*

His Greatest Hits, Babyface in November 2000 in Europe and Japan. Kenny gave them a song and video, "Reason for Breathing," which he cowrote and coproduced with songwriter-singer Joe (Thomas). We shot the video in Rio de Janeiro in October.

It was my fiftieth birthday. I was flying from New York, and Kenny and Andre were flying from Los Angeles. We met in Miami and flew on the same plane for our last leg to Rio de Janeiro. It was my first time in Brazil, and I fell in love with the culture, beaches, cuisine, music, and the most exotic and mixed blend of beautiful people I had seen on planet Earth. We stayed at the famous Copacabana Hotel and shot some scenes in several historic sites around the city, including the statue of Christ the Redeemer, Ipanema Beach, the colorful Selaron Steps, and a beautiful waterfall hidden away in a jungle area about an hour and a half drive from Rio. Marcus Raboy directed the video.

Kenny's new album was titled *Face2Face*, and "There She Goes," which he cowrote with the Neptunes (they produced it), became the debut single release on his Nu America label. It was funky, up-tempo, and danceable, and it marked the first time Kenny released a solo single he didn't produce. Pharrell was also a featured vocalist on the track and in the video, which Hype Williams directed.

It immediately got traction on the radio, and MTV had the video in rotation. It peaked at #31 on the Hot 100 and #10 on the R & B Singles chart. The single created substantial buzz for the album. His revamped image was getting mixed reviews. It caught people off-guard, but the fact they noticed and were talking about it was a plus.

Arista had stepped up and secured significant media coverage and promotion to support the launch. We set up a live concert event at the Apollo Theater in New York to launch the release on Tuesday, September 11, 2001, the in-store date for the album. I booked him on the *Tonight Show* the night before to perform and premiere "What If," which was lined up as the album's second single. After the Apollo show, we had about a week of media and promo activities set up for him.

Kenny and I were taking a red-eye flight to New York after the *Tonight Show*. Our stage personnel and production staff (over thirty people) were flying to New York for the Apollo event and staying at a hotel in New Jersey. We were scheduled to arrive around 6 a.m. Kenny was booked to appear as a celebrity guest at Dominican designer Oscar de la Renta's fashion show at 10:30 a.m., which was one of first shows kicking off New York Fashion Week.

We took a town car into Manhattan to drop him off at his apartment on East 62nd Street and me at my hotel in Midtown on the West Side. In a couple of hours, I'd pick him up, and we'd head to the fashion show. As soon as I got into my hotel room, I flopped on my bed and turned on the TV. A few minutes into watching the *Today Show*, a "Breaking News" notification flashed on the screen reporting that a small plane had crashed into the World Trade Center's North Tower. They couldn't confirm the size of the plane or the extent of the damage.

As speculation about the specific details began to escalate, I witnessed the second plane crash into the South Tower. I was aghast, emotionally overwhelmed, and couldn't believe what I had just seen. In the ensuing minutes, it became increasingly horrific and unimaginable. I tried calling Kenny and my family on my cell, then using the hotel phone, and couldn't get through. Then the news came that two other planes had crashed, one into the Pentagon and one in Pennsylvania.

In the hour and seventeen minutes since the first plane crash, my own little world had collapsed. I knew immediately we'd have to scratch everything we had slated for Kenny—the Apollo Show, media ops, and so on. A million things were racing through my mind beyond the sheer shock and dismay of a cataclysmic disaster on US soil. We had thirty-nine personnel stuck in a hotel in New Jersey, and I had no clue how long we could keep them there. Some of our crew had already started loading equipment at the Apollo. The airports were already closed, and Penn Station, Amtrak, and the Port Authority Bus Terminal would be shutting down soon as well. There were looming financial liabilities and expenses, and there was no way to find out if the label would cover them.

When my cell finally started working, I arranged to go to Kenny's apartment so we could conference and discuss options with our road manager, Marc St. Louis. We wanted to get everyone out of New York and back to Los Angeles as soon as possible. Marc thought he might have a shot at renting buses from privately owned tour bus companies. Within an hour, he found an available bus from a company based in Baltimore, and later a second one from a company based in New Jersey. The bus trip to LA was approximately 2,500 miles and would take sixty-five hours. The buses would arrive late evening in New Jersey. Kenny agreed to cover the rental costs.

I had to get Kenny to New Jersey before 5 p.m., which is when all the bridges and access in and out of the city would close. We barely made it, arriving in New Jersey in the early evening. Our personnel had been advised to check out of their rooms, so they were hanging out at the hotel bar and restaurant. It was 2 a.m. before the buses arrived. It had been a harrowing day, but everyone was thrilled to be going home. After I said goodbye to Kenny, our driver drove me home to Chappaqua, New York, and I ended my day at about 4 a.m.

Due to 9/11, the response to Kenny's *Face2Face* album fizzled out much faster than we had all anticipated—even though it was eventually certified platinum. But before "There She Goes" had run out of momentum, Arista released "Baby's Mama," which featured a guest appearance by Snoop Dogg, solely as a promotional single, before releasing the second commercial single, which was going to be a ballad. We shot the video for "What If" in Los Angeles. Billie Woodruff directed it, and we cast actress Sanaa Lathan to be Kenny's love interest. The song reached #28 on R & B Singles chart, but only #80 on the Top 100.

We didn't have much time to lament about the record being temporarily stymied, because I had booked Kenny's second tour in Japan. During rehearsals we heard that protests and demonstrations had begun in Japan after prime minister Junichiro Koizumi announced he was considering sending troops to Afghanistan to support the US global antiterrorist peace movement. It prompted a public outcry for the government to remain neutral. Kenny was freaking out and wanted to cancel the tour or postpone it, but neither was an option.

On top of that, Kenny and Tracey's relationship was spiraling downward. For the first time, Tracey was calling me directly about a range of problems she had with him, from his new image to his financial liabilities. She once vented about Kenny's hairdo being too unruly and long. I explained that Kenny never sought my input on his hair. However, I said, "You're his wife, so if he's going to listen to anyone, it's probably you. Tell him how you feel." Later, Kenny would ask, "I heard Tracey called you—what did she want?" I said, "She doesn't like your hairdo, so I told her to talk to you." He just said, "Thanks." It developed into a pattern, but luckily it was short-lived.

The Japan tour fortunately wasn't that long. It comprised seven cities and a two-day engagement at Zepp Tokyo, a thousand-plus club, to tape a music special for Wowow TV, one of Japan's top commercial television networks. Noted Japanese producer and director Dai Hirose fulfilled both roles for the special.

We kicked off the tour in late October, and on the way into Tokyo from the airport, we witnessed spirited protests within a short distance from our hotel, the prestigious Capitol Hotel Tokyo in Akasaka—a popular spot with international touring artists. Kenny was immediately unnerved. While we were attempting to check in, he was adamant about moving to a hotel in another area of the city.

It was a big ask, especially since the Japanese are traditionally reticent to make even minor changes in an artist's itinerary. But within a few hours the promoter made magic happen and arranged to move our entire entourage to the Westin Hotel in Ebisu, an upscale area of the city near Shibuya. It was far removed from the civil unrest, which quelled Kenny's anxiety.

The tour was phenomenal, and we pulled off the Wowow TV taping without any glitches. Personally, we all connected and bonded as a family, doing a lot of fun group activities together, such as night bowling and dinners on off nights or after the shows. The album reached #25 on Japan's Pop Albums chart, and the bonus single with Gwyneth Paltrow,

"Just My Imagination (Running Away with You)," reached #13 on the Pop Singles chart.

While we were in Japan, I was in touch with Al Haymon about packaging a couple of different concert tour packages. We were both keen on pairing Kenny with Gerald LeVert on a theater tour, but Kenny wasn't feeling it. Nor did he seem interested in touring at all. My sense was that the divisive fallout from 9/11 on his album project zapped all his energy and enthusiasm, and he needed some space and time to recalibrate and figure out his next move as an artist.

In the interim, he planned to focus on sustaining writing and producing for other artists, but he didn't need me to manage that area for him, so we ended our management relationship for the second time. Our split was amicable, and we've stayed friendly and have kept in contact occasionally over the years. He invited me to his fiftieth birthday party in New York, which L.A. put together for him, and he invited me to his Hollywood Walk of Fame ceremony and afterparty on October 10, 2013. It's an honor I felt he immensely deserved.

Kenny's relationship with fame embodies why I don't feel fame should be viewed as a destination. It shouldn't be an end goal—because after you achieve it, and then inevitably lose it, life goes on. Kenny never chased it, but he built up some minutes, which I feel I contributed to during my stints with him.

I don't know if Kenny is comfortable with the ebb and flow level of fame he has achieved, but I feel safe in saying that his success stems from the way he's utilized his natural gifts, along with perseverance, authenticity, and commitment to the art form. Those "it" factors are often overlooked, yet they're character traits that enabled Kenny to sustain comparable levels of success and relevance over several decades. Ultimately, they're more valuable to sustaining success than acquiring fame is.

10

FAME IS CURRENCY—
INFAMY IS A LIABILITY

Most of my former clients had achieved varied levels of fame before I met them. Many had also experienced one or two instances of infamy. Infamy is just as powerful and can diminish or bankrupt fame. There are numerous celebrities whose questionable acts are fueled more by infamy than by fame. Little did I know that one day I would represent, fall head over heels in love with, marry, and build a family with a client who faced the dilemma of balancing her fame and infamy.

Vanessa Williams achieved overnight fame in its purest form. On Saturday, September 17, 1983, she competed in the 57th Miss America Pageant, which was a two-hour broadcast on NBC watched by forty-five million people, while a live audience of ten thousand filled the Boardwalk Hall in Atlantic City, New Jersey. The show's final one minute and forty seconds arrived, and host Gary Collins is about to announce the winner. If he doesn't announce her name, she returns to anonymity. Instead, Collins says, "And our new Miss America is Vanessa Williams, Miss New York." In those ten seconds she achieved instant fame, accomplishing a historic feat by becoming the first Black woman to win the Miss America Pageant in its sixty-three-year history.

Vanessa came into my consciousness for the first time the next day, after I saw a small photo on the front page of the *Los Angeles Times* with a brief caption crediting her historic accomplishment. I always feel a sense of gratification, pride, and joy whenever a Black person alters the course of history and breaks a barrier by being the first at anything. In that moment, I quietly applauded her victory.

Several months later, Phoebe Beasley, a talented Black painter that I represented, called to tell me that one of her longtime friends and college buddies, Dennis Dowdell, was a neighbor and personal adviser for Vanessa and her family. He was building a team to orchestrate her transition into the entertainment industry once her reign ended. She wanted to recommend me to him and was seeking my permission. I told her I'd be happy to talk to him.

In our initial telephone conversation, I discovered that he was a high-ranking attorney at American Can and had assumed his advisory role for Vanessa at the behest of her parents. The pageant had never had a Black Miss America, and they were being besieged by guest appearance inquiries and offers from Black organizations around the country. Our introductory conversation led to a meeting in New York. He was likable and seemed to be reveling in his advisory role. He surmised that I would be a good fit for Vanessa and wanted to arrange for us to meet. He promised to contact me once he had a few options.

About three months later, in July, Dennis called. I presumed it was to set up a time to meet Vanessa, but he wanted my input on a problem. On Friday, July 13, Vanessa was doing a phone interview with a reporter from the *New York Post*. At the end of the interview, he quizzed her about a rumor circulating that Bob Guccione, the salacious founder and publisher of *Penthouse* magazine, planned to publish nude images of her. She didn't engage him other than to say she wasn't aware of the rumor. After hanging up, she called Dennis.

She confessed that during the summer of 1982, when she was nineteen years old, she worked briefly as a receptionist at the Mount Kisco Modeling Registry, which was about twenty minutes from her home in Millwood. Tom Chiapel, a photographer at the agency, had convinced her to take nude photos in their offices. She told Dennis she didn't sign a model release and had kept it secret from everyone and blocked out all memory of the incident—until the reporter sparked her recollection.

He wanted advice on what to do. I asked if they had seen the pictures. He said no. I advised him not to do anything until he found out if the story was true and saw the photos if they existed. The following Thursday he called to tell me the story was true. He had viewed *Penthouse* and didn't feel the images were extremely pornographic. He had not been contacted by the pageant, so I advised him not to say anything or take any media inquiries. He agreed to email a copy of the magazine spread so I could assess how damaging they were.

The pictures were candidly not Miss America—friendly, and neither he nor Vanessa had mentioned that a second nude woman was posing in simulated erotic and provocative positions with her. The cover featured Vanessa in a pageant-style gown standing next to George Burns (who had starred hit comedy *Oh God!* in 1977), who was holding a cigar. It commemorated *Penthouse*'s fifteenth anniversary issue with the banner headline "Miss America: Oh, God, She's Nude!" *Penthouse* scheduled it for the September issue, with an August 1 newsstand date.

As more evidence surfaced, I sensed the story could mushroom into an epic scandal. I just couldn't predict how much damage it would inflict on Vanessa. On Friday morning, July 20, one week after Dennis initially reached out, Albert Marks, the venerable thirty-five-year chairman and executive producer of the Miss America Pageant (known as Mr. Miss America), called him to demand that Vanessa relinquish her crown. He gave her seventy-two hours to respond. It was about 11 a.m. when he called. He had also announced his decision in front of television cameras while holding a copy of the magazine. But Marks had given us a chance to control the narrative, at least for the next seventy-two hours. Dennis asked, "What do you recommend we do?"

The first thing I sought was clarity that I had the power and autonomy to implement a strategic plan to manage the crisis on behalf of Vanessa. He confirmed that I did. I proposed we hold a press conference in New York to make a formal announcement as close to Marks's seventy-two-hour deadline as possible. I needed approval to set up the press conference for Monday, July 23, at 11:00 a.m., and to cover all the expenses for the press conference, renting a location, lights, and sound, and hiring a New York PR company to provide staff for the day-of management of the press conference.

I recommended that Vanessa make an official public statement to the world about her decision at the press conference, which would also serve as her official response to Marks's mandate. She would not field questions from the media after making the statement. We'd make printed copies of the statement available to the media. I reassured him that I'd oversee everything. In addition, I suggested he advise the pageant as to how and when they'd receive her response.

Dennis didn't know whether Vanessa would fight to keep her title or resign. I emphasized it wasn't necessary for me to know immediately. However, it was Friday afternoon, and we needed to plan the press conference posthaste. He gave me the green light to proceed.

I retained the services of Ed Callahan, a New York–based PR associate and friend of mine, to assist in setting up the press conference. I trusted him implicitly. Within hours, we set up the press conference at the Sheraton-Hilton Hotel on 7th Avenue in one of their salon rooms. We prepared a photo news alert to send to all major media in New York before the end of the workday so we could get RSVPs to estimate the turnout for Monday. The alert promoted that she'd make a historic statement announcing her decision.

I booked a red-eye flight to JFK in New York and planned on staying in a hotel, but Dennis insisted I stay with his family in Millwood and offered to pick me up at the airport, saying it would be more convenient for everyone. This was morphing into a momentous adventure. I had only met Dennis once, had never talked to or met Vanessa, had no clue what we'd announce on Monday. And I had just agreed to stay in house with strangers.

I didn't know how much input I would have in Vanessa's final decision, but my gut instinct was that she should resign and get on with her life. The magazine was coming out regardless of her decision. I didn't feel that Marks would permit her to act in an official capacity or appear on the national broadcast of the next pageant, which were the only meaningful things left for her to do.

Dennis met me at JFK, and en route to his home, he informed me that he had retained one of New York's top litigators, Peter Parcher, and his firm to sue Chiapel and Guccione, and *Penthouse* for publishing the photos. They planned to file the lawsuit based on Vanessa's emphatic statement that she had not signed a model release. They hoped to prove that the signature they alleged was hers was fraudulent. Parcher and a couple of his associates were coming to meet with us to ensure nothing in Vanessa's statement would incriminate her or have an adverse impact on the lawsuit. I had not accounted for this new wrinkle, but I felt if she had legitimate legal grounds to contest the rights to the images being published, it made sense to pursue a lawsuit.

MEETING VANESSA

Upon my arrival at Vanessa's house early Saturday, there were about four hundred media personnel, journalists, photographers, and television trucks bunkered at the edge of their front lawn and also spread across the highway directly in front of the house. They had been there for twenty-four hours, jockeying to catch a glimpse or grab a news bite of Vanessa entering or leaving the house. I suddenly realized that this story was significantly more sensational in New York than I had imagined.

The Williams' home was ranch style, with a pool on the left side. The driveway on the right was full of cars. It was quaint and homey, nothing lavish or extravagant decor-wise. As I walked up the stairs to the main floor, I noticed a wall filled with family photos of Vanessa and her brother, Chris, that captured all phases of their childhood.

Dennis introduced me to her parents, Helen and Milton, who were gracious. Helen was very petite, observant, and engaged in conversation almost immediately. Milton was lean, about six feet tall, with a beard and curly hair but not an Afro. Both were bustling about in the kitchen. Minus my presence, they gave the impression that within the sanctity of their home, this was just a normal Saturday morning. They offered me breakfast and coffee, which I happily accepted.

Minutes later, Vanessa appeared. She looked tired, with a blank stare like a deer caught in the headlights. Her cheeks were blotchy and slightly reddened. It was early, so she had on casual attire and looked like she had just woken up. She extended a polite hello but wasn't talkative. Helen and Milton fervently concurred that Vanessa should not resign, and Dennis had already expressed he was aligned with that view. They shared a disdain for Guccione and Marks—especially Helen. She vehemently resented Marks for not supporting Vanessa. Vanessa was present and listening but remained silent. My initial impression was that she'd accept whatever decision her parents and collective advisers felt was in her best interest.

When I met Peter and his associates, they were adamant about limiting Vanessa's statement to the absolute minimum. I argued that her statement needed to be heartfelt and substantive. I didn't feel it was worth risking any further public embarrassment by having her make a shallow statement. If that was their intent, I recommended we cancel the press conference and issue a legally framed press release that only announced the lawsuit and her decision.

We were racing against the clock, with around forty-eight hours left to craft a statement, get the lawyers and Vanessa to approve it, and allow her adequate time to rehearse it so she'd feel comfortable enough to deliver it convincingly. When I sat down with Vanessa, I spoke candidly and tried to reassure her that she was in control. My job was to help her craft a statement that was heartfelt, believable, and in her authentic voice. And I reminded her that it would shadow her for the rest of her life—so it had to be definitive.

The rest of the weekend I spent haggling with Dennis and Peter's team over different iterations of the release. It became a team effort to effectively integrate their input. Helen and Milton weren't heavily involved in the creative process but did share their opinions toward the end. Vanessa became more engaged and hit her stride during our rehearsals. I wrote the statement so that her decision not to resign would be announced at the end.

In my final session with Vanessa, I reminded her that the ballroom would be packed with frenzied and unruly media, and she needed to get in a zone, block out all the noise, and not let them throw off her rhythm—and avoid stopping at all costs. I recommended she get a good night's sleep, so she'd feel a little less stressed out in the morning. That night I felt wide-eyed and anxious. My handprint, reputation, professional integrity, and ass were on the line. I wanted our team to win—but mostly I wanted Vanessa to win. I was pumped and ready to go but still had seven hours to kill.

Monday morning came, and we followed our plan to drive into the city early and sneak a disguised Vanessa (wearing sunglasses and a baseball cap covered by a hoodie) into the hotel so she could get ready. It was a little past 9:30 a.m. I was doing the final edit on the statement at Peter's office before printing it for distribution. The lawyers were huddling, and a few minutes later, they revealed that their lead handwriting analyst couldn't verify "with no doubt" that the signature on the model release wasn't Vanessa's. They believed they needed irrefutable proof that it wasn't her signature for her to win the lawsuit, so they recommended Vanessa resign. She agreed. They committed to pursue the lawsuit anyway, which Vanessa's parents requested. I had to rewrite portions of the release, then get it approved and to Vanessa within the hour. Although it produced a whirlwind of untimely and intense stress, it pleased me that they flipped the decision. I gave the statement to Vanessa to review; she was stoic and miraculously unflustered and calm. We had less than thirty minutes left.

When we entered the salon, the media were screaming, yelling, pushing, and jockeying for better positioning. There was barely a clear lane in front of the stage and podium to walk. Mics were everywhere, and TV camera crews were stretched across the entire back wall. The atmosphere was over-the-top chaotic, the wildest press conference I had been a part of—and we hadn't said a word yet. I introduced the principals, and right before Vanessa took the mic, I whispered, "I told you it would be bedlam. Just stay in your zone, block out the noise, and you'll be fine." As soon as Vanessa began to speak, the room quieted down a decimal. She didn't miss a beat, remain composed, and masterfully delivered the statement. Vanessa acknowledged that she was culpable and erred in taking the pictures and briefly summarized the sequence of events that led to the incident. She thanked the pageant for their support throughout, and in closing she humbly apologized and announced she was resigning as Miss America. The room erupted with mostly boos and the media yelling and screaming to get her attention. As we walked out, the remnants of exhilaration and high energy still lingered in the room. It is an experience that has never waned in my memory. Vanessa finally got a chance to exhale and feel a momentary sense of closure to an ill-fated chapter in her life. She left with her integrity intact and her head held high.

THE AFTERMATH

Guccione released the issue the same day, and it became his best-selling issue of all time. The New York tabloids (the *Post* and *Daily News*) started running front page headlines like "Vanessa the Undressa" every day. Suzette Charles, the Black runner-up from New Jersey, filled the slot vacated by Vanessa as Miss America. As promised, her lawyers filed a $400 million suit. Vanessa was allowed to keep her $25,000 scholarship award but lost potential endorsement deals cumulatively worth over a million dollars with Gillette, American Greetings, Coca-Cola, and Disney World, and several high-paying personal appearances.

Dennis informed me that an old friend of his owned a small resort property, the Out Island Inn in Exuma, Bahamas, and had offered a complimentary stay for Vanessa and her mother. Vanessa invited me to join them.

Dennis was invited as well, but he had a prior business commitment. I had to fly to Buffalo to listen to some new songs Rick James was recording for his next album, but I let them know that I'd join them for a couple of days.

Exuma is a quaint island getaway. The hotel resort was right on the ocean, and my room was twenty yards from the beach. The weather was perfect. It was not fancy but comfortable and idyllic. The first night I joined Vanessa and her mom for dinner. It was nice to be in their company in a casual setting with no impending stress and anxiety hovering over us—but a little awkward. I had only met them the week before. Helen was disappointed that Vanessa had resigned and mentioned it—but I wasn't in the mood to rehash everything, so I didn't take the bait. Helen called it a night, and Vanessa and I had nightcap and took a walk on the beach and had a chance to talk casually for the first time.

The next day Helen flew back to New York in the early afternoon, and I met Vanessa for dinner. She was wearing a long off-the-shoulder black cotton sundress. She had on a touch of makeup, and her hair was done. She looked stunning and drop-dead gorgeous. It was the first time I had looked at her as just a woman, not a victim or a client. We ate a delicious Bahamian meal, drank some wine, and walked around town. When we returned to the hotel, we sat on the beach talking for a couple of hours.

We connected on multiple levels even though there was a twelve-year age difference between us. We shared an affectionate hug and gently kissed before saying goodnight. The next morning, we reminisced about the special day we had shared. We agreed that we might be lunging past those imaginary lines that business associates aren't supposed to cross. I was torn and not sure how I felt. In the back of my mind, I was hoping we had just shared a moment.

THE COLLATERAL DAMAGE OF INFAMY

Two weeks later, just as the fallout had started to ebb, we were blindsided when a story broke about a second nude photo shoot Vanessa had done in

Manhattan with the photographer Gregg Whittman after the Chiapel shoot. They met on the subway in the city, and she impetuously did the shoot with him and signed a model release. After realizing she had made a mistake, she went back to Whittman and convinced him to give her all the negatives. After hearing about her *Penthouse* spread, he sent a telegram to Guccione advising him that they existed. Guccione purchased them and planned to publish them in January 1985. Vanessa didn't find out that Whittman had kept several negatives until *Penthouse* published them.

I asked her bluntly, "This is it, right? There are no more photos? If you're hiding anything else, it's best to come clean now. I can't help to restore your image and put this ordeal in the past if more indiscretions surface." She confirmed that her closet was empty. I set up an interview for her with UPI and the *New York Times* to give her own account of what had transpired. After her admission, luckily the story petered out.

Vanessa finally got an offer to guest-star on the short-lived series *Partners in Crime*, starring Lynda Carter and Loni Anderson as private detectives. She played a rock 'n' roll star who was being chased by a stalker. It was shot in San Francisco, and Helen and I were both there. We were sitting about four feet apart on a shuttle boat back to shore and weren't talking. Vanessa had told her she was seeing me. She turned, looked at me, and said very matter-of-factly, "You know, Vanessa has a tendency to get bored with men quickly." I said, "Thanks for the tip. That's not so strange, because the same thing happens to me with woman. We'll just have to wait and see who gets bored first." She turned away and ignored me for the rest of the ride. I sensed that Helen had elected to be divisive. This was just a preview of shots she'd tactically fire in the days, weeks, and months ahead.

When I was an outlier from Hollywood who had swooped in to help Vanessa get through the most challenging ordeal in her young life, her parents were warm and grateful. Once Vanessa had developed feelings for me, it stoked animosity toward me—mostly from Helen. She harped on our age disparity and scolded Vanessa for getting involved with me. I respected her desire to protect their daughter, but we weren't far enough along to warrant her becoming adversarial.

Vanessa got excited about Tommy Tune wanting her to take over the starring role played by Twiggy in the Broadway hit *My One and Only*. He was a fan and was prepared to champion her. But the Gershwin estate emphatically quashed the idea. They firmly denounced Vanessa as a person they would not allow to be associated with their name or the production. Their harsh rejection deflated her momentarily, but it also alerted her and her inner circle about the uphill battle she faced to change how she was viewed and become the person she wanted to be.

International Creative Management (ICM) agreed to represent her. Dennis had positioned himself to be her long-term manager, and for whatever reason, I didn't realize that was his end goal. I saw a management agreement he had submitted that I didn't feel was artist-friendly. I advised Vanessa not to sign it without having an entertainment lawyer review it. Dennis continued as an adviser to her for a while longer, but she never signed a management agreement with him.

The closer we became, the more she trusted me and wanted my input and counsel. I explained to her that she represented two starkly different images, one as the deposed former Miss America, and the other, the provocative soft-porn vixen portrayed in the published images. Neither persona aptly embodied or represented who she was. She needed to create an authentic persona that dispelled both, which she could commit to and sell to the public.

The strongest advice I gave her was to pursue a career as a recording artist and performer. It would give her a chance to establish her own artist brand, control her image and products, build a loyal fan base exponentially faster, and hopefully leverage her superstar power to eventually cross over into other entertainment mediums like Broadway, television, and film.

We were still sneaking around trying to keep our growing affection for each other under wraps. I didn't want to create a scenario where she felt she had to pick me over her parents. But my nose was so wide open you could drive a Mack truck through it. All the divisive outside noise just helped to crystalize our belief in each other. We took on an "us against world" attitude and were building genuine love, with more trust and less doubt in each other.

WE'RE OUTED

I had arranged for Vanessa to do an interview with *People*. I set it up at a restaurant in New York for the early evening. I planned to be there to broker the introduction and then leave and come back once she finished the interview. When I asked her how the interview went, she said it went fine except that the writer busted her. She said he saw the way we looked at each other and knew. My initial reaction was, "Damn, *People* magazine, the biggest tabloid in America, is going to expose our secret. Well, so much for staying under the radar. It was bound to happen at some point, so we'll just have to deal with it." Once the story broke, the other tabloids ran stories as well. For a few weeks, the paparazzi stalked us everywhere we went and made themselves a nuisance. It was an especially bizarre twist for me, because I had dealt with paparazzi for years—but I wasn't the subject. Vanessa was used to it, but she didn't like it either. Fortunately, our heat as a flavor-of-the-month couple eventually subsided.

She was trying to get her life together and convinced her parents to cosign on a one-bedroom apartment on East 54th and Sutton. It thrilled Vanessa to finally have her own place. I helped her decorate and laid carpet for her living room, which I had never done. It made it convenient and cheaper for me to visit, instead of booking hotels. She was socializing and building her own independent lifestyle. But she was unemployed and wasn't generating a steady income. After several months, facing escalating financial challenges, her parents told her they couldn't afford to pay for the apartment, so she had to move back home.

FIRST BREAK ON BROADWAY

She felt miserable living at home again. Then she got a break, landing a minor role in the original musical *One Man Band*, starring actor James Lescene and written by D. J. R. Bruckner. It was produced by Willa Shalit (daughter of Gene Shalit, the longtime colorful entertainment correspondent on the *Today Show*) and Robert Levithan and was set for a limited engagement at the off-off-Broadway South Street Theater on 42nd Street, in June–July 1985. Willa was immensely supportive of Vanessa, and they forged a friendship. Willa had a spare room in her apartment on 106th Street and Riverside Drive. She offered it to Vanessa for free during the run of the play. Vanessa jumped at a chance to escape, and it saved her time and money on commuting every day into the city. I stayed with Vanessa a couple of times and became friends with Willa as well.

Vanessa was cast as one of three singers and had a featured solo performance as well. The play generated a good buzz, and several celebrities turned out, including NBA superstars Magic Johnson and Isaiah Thomas, as well as Andy Warhol, for shows I attended. The *New York Times* review noted, "And Miss Williams, who was Miss America last year, does just fine; she is especially effective in the comic sequences where one might expect a newcomer to be a bit awkward." It was a triumphant debut, not so much as a major career move, but as a positive step toward giving people a taste of her talents.

Warren Beatty met with her and cast her in a minor role for his film *The Pickup Artist* (1987), which he produced for 20th Century Fox, starring Molly Ringwald and Robert Downey Jr. They shot it in New York. It didn't trigger any hoopla, but it was a job. I stopped by her trailer on the Upper West Side and had time to meet and talk to him briefly. I was a legit fan, so I enjoyed meeting him.

Once the play ended, she dreaded the thought of living at home, so she asked if she could come live with me in Los Angeles. We were seeing each other exclusively, and I knew she was frustrated. I wasn't sure if she'd feel comfortable living in my space, but I figured it would be a good test for our relationship, so I encouraged her to come.

Once she moved to Los Angeles, a few opportunities began trickling in. She costarred with Sam Jones (who starred as Flash Gordon) in Marquis Films's low-budget action-adventure film *Under the Gun*, which went straight to video. Her appearance in indie B films drew more attention than if she was just an unknown twenty-two-year-old actor pounding the pavement and paying her dues. It was a positive step forward. Doing the movie didn't help or hurt her, and she got a paycheck.

I consulted Vanessa on everything. I wasn't her manager, and I felt she needed to secure one. A few months later, Dolores Robinson, one of the few Black female managers in the business (who represented LeVar Burton, Martin Sheen, Emilio Estevez, Elisabeth Shue, and Wesley Snipes), expressed interest in working with Vanessa. We were friendly, and I respected her, so I encouraged Vanessa to give her shot. They agreed to test the waters and work without a contractual agreement. She got Vanessa a guest appearance on ABC's short-lived series *He's the Mayor*, starring Kevin Hooks. But after a few months Vanessa didn't feel their personalities meshed. She decided to end the relationship without my input. Learning when to make decisions is just as important as making them.

I committed to finding her a credible music manager. I had an association with Shep Gordon when I worked at his Alive Management offices (handling Alice Cooper and Luther Vandross), so I asked him if he'd like to take over, but he passed. I made several other inquiries, but no one was willing to take a leap of faith.

After a few weeks of getting rejected, I wanted to give Vanessa a status update. She stopped me midstream and said, "Why don't you manage me? I wouldn't make decisions without getting your input anyway. I want you to do it." I had a laundry list of reasons why I didn't want to be her manager, but I had already broken several of my ethical rules of business by falling in love with her, so I thought breaking another one wouldn't be a major concession. Everything we were doing was uncharted, but I was motivated by love and wanted to make her happy. So I agreed to do it.

My top priority: getting her a record deal. Over several months, I got rejected by eight to twelve labels, mostly from the heads of the labels. They were my friends: Bob Krasnow, president of Elektra Records; Randy Jackson, head of A & R at Columbia; Jheryl Busby, president of Black music at MCA Records; Clive Calder, founder and CEO of Jive Records; and other A & R reps from Arista, Epic, and Manhattan Records. A few offered demo deals, but others felt that because of the stigma attached to her, no one would take her seriously.

GEORGE CLINTON: "DO FRIES GO WITH THAT SHAKE"

In the interim, Debra Barsha, one of Vanessa's friends and a fellow cast member in *One Man Band*, contacted her. She was working on a project with George Clinton, the legendary funkster and founder of the funk band Parliament Funkadelic, and she wanted to refer Vanessa to him. We met with him; he was eccentric and uniquely engaging. He took an immediate liking to Vanessa and was enthusiastic about using her as a vocalist on a couple of songs on his forthcoming album, *R & B Skeletons in the Closet*. She cut two songs: "Do Fries Go with That Shake" and "Hey Good Lookin'." George wanted to feature her in the video for "Do Fries Go with that Shake," wearing a natural-colored body suit and climbing down a straw into a giant chocolate milkshake. Being portrayed in an erotic scene as a video vixen would overshadow the legitimacy of her vocal collaborations. We passed. George replaced her vocals with another singer (whom he featured in the video) but kept her vocals on "Hey Good Lookin'," which featured Bootsy Collins on vocals and bass guitar. The song was released as a single and marked her professional debut as a vocalist.

SPIKE LEE: SHE'S GOTTA BE NUDE

In the same time frame film producers and directors were trying to exploit the image suggested by her nude photos. Spike Lee wanted Vanessa to play the lead role of Nola Darling in his directorial debut, *She's Gotta Have It*, but emphasized that the role required full nudity, which was nonnegotiable. We passed. Director Bill Duke, whom I had profound respect for, wanted her to be in *Harlem Nights*. He issued the same nonnegotiable must-be-nude ultimatum. I passed.

She auditioned to be Eddie Murphy's love interest in two films, *Coming to America* and *Boomerang*. The director of *Coming to America*, Jon Landis, told us on the phone he thought she had a good chance of getting the role. She didn't get it. He chose Shari Headley. Eddie and I were friendly, and one night at R & B Live, he told me he wanted Vanessa to be in his next film, *Boomerang*. He made good on auditioning her but gave the role to Robin Givens. She was newly single after divorcing Mike Tyson. The uncertifiable rumor was that Eddie preferred his female leads to be single.

The rejections were piling up. I told her we might need to settle and accept one of the demo deals, even though I wasn't keen on the idea. Then I received a surprise call from my friend Ed Eckstine. We hadn't talked in quite some time, so it was a catch-up call. He had exited Quincy Jones Productions after an eleven-year tenure as the company's general manager and landed safely with his own custom label deal, Wing Records at Polygram. He had called to give me a heads-up to keep him in mind if I came across any talented artists.

I joked and said I hope they gave you a bunch of money. He countered, "I wish!" Instead, they gave him a lot of autonomy and a chance to put his signature on the label. He mentioned he was close to signing a couple of artists but couldn't reveal them yet. Right before he was about to hang up, he asked, "How are things going with Vanessa?" I responded, "Funny you should ask. I've shopped her to few places, got a few rejections and offers to do demo deals." Without a pause he said, "Bring her here, and we'll do it." I was surprised. "Seriously?" He affirmed, "If you're looking for a big artist advance, I can't give you that, but I'm definitely interested." I was thrilled and told him I'd discuss it with Vanessa and arrange a meeting.

Finally, I had some uplifting news to share. I had been repeating incessantly that it doesn't matter how many labels reject you—you only need one to say yes. I gave Vanessa an overview of Ed's history with Quincy, our history, and the little he had shared about his new label. I emphasized that I couldn't vouch for his new venture, except he said it wasn't heavily funded.

Her meeting with Ed went fabulously well. He understood our goal to make her a legitimate artist. She was enamored with him and respected his musicality and lineage as a son of jazz great Billy Eckstine working with Quincy and being around famous people and artists his whole life. He understood the fragile nuances of artist egos but was also shrewd and didn't pander to them.

Financially, the deal he offered was in the low six digits, which was not surprising. Vanessa was an unknown commodity and didn't have a track record I could leverage. He agreed to bump up the deal by 10 percent. We shared a vision of establishing Vanessa as a legitimate artist, and that was more important than the money. I thanked Ed and said, "You know if we fuck this up for Vanessa and don't win, everyone is going to blame us, right? So we can't let that happen." Securing a record deal for an artist gets them in the game, but what happens after is much harder.

Vanessa and I had fallen madly in love and started contemplating marriage. While visiting New York, we were upstate running an errand for her mom and stopped in a small jewelry store, where we saw a stunning antique diamond ring that Vanessa loved. They had the original certification documents. A few days later I went back and purchased it. I stopped by her parents' as a courtesy to ask for her hand in marriage, which was a disastrous idea. Milton was under his car fixing something. When I told him why I wanted to talk to him and Helen, he refused to get up and told me to talk to Helen. When I told her, she was disgusted and angry and just said, "Vanessa should be telling me this." I reminded her that Vanessa didn't know; I planned to surprise her that night. The outcome could not have been worse. Deflated and disgusted I headed back into the city.

I made dinner reservations for my surprise at Central Falls restaurant on West Broadway in Soho. I had written a poem and asked her to read it. While she was reading, I slipped the ring box under the paper, so when she finished, she'd see it. She cried when I popped the question. Happily, she said yes, and the other patrons realized what had transpired and applauded. A couple sitting nearby stopped by to congratulate us and said, "We sat next to David Letterman last time, now this!" It was a momentous evening and a great recovery from my earlier debacle with her parents.

When Vanessa told her mom, she remained dogged in her attempt to convince her not to marry me. On another call, after realizing she'd lost the battle, she proposed hosting the wedding at their home in June of next year. Vanessa didn't agree but said she would think about it. Within a month, Vanessa surprised me at dinner and told me she was pregnant. It was a twist neither of us expected. We shared a mutual desire to have children but not this soon. We embraced it with effusive joy.

Vanessa's projected delivery date was June 30, 1987. When she told her mom, it infuriated her even more. She wanted to get married before the baby was born and before she started to show, so we set January 3 as our wedding date. When Vanessa shared our plans with her parents, Helen said they would refuse to attend. I felt bad for Vanessa, but she didn't relent, and we began planning the wedding without them.

Meanwhile, Vanessa's recording deal had been inked. We agreed the album needed to be driven by catchy R & B songs with great melodies, hooks, and crossover appeal. Ed found a core group of up-and-coming affordable songwriters and producers he felt could help Vanessa develop her artistic brand. He found a few other songs that came from outside that group. The core writers and producers included Amir-Salaam Bayyan, David Paul Bryant, Lewis A. Martineé, Donald Robinson, Larry Robinson, Darryl Ross, and Rex Salas. Ed served as executive producer.

Ed was cool and congratulated us on getting married. When we told him she was pregnant, he didn't freak out, but it threw an untimely wrench into the release strategy. He had learned from Quincy that a woman's voice usually changes during pregnancy, so he wanted to wait until Vanessa had the baby before she recorded any of her lead vocals. We pushed the album release back to early 1988. It took some pressure off Vanessa, and we continued to search for hit songs.

We planned for over two hundred guests to attend our wedding and found a Catholic church downtown in the West Village, the Church of Saint Francis Xavier on 16th Street. It was established in 1851 and adorned with beautiful stained-glass windows throughout. We set the wedding for 3:00 p.m. Then we picked a cool restaurant for our reception in walking distance from the church. We did a buyout deal with the restaurant for the night. Putting it together ourselves was a major undertaking and more time-consuming than I anticipated. We collaborated on everything—all the decorative elements, flower arrangements, the dinner menu for the reception, the rehearsal dinner, the calligrapher, dresses, tuxedos, the wedding photographer, the videographer, press/paparazzi, security, limos, music, the DJ, a late afterparty for close friends, and the honeymoon.

There were just three days left. Vanessa called to tell me her parents had reconsidered and suddenly wanted to attend the wedding. I was surprised but happy for her. I said, "Congratulations." She said thanks, but that wasn't everything. "They also want to invite twenty-five couples to the wedding and the reception." I was dumbfounded, "You're kidding, right?" She said, "No, they're willing to contribute $3,000 for them." I remarked, "I don't care about the money, but this is extremely inconsiderate timing." It required redoing the seating chart, moving the piano to add more tables, going back to the calligrapher—and more. The night before our wedding I was up until 5 a.m. By early afternoon I was in a fog and could barely keep my eyes open.

Watching Vanessa walk down the aisle was exhilarating and woke me up. I was awestruck! She looked stunning, marvelous, and worthy of every superlative known to man, but more than anything else—she looked happy. The wedding was fabulous and came off without a glitch.

The highlight of the reception for me happened when Helen approached me. I was expecting a snide remark. Instead she smiled and said, "Congrat-

ulations, she's all yours now." I wasn't sure how to respond. Was she waving
a white flag or being coy? I chose the safest route and just said, "Thank
you." She turned around and went back to her seat. But from that moment
on, she became the model mother-in-law and grandparent. Throughout
our marriage and all our ups and downs she championed and stood by me
and I've appreciated and have loved her for years.

The next eight years were a whirlwind, and we barely had time to breathe.
Every year Vanessa either released an album or gave birth to child. We had
three children, Melanie, born June 30, 1987; Jillian, born June 19, 1989
(both in Los Angeles); and Devin, born April 14, 1993 (in Mount Kisco,
New York). During my stint as her manager, Wing/Polygram released four
albums, *The Right Stuff* (January 1988), *Comfort Zone* (August 1991), *Sweetest
Days* (December 1994), and *Starbright* (November 1996), which was her
first Christmas album.

We discovered very early in the process that sustaining an equitable
balance between our multiple roles as wife, husband, mother, father, parents, and business partners (manager and publicist) would be daunting.
But we embraced the challenge and took our children with us on trips
around the country and the world whenever possible.

THE RIGHT STUFF

Three days prior to Melanie's first birthday, Wing/Polygram released
Vanessa's debut solo single, "The Right Stuff" (January 27, 1988). It reached
#4 on *Billboard*'s Hot R & B/Hip-Hop Songs list, #44 on the Hot 100 Singles
charts, and #1 on the Dance/Club chart. Her album *The Right Stuff* generated
four hit singles with well-received videos. "(He's Got) The Look," written
and produced by Amir Bayyan, peaked at #10 on the R & B Singles chart.
Alek Keshishian directed the video. "Dreamin'," written by Lisa Montgomery and Geneva Paschal and produced by Donald Robinson, became
her first #1 on the Hot R & B/Soul chart, and her first track to break the
Top 10 on *Billboard*'s Hot 100 Singles chart, peaking at #8. Internationally

it charted in the UK, the Netherlands, and New Zealand. Alek Keshishian directed the video. "Darlin' I," the album's fourth single, was released in January 1989. Kenny Harris and Rex Salas wrote "Darlin' I," which peaked at #10 on the Hot R & B/Soul chart, and #10 on the Adult Contemporary chart. Alek shot the video in black-and-white (inspired by *I Love Lucy*). Vanessa was three months pregnant with our second daughter, Jillian, so he came up with intriguing angles designed to hide her pregnancy.

The Right Stuff was released on June 6, 1988. It reached #18 on the R & B Albums chart and #38 on the Top 200 Albums chart. *The Right Stuff* was an auspicious debut for Vanessa. It fulfilled most of our goals, especially legitimizing her artist brand—our main priority. It was initially certified gold and later platinum. She earned Grammy Award nominations in 1989 in the prestigious Best New Artist category and for Best Female Vocal Performance, and won the NAACP Image Award for Outstanding New Artist, which was especially gratifying. That win helped solidify her artist brand and further galvanized support within the Black community. She gave a heartfelt and emotional acceptance speech that touched me and elicited some tears of joy.

While promoting *The Right Stuff* Vanessa made her theater debut in Los Angeles in a four-week run of the play *Checkmates*, written by Ron Milner and directed by Woodie King Jr. The play centered on two cross-generational Black urban professional married couples. The original cast comprised Denzel Washington, Paul Winfield, Rhetta Greene, and Gloria Edwards. Vanessa and Richard Lawson replaced the young couple, and Marla Gibbs was cast to play opposite Paul Winfield. Vanessa was also cast to play a small role in *Harley Davidson and the Marlboro Man*, costarring Mickey Rourke and Don Johnson. They were both considered stars, but the film was an instant flop.

A few months after, Jillian was born and Vanessa started recording songs for her sophomore album. We received interest from MTV to develop a Black video show for VH1. After a couple of months of negotiations, the network green-lit *The Soul of VH1* with Vanessa as the host. Her fee was low, but the show offered her higher visibility on the network, elevated her brand identity, and was strategically timed to support her new album. She hosted the series for two seasons.

THE COMFORT ZONE

The level of enthusiasm about the potential of Vanessa's album *The Comfort Zone* was off the charts. Vanessa had matured vocally, the songs were soulful, well written, and well produced, and the album had a distinctive vibe. After having two kids, she looked more beautiful than ever. Ed got Polygram to contribute more funds to her album packaging, photo shoots, and videos. Dawn Bridges, VP of corporate PR, and Walter Green, who headed urban publicity, did a lot of heavy lifting getting her publicity, and the entire Wing staff were collectively on board. I was coordinating promotion and marketing in all the major international markets, including Europe, Japan, and Australia.

Wing/Polygram released "Running Back to You," an up-tempo, funky dance tune as the lead single in July 1991. Trevor Gale and Kenni Hairston wrote the song and produced it with DJ L.A. and Rob Arx. It reached #1 on of Hot R & B/Hip-Hop Songs chart, #2 on the Dance/Club chart, and #18 on the Hot 100. The video, directed by Ralph Zimon, was a powerful performance featuring a handful of dancers against colorful '60s psychedelic, hippie-flavored backdrops. It achieved the highest chart numbers of her first five single releases to date.

Because "Running Back to You" was a smash out of the box, Wing opted to release the album next, rather than another single. *The Comfort Zone* was released a month later, on August 20. It reached #1 on the Billboard Top R & B/Hip-Hop Albums chart and peaked at #17 on the Top 200 Albums chart. It also charted in the UK, Australia, Canada, Holland, Germany, Switzerland, and Japan.

Vanessa received a producer credit and shared an executive producer credit with Ed. She had an engineering credit as well. Seventeen producers were credited on the album, along with luminary featured guest musicians and singers, including Brian McKnight, Stanley Clarke, Hubert Laws, Gerald Albright, Paul Jackson Jr., Harvey Mason Jr., and Wah Wah Watson.

At the end of October, Wing/Mercury released the title song, "The Comfort Zone," as a single. Kipper Jones and Reggie Stewart wrote the song. Jones and Gerry Brown produced it. It reached #2 on the R & B/Soul chart and peaked at #62 on the Hot 100 Singles chart. The video was shot in the desert with Ralph Zimon directing. It stands as my favorite song and video from her catalog.

At the top of 1992, Wing/Mercury released the third single, a lilting ballad, "Save the Best for Last," penned by veteran songwriters Phil Galdston, Wendy Waldman, and Jon Lind, and produced by Keith Thomas. It became Vanessa's third #1 on the Hot R & B/Soul Singles chart and kept the top slot for five consecutive weeks. In addition, it became her first #1 on the Hot 100 Singles and Adult Contemporary charts and stayed at the top of each chart for three weeks. Internationally, the single charted in the top five in over twelve countries and reached #1 in Canada and Australia.

Wing/Mercury released two more singles, including a moving ballad called "Just for Tonight," written by Cynthia Weil and Keith Thomas, and produced by Thomas. It peaked at #2 on the Adult Contemporary chart, #11 on the Hot R & B/Soul chart, and #26 on the Hot 100.

Wing/Polygram released the fifth and final single and video from the album in July. Vanessa covered the Isley Brothers' classic hit, "Work to Do," which they collectively wrote. Vanessa produced it with Gerry Brown, Dr. Jam, and Phase 5. Pam Thomas directed the video, which also featured the rapper Dres. It reached #3 on the Hot R & B/Soul chart and was released in several twelve-inch remixes for clubs.

"The Comfort Zone" and "Save the Best for Last" propelled Vanessa to superstardom as an artist. The 1993 awards season for Vanessa was phenomenal. *The Comfort Zone* was nominated for five Grammy Awards, including two of the most coveted, Record of the Year and Song of the Year for "Save the Best for Last."

The song earned a nomination for Best Pop Vocal Performance, Female. She was also nominated for Best R & B Vocal Performance, Female, for "Running Back to You," and Best R & B Vocal Performance, Female, for "The Comfort Zone." The latter was her third nomination in that category. She performed "Save the Best for Last" at the Grammy Awards ceremony, sitting on a stool while she was thirty-three-weeks pregnant with our son Devin. ASCAP named it its Song of the Year for being performed more than any other song in 1992, and *Billboard* ranked it #4 on its year-end Top 100 Hits of 1992. *The Comfort Zone* was certified triple platinum and remains her all-time best-selling album. It was a stellar success, but I was genuinely disappointed she did not win at least one Grammy Award—that would have been the icing on the cake.

When Vanessa wasn't promoting the album, we looked for other TV and film projects she could squeeze into her schedule. She played the legendary Motown executive and producer Suzanne de Passe in *The Jacksons: An American Dream* (also known as *The Jackson Five*), a five-part miniseries broadcast on ABC-TV that De Passe produced. *The Jacksons: An American Dream* became one of the most popular and successful music biography miniseries of the 1990s and was viewed by over thirty-eight million people. I had worked at Motown, had represented the Jacksons, and had known Suzanne for over a decade, so it was a special treat for her to cast Vanessa to play her.

"LOVE IS"

Ed had firmly established Vanessa and the group Tony! Toni! Toné! as burgeoning stars on Wing Records. He had also signed Brian McKnight, a talented young singer-songwriter, as his first male solo artist for the label. He shared a lilting ballad titled "Love Is" that Brian was set to record. Ed wanted Vanessa to duet with Brian on the song, and make it the lead single for his debut album.

I knew and liked Brian and the song, and Vanessa loved the song and was excited about dueting with Brian. Tonio K, Michael Caruso, and John Keller wrote the song, and Gerry Brown produced it. The single first appeared on the soundtrack for the hit series *Beverly Hills 90210*, released by Giant/Reprise Records (and later featured in the show's spin-off series, *Melrose Place*). Wing/Mercury released the single on March 16, 1993, two days before Vanessa's thirtieth birthday. It reached #1 on the Adult Contemporary chart, #2 on both the Mainstream Top 40 and Rhythmic charts, #3 on Top 100 Singles chart, and #5 on the Hot R & B/Hip-Hop chart. The video was shot in black-and-white. It zoomed in on Vanessa's upper torso, to hide she was pregnant with our son Devin. The song was nominated for a Grammy Award for Best Pop Performance by a Duo or Group with Vocals.

FIRST ENDORSEMENT DEAL

The success of "Save the Best for Last" helped elevate Vanessa's brand in Japan, her second-biggest market. I met a couple of agents in New York who specialized in securing sponsorship deals in Japan, and we agreed to work together. They secured interest from one of Japan's oldest and largest pharmaceutical companies, Shionogi and Company, based in Osaka. Shionogi manufactured a fast-acting tablet to relieve pain symptoms associated with young women's menstruation cycles. The company felt that Vanessa's image was perfect for their demographic and signed her to a lucrative six-figure endorsement deal spread over multiple years. They incorporated footage from the video for "Save the Best for Last" in their national television commercial campaign, extending the life of her album and broadening her fan base in Japan.

SEEKING COUNSELING

Behind the scenes we were struggling as a couple. We had sunk into mediocrity and weren't aligned on anything. I couldn't seem to make her happy as a husband, a manager, or a father. It was depressing. We had been showered with abundant blessings and success and should have been floating on a cloud of contentment. Our mantra was no longer "Us against the world"; it was "Our worlds against each other." We tried a couple of different marriage counselors. They helped to enlighten but not empower. We discussed separating.

Vanessa was insisting we move to New York so she could be closer to her parents. She wanted the girls to go through the Westchester public school system, which was rated among the best in the country. We moved to New York and purchased a house in Chappaqua on four and a half acres of land for just under a million dollars. It was about twenty minutes from Millwood, where her parents lived. I gambled and hoped Vanessa would feel much happier being back in New York and closer to her parents. About a year later our son Devin was born, and I felt immensely blessed and happy that we had stayed together.

In the summer of 1994, she played the lead role as Rosie in the RHI Entertainment and ABC television production of the musical comedy *Bye Bye Birdie*, based on the screenplay and book written by Michael Stewart. Stewart wrote the book for the original Broadway production of the work in 1960. Directed by Gene Saks, the cast included Vanessa and Jason Alexander, and featured Chynna Phillips, Tyne Daly, Marc Kudisch, George Wendt, and Sally Mayes. We moved to Vancouver where it was being shot during the summer, and I shuttled back and forth every week. We found a nice summer camp for the kids, and Melanie and Jillian connected with two sisters, Yasmine and Leila, their same age at camp. They bonded, and we've stayed lifelong friends with them and their family.

KISS OF THE SPIDER WOMAN

The biggest breakthrough for Vanessa came when Emily Gerson, her New York–based agent at William Morris, connected her with the noted Canadian theater producer Garth Drabinsky. Drabinsky had relaunched a revival of the legendary musical *Show Boat* in Toronto, directed by Hal

Prince. Garth was interested in Vanessa assuming the role of Julie, played by Lonette McKee, who was leaving the show. We went to see the show, but Vanessa was not thrilled with uprooting our family and moving to Toronto.

Garth wanted to work with Vanessa, so he came back with an offer for her to take over Chita Rivera's lead role as Aurora in the Broadway production of *Kiss of the Spider Woman*, which had stormed Broadway, winning seven Tony Awards the year before, including Best Musical and a Best Actress award for Rivera. Vanessa was thrilled with the idea of starring on Broadway, which was a dream of hers. Emily worked out a limited engagement from June 24 to September 24 and secured a respectable weekly salary which amounted to five digits. It was considered high for a replacement lead in a play for an actor with Vanessa's limited Broadway experience. Garth became one of the first producers to cast a nontraditional Broadway star from television, film, or music and a Black female in a lead role for a Broadway play.

Vanessa's opening night was June 24, which marked ten years and a day since she resigned as Miss America. *New York Times* theater critic David Richards raved, "Whenever she's onstage, the temperature in the Broadhurst Theatre shoots up about 20 degrees. The air-conditioning bills are going to be hell to pay, but the box office is bound to start jumping as word of her performance gets around." I was grateful that David had opted not to run the infamy identifier "deposed Miss America who posed nude." It had taken ten years, but she had finally gotten her name back. The play was extended for another three months (through January 1995), and a second *Kiss of the Spider Woman* cast album was released featuring Vanessa. It was the happiest I had seen her.

THE SWEETEST DAYS

Kiss of the Spider Woman threw off the scheduled release of her third album, *The Sweetest Days*. It was supposed to be released in the fall but I felt we should wait and release it early in the first quarter. I pleaded my case, but Ed and David Leach, who was VP of pop radio, wanted to release the title song, a ballad, as the first single in early December. I wasn't excited about leading with a ballad either, but I lost the battle on both issues.

Wing/Mercury released "The Sweetest Days" on October 18 (my birthday). Phil Galdston, Wendy Waldman, and Jon Lind wrote the song, and Keith Thomas produced it (the same quartet who created "Save the Best for Last"). It peaked at #3 on the Adult Contemporary chart, #18 on the Hot 100, but only #40 on the R & B Singles chart. They opted to release a romantic-inspired and urban version of the video, directed by Kevin Bray.

Wing/Polygram released the album on December 6. Vanessa was given the freedom to stretch her creative muscles and put her signature on the album. She coproduced seven tracks with Gerry Brown, and shared an executive producer credit with Ed. It was her most varied project as far as genre, including R & B, pop, jazz, and Latin styling. I had encouraged her to expand her creative contributions as a songwriter and producer, so I was happy to see it finally happen. Babyface wrote and produced two songs on the album.

At the end of January Wing/Mercury released the album's second single, "The Way That You Love," a dance/R & B track penned by J. Dibbs and Abena and produced by Vanessa and Gerry Brown. It peaked at #6 on the Dance chart, #23 on the R & B chart, and #26 on the Hot 100 chart. Noted photographer and director Matthew Rolston shot a cool black-and-white video that featured Vanessa sporting high-fashion glamorous looks, including one with long black braids. "You Can't Run" was the third single released, and it peaked at #40 on the R & B chart.

The album was certified platinum, the last album in her career to be certified platinum. In addition, it received two Grammy Award nominations in 1995, "The Way That You Love" for Best R & B Vocal Performance, Female, and "You Can't Run" for Best R & B Song.

"COLORS OF THE WIND"

While the album was being promoted, I received arguably the best offer in her career. Disney wanted Vanessa to sing the end title song, "Colors of the Wind," for its next animated movie, *Pocahontas*. Stephen Schwartz and Alan Menken wrote and produced it, two award-winning songwriters who were collaborating for the first time. Disney was also offering a high-six-figure number, the highest fee Vanessa had received as an artist. I was elated, and Vanessa was elated. It was a ringing endorsement that our strategy had worked. Getting a stamp of approval from Disney and becoming a part of their monolithic animated film franchise left us euphoric. I couldn't wait to share the news with Ed.

Ed instantly zapped all my enthusiasm by nixing the idea, claiming it would interfere with the label's marketing campaign for her album. The all-mighty Disney was gifting us with a hit song served on a platinum tray and a chance to be part of their mega box office and Academy Award–winning song franchise, and Wing/Mercury couldn't figure out a way to capitalize on it. His response stunned and baffled me. I felt arguing with him would be futile, but I wouldn't accept no as an answer—at least not without a fight.

For the first time, I went over his head and contacted Alain Levy, the chairman of Polygram. We had met and talked cordially on several occasions, but not about Vanessa. When I connected with him, he deferred to Ed's decision. Strike two! I felt the only shot left was to have Vanessa plead her own case to Alain. We were attending an industry event at the Biltmore Four Seasons Resort's beachfront property in Santa Barbara. I updated her on the situation and told her she'd have to beg, cry profusely, and do whatever was necessary to convince him that as an artist she needed to do the song and guilt him into approving it. I felt we needed to do it ASAP, and I offered to leave the room so she could express her feelings privately.

Their call went well; Alain acquiesced, giving approval to record the song. While I was coordinating everything with Disney, I found out Alain wanted Vanessa's entire fee paid to Wing/Mercury and applied to the un-recouped balance she owed. It infuriated me, so I called him again. His only retort, in his signature raspy French accent, was, "She said she really wanted to record the song, but she didn't mention anything about the money." I thought to myself, duh, of course she wants the money. With a little more coaxing, he agreed to let her keep the full fee.

Ed was not pleased, and it altered our business relationship and friendship. I felt personally indebted to him for taking a risk and signing Vanessa, and I was tremendously loyal to him. But I was sad that we were at odds about an opportunity that should have a been a no-brainer.

Disney Records released the song on May 23, 1995. The *Pocahontas* soundtrack came out a week later. It peaked at #2 on the Adult Contemporary chart, #4 on the Top 100, #10 on the Hot Adult Top 20 chart, and #53 on the Hot R & B/Hip-Hop chart. It was certified gold, selling seven hundred thousand albums. Dominic Orlando directed the video. Raisa Bruner of *TIME* noted, "Williams' rendition was performed flawlessly . . . painting a vision of 17th-century Native American life—and the importance of the environment—that still resonates with audiences today." It swept the Oscars, Grammy Awards, and Golden Globes in the Best Original Song category. Vanessa performed it on the Oscars telecast on March 26, 1996, which was another first for her.

The last album I worked on with Vanessa was her first Christmas album, *Star Bright*, her fourth studio album. Wing/Mercury released it on November 5, 1996. It was certified gold and earned a Grammy Award nomination in 1997 for Best Pop/Contemporary Gospel Album.

TOUR CANCELED

The one area Vanessa had not conquered to elevate her fame was touring and becoming a superstar live attraction. We had purposely bypassed touring to build her artist brand and hopefully increase more of the demand for her. Touring would solidify her artistry, boost her fan base, and hopefully help sell more records. My goal was to launch the tour in Japan with eight to ten dates and then follow up with a US leg in the major markets. I hired Alan Zullo, a veteran tour manager, to help put the production team together (he had served in the same capacity for Natalie Cole when I represented her). We had booked rehearsal space downtown, and had three weeks left before leaving for Japan. The Japan tour had already been announced, and the dates were sold out. The US leg was a work in progress.

I was meeting with Alan in my New York offices when I received a fateful call from Vanessa. It triggered a disastrous turn of events that forever altered our lives. She revealed that her West Coast film agent, Michael Gruber, had received interest from someone in Arnold Schwarzenegger's camp for her to costar in his next film, *Eraser*. She was understandably thrilled, but I wasn't—for a plethora of reasons.

Pausing briefly, I asked her when the film was slated to start. She said in a month. Confused, I said, "You'll be in Japan and all the dates are sold out." She added, "I already told him if they make a firm offer, I'd do it." It appalled me. "That's crazy—it's too late! The promoter will sue us. Plus, I'll have to negotiate cancellation fees and settlements with all the personnel."

I called Michael to get more specifics. He had not discussed the fee but speculated it might be $500K. I asked him if he had given any thought to the financial liabilities Vanessa would face by canceling the tour. I knew the answer. I didn't trust him. I thought he was a grandstander who talked a better game than he delivered. But he had captured Vanessa's ear. Vanessa assailed me (as her husband and her manager) for not agreeing to support her doing the film. I fully understood her excitement. Schwarzenegger was a megastar and one of top box office attractions in the world. It would be the biggest movie of her career.

We were partners and had committed financially to a strategy to attain our goals. As her husband and her manager, I didn't feel it made ethical or practical sense to throw everybody under the bus and incur major financial liabilities to do the film. I personally wished the offer would have come at a more opportune time. This was not an inflection point in her career or a do-or-die scenario. And it wouldn't be the first time a star had to reject an offer they wanted to do due to a prior commitment—it happened all the time.

Walking out of my office after the call, I felt disheartened and betrayed—and like a mop waiting for a flood. Alan and I walked to a local bar to blow off steam, have a few drinks, and figure out our strategy if Vanessa bailed. When we got to the bar, I called her from the bathroom. Our conversation was horrendous and only made matters worse. I told her I was having drinks with Alan and wasn't sure when I'd be home.

BUSTED

By the time I got home, it was about 2 a.m. When I got to the bedroom, Vanessa appeared to be asleep. As I was easing my way into the bed, she startled me by asking if I had looked at our refrigerator door. I said not really. She insisted I go look at it. The refrigerator was plastered with images of our children and families. I was tired, a little buzzed, and had no inkling of what she had planted for me to see. After staring for ten to fifteen minutes, I noticed a handwritten note on a card. When I read it, I realized it was from a woman I knew. I returned to bed and acknowledged I had found what she wanted me to see. I didn't want to talk about it and promised I'd talk to her the next day.

The note she pasted on the refrigerator was not graphic, but it was suggestive. It was an old note that I didn't remember keeping. Vanessa thought the woman who wrote it was too familiar and friendly with me. And she presumed right. I had cheated. I couldn't rationalize why I did it, nor had I seriously contemplated the consequences of her finding out. There aren't any valid excuses to justify cheating. It's wrong and selfish, breaks a seal of trust, is a sign of weakness, and in most cases is unforgivable. I created my own infamy and a stigma that couldn't be erased. I've accepted it as my worst failing, and always regretted the hurt and pain that could have been averted.

The next morning after the kids left for school, I confessed, accepted culpability, apologized, and said I was sorry. I didn't make any excuses and told her I regretted it. I didn't beg for forgiveness. I said if she wanted a divorce, I would respect her wishes. At that moment, I knew she felt hurt and angry. Over the next few days, her hurt mushroomed into hate—and she told me she intended to destroy me. The first thing she did was fire me as her manager. It was understandable, and I accepted it. I had fueled the ultimate provocation, but even without it, I felt we'd need a miracle to resuscitate our relationship. She faxed the note to my employees, and a few weeks later I discovered she had stuffed copies of it in every single folder in my filing cabinet. I was shocked that she indulged in such a painstaking and time-intensive endeavor to express her angst.

She surprisingly didn't want to get divorced and preferred to separate. We tried a last-gasp effort to salvage our marriage. We planned a few dates, and our last professional and family event together was attending Super Bowl XXX in Tempe, Arizona, for her performance of the national anthem. There were only a few dimming embers left in the fire—so we stopped trying. One day she left me a written message that she was filing for divorce.

When I moved out, I rented a three-bedroom house less than ten minutes from the house we were renting. It made it quite easy for the kids and for us as well. We never spent a day in court; she filed for divorce and we agreed to share mutual custody of our children. We were legal co-owners of the house and had cosigned on a six-figure construction loan to facilitate the expansion. I later decided to relinquish my financial equity in the house to her so we weren't liable to each other.

Over the years, Vanessa and I established a peaceful coexistence. Although our marriage failed, we didn't fail as parents. I'm most proud of the splendid job we've done coparenting and sustaining a loving family unit for our children. We have mastered the art not letting the inherent dysfunctional components undermine a functional family unit that thrives on love and respect. We've shared most of the holidays, milestones, and birthdays over the past two decades as a family. As a bonus, I also developed a loving relationship with Sasha, her daughter with Rick Fox.

Watching Vanessa mature and spread her wings as an entertainer has been gratifying. She has crafted a diverse career that encompasses television, music, theater, film, commercial endorsements, signature branded apparel products, philanthropy, social activism, and to a lesser degree contemporary music, which makes her unique. Every career has successes and failures, but it's how you face and manage them that determines your longevity and ability to keep moving forward. That's where I feel Vanessa has learned the most and been exceedingly triumphant and resilient in sustaining her fame.

In retrospect, I'm proud of the contributions I made to her first decade of superstardom, and I learned a few vital lessons as well. No matter how deeply you love someone and channel that love to help them achieve happiness, you can't rely on their happiness to make you happier. Be happy for them, be happy with whatever you did to help them be successful, but never stop seeking your own happiness. Unquestionably, the most valuable lesson I learned is that I know more about fame than women.

11

SHORT FAME TALES

I've learned that cultivating fame and collaborating with famous people are inherently unpredictable. Unforeseen circumstances can arise with no warning and require immediate action. As I publicist I was customarily retained for three to six months, and as a manager usually a year. But occasionally I was engaged spontaneously to assist with time-sensitive matters that necessitated making a few phone calls or working as little as one week to a month.

Here are five short tales of my experiences as publicist and manager that were challenging, rewarding, or fell short of my expectations.

TALE ONE: CRISIS INTERVENTION

Last year, August 25, 2021, marked the twentieth anniversary of the untimely and tragic death of superstar songwriter, singer, and actor Aaliyah (Aaliyah Haughton), which totally depressed me. I had spoken to her once on the phone in the 1990s and still hoped to meet her one day.

On August 25, 2001, at 6:50 p.m., Aaliyah and six members from her entourage and label boarded a chartered Blackhawk International Airways twin-engine Cessna 402 light aircraft piloted by Luis Morales III for what should have been an hour and ten minute flight from Marsh Harbour Airport in Abaco Islands, the Bahamas, to the Opa-Locka Airport in Florida. They had just finished filming a video for her song "Rock the Boat."

The plane crashed and caught fire shortly after takeoff, about two hundred feet from the end of the runway. Aaliyah and the eight others on board (which included the pilot) all perished in the crash. The National Transportation Safety Board later reported that in addition to the plane being seven hundred pounds overloaded, the flight was carrying one more passenger than its certified allowance. In addition, the pilot was not approved to fly the plane. He had fraudulently obtained his FAA license by falsifying hundreds of hours never flown, had lied to his employer, and toxicology tests revealed traces of cocaine and alcohol in his system. Based on detailed reports of what had transpired, the accident could have been averted—at least from my assessment.

On August 18, 2021, the week before the twentieth anniversary of the crash on August 25, 2001, a federal trial commenced in Brooklyn. R. Kelly faced one racketeering charge and four violations of the Mann Act, which criminalizes transporting woman and girls across state lines for the purposes of illegal sexual activity.

Two weeks prior to that, on August 5, Barry Hankerson, Aaliyah's uncle, former manager, and founder of Blackground Records, announced plans to rerelease the label's entire catalog, including Aaliyah's four albums recorded while signed to the label, on streaming services worldwide after entering a new partnership with the independent label Empire. On August 19, the second day of Kelly's trial, Spotify announced Aaliyah's 1996 album *One in a Million* was available for streaming, and the other albums were queued up in their streaming pipeline.

For the past twenty years none of her catalog, for which Blackstone owns the masters, was available for streaming due to conflicts between Hankerson and Aaliyah's estate, represented by her mother, Diane Haughton, Hankerson's sister. In response to the announcement, Ms. Haughton remarked, "Now, in this twentieth year, this unscrupulous endeavor to release Aaliyah's music without transparency or full accounting to the estate compels our hearts to express a word—forgiveness."

These events rekindled my memories of the late summer of 1994, when

I unexpectedly got involved with Barry, Aaliyah, her mother, and R. Kelly at a threshold moment that forever altered their lives. I had known Barry for over a decade and had interfaced with him when I managed Andraé Crouch, who had signed his clients, the Winans, to a production deal. We connected again in the 1990s, when he managed R. Kelly, who wrote and produced "It's a Woman's Thing" for Ex-Girlfriend, an all-girl group based in New York that I was managing. They recorded the track at the Chicago Recording Company, the same studio Kelly used to record his debut solo record and Aaliyah's as well.

Meeting with Barry Hankerson

In the first week of September 1994, Barry Hankerson called me unexpectedly and said he had an urgent and highly sensitive matter that he wanted to meet about. When we met, he revealed that R. Kelly and Aaliyah had eloped and married three days earlier. Barry had introduced Aaliyah to R. Kelly when she was fourteen years old. Kelly mentored, wrote, and produced all the songs for her debut album. Barry managed both Kelly and Aaliyah.

What I didn't realize was that Aaliyah's mother, Diane Haughton, was Barry's sister, and he was Aaliyah's uncle. Aaliyah and Kelly had been secretly engaging in a clandestine intimate relationship for quite some time. Barry emphatically confessed that he had no clue it was going on.

He said his sister was devastated, shocked, and angry. She felt he was culpable for letting this happen to his fifteen-year-old niece while she was under his watch. He wanted me to consult with his sister and Aaliyah about the best way to curb a media frenzy and prevent severe damage. He offered to pay me and gave me complete autonomy. It was an unusually difficult family/business cataclysm where they all felt victimized. And a tragedy for Aaliyah, considering she was a minor. I agreed to talk to his sister and Aaliyah, and hoped I could help them out. He mentioned that a small rumor about them being married had appeared in a magazine.

I had no idea whether Aaliyah and her mother had done anything yet, or whether they already had a strategy in place. I hoped to mediate the crisis and ward off a potential media maelstrom. Barry wanted to get his sister's blessing first. He notified me that she had agreed to speak to me and expected me to call the next day.

Aaliyah was in the embryonic stages of her career but had been dabbling in the industry for five years. She appeared on *Star Search* at age ten and sang with her aunt, Gladys Knight (who was formerly married to Hankerson), at one of her Las Vegas concerts at age eleven. When she was twelve, Barry set up his own label, Blackground Records, signed her to his label, then cut a distribution deal for his label with Jive Records. He also managed R. Kelly and signed him to Blackground/Jive Records. He wanted Kelly to write and produce songs for her debut album.

Aaliyah was introduced and featured in March 1994 on a remix of "Your Body's Callin'," which was one of the biggest songs on Kelly's debut album, *12 Play*. A little less than five months after her fifteenth birthday on January 16, Aaliyah's debut single, "Back and Forth," was released and reached #1 on *Billboard*'s Hot R & B/Hip-Hop Songs chart for three weeks. Her debut album, *Age It*, debuted at #24 on the *Billboard* 200 chart and sold thirty-eight thousand copies in its first week.

A Call with Aaliyah and Her Mother

When I spoke to Aaliyah and her mother, they were friendly and warm. I asked them to give me a transparent account of what had transpired, if they had shared what happened with anyone outside of their family, and whether they intended to pursue any legal actions since Aaliyah was a minor. I wanted to know if he had forcibly kidnapped her or raped her. I explained I couldn't give them meaningful input or advice without a comprehensive account of what occurred.

Just hearing those questions changed Ms. Haughton's demeanor. She understandably felt distressed and was fighting off tears. She was trying to respond in a quivering voice, so Aaliyah stepped in and spoke calmly and deliberately. She said Kelly had not coerced her or sexually abused her. She accepted full culpability for making a grave error in getting involved with and marrying Kelly. She spoke like a mature young woman rather than a naive teenager. They had no plans to file charges against Kelly, and Aaliyah firmly expressed her desire to get on with her life.

I expressed my empathy and recommended they do three things. First, have the marriage annulled as soon as possible. I suggested they retain a lawyer to make sure it was filed correctly. It didn't make sense for her to be legally connected to Kelly as wife. Secondly, I recommended Aaliyah terminate her personal and business relationship with Kelly if they had not made that decision already. Ms. Haughton stated emphatically that they had reached that conclusion and were proceeding to cut all ties to him.

And finally, I recommended that they not refute the rumor, make any official statement to the media, or discuss it with any close friends or family members who might leak it to the media. I stressed that they were under no legal obligation to alert the media about what had transpired, now or ever. No one needed know it ever happened.

Neither party had acknowledged they were married, so I emphasized that rumors can dissipate if you don't fuel them. I advised them that I would get a firm commitment from R. Kelly's publicist, Dan Klores, to adhere to a mandate of silence. They had every reason to honor it, since Kelly faced potential legal incrimination for his actions.

If at any point they changed their minds and wanted to make a public statement, I offered to oversee issuing it to the media. It would be a simple story. After the marriage, Aaliyah confessed and consulted with her parents. They took steps to protect her from enduring any further self-incrimination and to rectify the areas they could control, by getting the annulment and letting Aaliyah move forward with her life.

We talked on the phone for thirty to forty-five minutes. Ms. Haughton was emotionally distraught throughout, but by the end she seemed fine. They promised to heed my advice and get the annulment processed right away. I told them I understood this was an extremely stressful and emotional time for their family, but I admired them for their courage and desire to put this crisis behind them.

I immediately contacted Dan Klores, who was a respected entertainment publicist. He had launched his own firm after working under Howard Rubenstein, one of New York's most influential PR mavens. He agreed to maintain silence and said Kelly had agreed not to make any statements about it. I called Barry, and he agreed to do the same. After I let Ms. Haughton know I had worked things out with Dan and Barry, I never spoke to or heard from her or Aaliyah again.

The Aftermath

In 2021, I followed Kelly's court case and found out specific details about the marriage that they had never shared on our call. Kelly and Aaliyah had flown to Chicago, where they had procured a fake identification card showing that Aaliyah was eighteen years old. Kelly was twenty-seven. They were married by Nathan Edmond, a Baptist minister, in a room at a Sheraton Hotel in Maywood, a suburb near Chicago's O'Hare Airport. The marriage license was dated Wednesday, August 31, 1994. *Vibe* published a copy of the license for the first time in the December/January 1994 edition. Neither party commented on it.

According to Kathy Landoli, the author of *Baby Girl: Better Known as Aaliyah* (Simon and Schuster, 2021), they annulled the marriage on September 24, 1994. Aaliyah immediately cut professional ties with Kelly, and the two never worked together again or were seen together in public. That aligned with the time frame when I talked to them. Kelly's lawyers indicated that they both signed a nondisclosure agreement stating that neither would ever speak of the marriage or relationship. They sealed the agreement from being publicly exposed but honored the terms.

Barry stopped managing Kelly well before the end of the year, and Aaliyah's father, Michael Haughton, assumed the role of manager for her in early 1995. Barry had signed Aaliyah to his record label for multiple years, so he still owned her artist rights when she died. He served as executive producer on her third and final solo album, *Aaliyah*, released by Blackground/Virgin in July 2001, just over two months before she died.

I always felt touched by my brief interaction with Aaliyah and her mother, and remain inspired by my favorite song of hers, "Try Again," released as the lead single of *Romeo Must Die: The Album* on February 22, 2000, about a month after her twenty-first birthday. Stephen Garrett and Timothy Mosley wrote it, and Timbaland produced it.

I wish I could have met with Aaliyah before she died, just to commend her and her mother on how they turned her life around after our call. I was pleased they had taken my advice and not allowed what transpired to become an albatross around her neck for the rest of her life. In her short time on the planet, she embodied the essence of art imitating life in her song "Try Again." The hook is, "And if at first you don't succeed (first you don't succeed), / Then dust yourself off, and try again."

TALE TWO: "DON'T LISTEN TO THOSE WHO SAY YOU CAN'T. LISTEN TO THE VOICE INSIDE YOURSELF THAT SAYS, I CAN."

In 2003, I received a call from a good friend of mine, Kendall Reid, a programming executive at HBO. She said she was on the board of advisers for a talented young Black female producer and director, Shola Lynch, who had secured the rights to develop a documentary film based on the life of Shirley Chisholm. Shola was an optimistic first-time director and aspired to produce a platinum-selling soundtrack album as a companion to the film. Kendall hyped me up and suggested she meet with me to discuss her vision for the music.

When I was attending Whittier College, Chisholm was a featured guest speaker. She had an unflinching fighting spirit and willingness to buck the system. She understood that being Black and a woman were political liabilities, but they also heightened her resolve and sense of self-worth.

As an orator, she spoke unapologetically and from the heart, and her un-polished, no-nonsense persona left an indelible impression on me. The title of this short take is one of her most famous quotes.

Meeting Shola Lynch

I arranged to meet Shola for drinks at the Royalton Hotel in New York. It took only five minutes to understand that she was intelligent, charismatic, enthusiastic, and committed. She was also effusive and high-energy, a contrast to my laid-back demeanor—but I viewed those characteristics as strengths. She believed in and wanted her film, *Chisholm '72: Unbought and Unbossed*, to be a huge success. From my perspective, self-belief is a pre-requisite for any talent I opt to represent. When you're a manager, there's a fine balance between being an enthusiastic advocate and a dream slayer. After hearing that she had little or no budget to fund a major soundtrack, I gingerly encouraged her to lower her platinum expectations. I proposed taking a more practical route: license two or three well-known songs from the period, hire a composer to create original music, and create an end title song that could be released digitally as a single.

Shola had hustled and secured a deal with POV/American Documentary, funded by International Television Service (ITVS) and PBS for television broadcast. POV had committed $366,000 of finishing funds to complete the film but wouldn't disburse the funds until a rough cut of the film had been approved. She had additional fiscal sponsors who donated funding, including Women Make Movies, the National Black Programming Coali-tion, the New York State Council for the Arts, and the Paul Robeson Fund for Independent Media. Her dilemma was that the minimal funding she received from her fiscal sponsors was not sufficient to initiate and com-plete production of the film.

I shared my memories of seeing Chisholm speak and said that I respected her courageous spirit. I expressed my willingness to oversee the music.

I then proposed that I play a bigger role in the film—including raising funds. We worked out an arrangement for me to serve as the film's executive producer. It was my first film project serving in that capacity, and I viewed it as a gateway to the film business. I wouldn't make any money, but if the film did well, it might trigger more opportunities for me in the future.

Shola's documentary had a hook and a political storyline of historical value driven by a magnetic and unscripted character. Her vision was to chronicle Chisholm's historic run in 1972 to become the first African American major-party candidate to run for president of the United States. Four years prior, Chisholm had made history when she became the first Black woman elected to Congress in 192 years. The film would highlight the important moments of her milestone run from January 25, 1972, when she publicly declared her candidacy at Brooklyn's Concord Baptist Church, to the National Democratic Convention, held July 10–13 at the Miami Convention Center in Miami Beach. Chisholm captured only 152 first-ballot electoral votes for the nomination during the July 12 roll call, which wasn't enough to keep her in contention. She finished in fourth place behind George McGovern's winning total of 1,728 delegates.

Her campaign slogan was "Bring U.S. Together, Vote Chisholm 1972, Unbought and Unbossed," which inspired the title of the film. Chisholm had built a reputation as a fearless fighter for education, voting rights, and equality for marginalized Americans. She solicited people of color, women, feminists, gay people, and newly empowered eighteen-year-old voters to join her "on the 'Chisholm Trail' to reshape our society and take control of our destiny."

Her bid fueled racist opposition and polarization among Black political pundits who thought she was divisive, siphoning votes from the designated leading candidates when she had no chance of winning. But her fight to get as many Americans as possible to vote resonated with her supporters in Black communities.

In addition to making her debut as a director, Shola wrote the film and coproduced it with Phil Bertelsen. Her responsible executive partners at PBS were Cara Mertes, executive producer for POV/American Documentary, and executive producer Sally Jo Pfifer for ITVS.

In my role as an executive producer, I became a confidant for Shola and worked closely with Phil Bertelsen. We believed securing a theatrical release for the film was paramount to prepromote the broadcast, qualify it for submission to the Oscars and the Independent Spirit Awards, and platform Shola as a director. Leading with a television broadcast would disqualify the film from consideration for both film awards. In addition, the Academy of Motion Pictures mandated that a film be commercially released in a theater in New York and Los Angeles for one week before their required deadline.

POV had the distribution rights, so we needed them to agree to push back the national broadcast on PBS and allow us to pursue a separate film deal and release. Our optimum strategy was to premiere at the Sundance Film Festival, which Robert Redford had developed into the top festival in the US and one of the most prestigious film festivals in the world. The festival ran in January in Park City, Utah. The cachet value of being in the festival and premiering your film there as a first-time director was monumental from a marketing, PR, and acquisition vantage point.

Raising Money and Starting Production

That was our dream scenario, but the first step was to fundraise and get the film into production. I volunteered to pursue my celebrity friends to serve as private benefactors and make donations to the film as tax write-offs rather than investments. I decided to send open pitch letters to give them the option to donate or enlist as an investor. After a couple of months of solicitation, I secured donations from Oprah Winfrey, Bette Midler, Bill and Camille Cosby, and Halle Berry. They gave us permission to use their names in publicity as donors, but we agreed not to publicize the amount they donated. Shola was able to start production with the funding raised.

Additionally, I agreed to assume the role of music supervisor and solicited potential composers to write and produce the soundtrack. I also pursued licensing rights for existing songs that Shola wanted to feature in the film. I presented three or four composers for her consideration, and she opted to hire one of my longtime friends, Grammy Award–winning songwriter and producer Barry Eastmond. We asked Barry to write original music for select cues and create a title song that reflected the music of the early seventies, which he titled "Shirley's Theme."

Shola was able to pull together a rough cut to submit to Sundance. It was the pillar of our release strategy, so playing the waiting game was nerve-racking. The festival accepted the film, leaving us just one month to complete the final cut. On the evening of December 31, they were still editing the film to meet the last Fed Ex special delivery deadline for that day. It was a joyous occasion, so we popped champagne and brought in the New Year on a celebratory high.

Attending the Sundance Film Festival was a rewarding experience. As an official entry in the festival, we had access to major events, cocktail parties, film screenings, receptions, and late-night parties with celebrity live entertainment every night. I managed to squeeze in time to ski at the Deer Valley and Park City ski resorts. Meeting the wide range of filmmakers and creatives who were not famous but shared heart-wrenching sagas about their passion and unrelenting spirit to get their films completed made being there more inspiring and special.

The Premiere at Sundance Film Festival

The film premiered on January 18 to a packed house in a normal-size theater in Park City. I had only seen the film on small television monitors, and none were larger than thirty inches. Seeing it on a big screen for the first time was formidable and beyond my expectations. It was an emotionally moving experience that caused me to shed tears of happiness. I felt immense joy that Shola had given birth to her baby. And I was ecstatic about what we accomplished as a team.

The reviews and feedback were uplifting and uniformly positive. Almost immediately after the screening, we started receiving interest from a handful of film companies who wanted to acquire distribution rights. A couple lost interest after finding out we had a commitment to PBS and they wouldn't have distribution rights across all platforms.

Securing acquisition deals at Sundance or any of the other major film festivals is the reason filmmakers desperately hope their film gets accepted. Without a meaningful distribution deal, documentaries can end up as vanity projects—at least in terms of generating revenue and snagging a few minutes of fame.

Film Movement, founded by producer Larry Meistrich in 2002, aggressively pursued us. It was one of the first-ever subscription film services, and its core feature was a DVD-of-the-Month Film Club. Meistrich had previously founded the Shooting Gallery production company, which produced the critically acclaimed independent films *Sling Blade* and *You Can Count on Me*, which helped reinvigorate the indie film scene in New York.

Signing and Exiting a Deal with Film Movement

He offered to distribute the film for limited runs in art theaters in twenty major markets, supported by a half-million-dollar marketing budget. We decided to accept his offer, but we would still need to negotiate and execute the contract. On January 24, a week after our premiere, the deal was announced on Indie Wire. It capped an exhilarating and encouraging trip—but it was short-lived.

About a month later, Meistrich reneged on his offer after he realized PBS owned the exclusive on-demand rights to the film. However, we had already advised him that PBS had those rights. His tune had changed dramatically, and suddenly he couldn't deliver on any of the key deal points. He made a paltry counteroffer that was unacceptable. We had lost time but not hope.

We asked Cara Mertes if she would push the broadcast back again to give us time to find another distributor, which she obliged. I immediately began making calls and got connected to Lori Henry, who wears many hats. She consulted and had her fingers in politics, film production, and major television events. She brokered an introduction for me to David Garber, founder of Lantern Lane, an indie distribution and production company that had contributed to the distribution team for *My Big Fat Greek Wedding*, which was a monstrous success in 2002. David believed in the film's potential, so we made deal with him. He secured distribution with 20th Century Fox Home Entertainment, which agreed to set up film screenings at some major film festivals and to release a DVD in tandem with the broadcast. We were back in business.

In the summer and fall the film screened at film festivals in Lake Placid, Nantucket, Los Angeles, and Dallas, along with the American Black Film Festival in Miami, the New York Film Festival, and BFI London Film Festival. We had planned a major premiere in conjunction with the opening in New York at Brooklyn Academy of Music Rose Cinema on September 24, 2004. Shirley Chisholm had agreed to attend, but a few days before the opening, we received notification that due to failing health she had to cancel.

On February 7, 2005, during Black History Month, the film was finally broadcast nationally on PBS. It received favorable ratings and reviews, and later earned two nominations at the 2005 Independent Spirit Awards for Best Documentary and their Truer Than Fiction category. We attended the event in Santa Monica, and although we lost in both categories, it was still a fun night and gratifying to have been nominated. In 2006, it received a nomination from Black Reels for Best Documentary and won a prestigious Peabody Award. That was the icing on the cake—a lovely event and a great way to cap the award season and run of the film.

TALE THREE: BRANDING . . . THE BIG PICTURE

By 1990, I was entering my second decade as a thriving entrepreneur and had successfully transitioned from public relations to personal management. A lawyer friend of mine, Ken Hertz, unexpectedly called and asked if I would meet with his friend Bill Hammond, who aspired to get into the entertainment business, knew about my background, and wanted to meet me. I met Bill; he was Black, about a decade younger than me, and I liked his energy. He didn't have the skill set or experience that I needed, but I felt if I mentored and trained him, he might develop into an employee. So, I offered him an unpaid internship. After a few months, things weren't jelling, so I let him go. We stayed friendly, and several months later he approached me with the germ of an idea to create a live music jam night featuring Black musicians. It was an interesting idea, but he didn't have a creative or business strategy, or the finances to launch and sustain it, which I conveyed to him.

I let it go, but then one day I had an epiphany about my time living in London in 1973–77, and remembered the Bailey's Supper Club, which was a well-respected franchise of supper clubs established in the UK's northern cities (Liverpool, Manchester, and Sheffield). The clubs attracted predominantly white audiences but regularly featured top second-tier R & B groups of the '70s, Edwin Starr, the Chi-Lites, and Three Degrees. I felt an updated R & B supper club franchise like that might work. My idea was to launch clubs in Los Angeles, New York, London, and Tokyo and book tours for the featured artists to perform at each location.

I'd use the one-night live event as a pilot and marketing tool to get investors excited about the bigger brand concept. The event would comprise a ninety-minute show featuring three or four name artists backed by a top music director and an all-star band, which we'd rotate weekly. Each artist would perform two or three songs. An impromptu finale featuring the guest performers would cap the show, and artists in the audience would be invited to join in. From a marketing perspective, the hook would be not to pre-announce or advertise the featured guest artists, so every show would be a total surprise to the audience. By making the brand the star and a must-attend event, I felt artists would be clamoring to get booked rather than me having to chase them.

My altruistic goal was to pay homage to the R & B artists and musicians who had been carrying the torch to keep the genre alive and culturally relevant as one of America's and the world's revered indigenous African American music genres. I came up with the name R & B Live for the brand and remember sketching the logo design on a napkin during a flight. My good friend and graphic designer Marc Bennett rendered the final logo. The *R* and *B* had a grand music staff in the middle and was placed above *LIVE* in a square format. I reconnected with Bill and shared my vision. He liked it, so we hashed out an agreement for our collaboration.

The final step was securing a great venue. I wanted to re-create the ambiance of a classic supper club with the aura and panache of the legendary Cotton Club in New York (without the dressy attire)—a place that would appeal to artists and target an upscale, culturally mixed demographic. We found out the Tramps of London Night Club, in the Beverly Center, was booking one-night events. Tramps had originated as a high-end celebrity private club in London, which I had been to a few times when I lived there. Giancarlo Parretti, an Italian mogul and the CEO of MGM-Pathé Communications, opened the club and used it as his private playground to hobnob with Hollywood's rich and famous.

We met with Miki, the club's manager, and liked the ambiance and feel of the club. Just to get a feel for the place and their team, we put together a teaser event in the guise of a party for my birthday in October 1990. We had a great turnout of industry folk and celebrities and announced we had a surprise planned for them coming in early 1991. For R & B Live I'd have to cover all shortfalls and wouldn't make a dime. But if we sold out (three hundred–plus capacity) I could feasibly break even. We agreed to present the event on Wednesday nights on a trial basis.

R & B Live Opens at Tramps

The headliners for our launch on Wednesday, January 16, 1991, were all my clients: Al Jarreau, Andraé Crouch and Sandra Crouch, and singer Thelma Houston, an artist I had worked with while I was at Motown. Our musical director was keyboardist Jerry Peters, and the band included the noted musicians drummer Ndugu Chancler and bassist Freddie Washington. We received a tremendous number of RSVPs and thought we might even have to turn people away.

Around 5:30 p.m., while I was finishing the final script for the show, a breaking news story announced that the Gulf War had erupted with US bombings in Iraq. The timing was horrible, but we decided "the show must go on." We packed the room to the gills. The show was electric, the band was tight, and the artists were all phenomenal. We had to endure a faulty air conditioning system, but it didn't dampen the crowd's enthusiasm. The postshow buzz was nothing but raves, and we sold out all the tables for the next show before I had secured any artists.

R & B Live quickly became a favorite haunt for famous entertainers, sports figures, and L.A.'s finest music-loving in-crowd. My strategy worked, because of the artists, musical directors, and musicians who embraced and supported our mission and delivered phenomenal performances every week—without them, it would have tanked. We weren't getting rich, but we created a special experience you couldn't get anywhere else in LA.

Although we didn't pay the artists, we did provide them with a complimentary meal and drink tickets. Chaka Khan, one of my favorite artists and supporters, held the record for the highest bar tab: $2,500 plus tips. One night when she performed, she ordered ten bottles of Cristal champagne at $225 per bottle. I was mortified—I hadn't known about it until her waiter told me right before she ordered the tenth one. I went over to her table and whispered in her ear that I would continue to pay for her drinks, but that I had to cut her guests off. She was understanding and obliged.

We had a nice run at Tramps, but the club was looking for us to do buy-out, which was way beyond our means, so we started looking for another venue.

R & B Live Becomes Famous

We made a deal with the 20/20 Club in Century City. In 1988 it took over the property space vacated by the Playboy Club. It was a much bigger space, with a capacity of eight hundred (seated and standing). We had doubled our weekly expenses to $6,000 per show, so we had to make $25K a month to break even. I felt we needed to bring in our own house manager to deal with the owners to make sure we were getting credited for the bar and to handle cash and credit receipts, and our weekly out-of-pocket expenses. We hired a seasoned veteran, Dana Gonzales, who was a savior for our team.

R & B Live's legacy was firmly established at 20/20, and we were attracting major superstars. We ultimately sustained the brand over a four-year span and featured a legion of the industry's elite contemporary R & B music stars, including Stevie Wonder; Prince; Bill Withers; Earth, Wind & Fire; the Ohio Players; Joe Sample; Lenny Kravitz; Chaka Khan; David Sanborn; the Emotions; Natalie Cole; Les McCann; Brian McKnight; Vanessa Williams; the O'Jays; the Temptations; Gerald LeVert; Heavy D; Babyface; George Benson; BeBe and CeCe Winans; Grandmaster Flash; Dougie Fresh; Lisa Stansfield; Mick Hucknall and Hamish Stuart (from Average White Band); Keith Washington; Cherelle; Lisa Taylor; Sheila E.; Angela Bofill; and Terri Lyne Carrington.

Our music directors and musicians included Greg Phillinganes and Marcus Miller. Occasionally, we booked comedian guest hosts like Jamie Foxx, Sinbad, and Tommy Davidson. Our list of the celebrities and industry luminaries who supported the club included Quincy Jones, Eddie Murphy, Barbra Streisand, Magic Johnson, Andre Harrell, Russell Simmons, Paul Mooney, Steve McKeever, Sylvia Rhone, Suzanne de Passe, Jan Gaye, Mike Tyson, MC Hammer, and Martin Lawrence. Steve McKeever, who founded Hidden Beach Recordings (and discovered Jill Scott), booked a table for six months after seeing one of early shows. I said, "Steve, I don't know if we'll be around in six months," but it was great to have that level of faith and reinforcement out of the gate.

The *Los Angeles Times* featured us in the calendar section, and we were frequently cited in the music trades. We were surviving but only making enough to get by. We had attracted a few sponsors—American Express and Pepsi—but only for one-off shows. I got nibbles from a few investors—but it was all talk and no checks. A Chinese friend of ours, Richard Huang, who was an avid supporter with deep ties in Japan, orchestrated a business trip to Tokyo to meet with a half-dozen potential investors. We had a blast on the trip but came home empty-handed.

Pivoting to Make R & B Live a TV Series

My A-plan had not come to fruition, so I decided to shift gears and see if we could get interest in packaging a music series for television—which would help create a national platform for the brand and give me a chance to re-coup some of my investment. Over the next year I contacted several noted producers and friends who were all enthusiastic, but I couldn't secure a deal. Russell Simmons and Stan Lathan, who launched the *Def Jam Comedy Hour* on HBO, were my first choice. I knew the VP of programming, Betty Bitterman (from working on Bette Midler's HBO specials), so we set up a pitch meeting with her and suggested programming R & B Live to follow the *Def Jam* series on HBO, but she passed.

We later moved to the Roxy Theatre on Sunset, and Lou Adler, who owned it, loved R & B Live. He introduced me to Peter Roth, who headed up 20th Century Fox Productions. He agreed to take us on. He secured interest from Bob Banner, the head of music programming at Fox. He came to a show with some associates and loved it. Afterward, he gave me a hand-shake commitment that Fox would do it. But the following week, after dis-mal ratings on one of their music specials, the network announced that it had ceased production of all music programming.

One of the highlights of our run included producing a pre–Grammy night party at the Supper Club in New York in 1993. Our finale alone had twenty-five artists performing on stage, and people were standing on the tables dancing. One reporter noted, "If a bomb went off in the Supper Club last night, it would have wiped out the entire R & B music industry."

We also produced a string of US tours sponsored by AT&T and presented shows for US armed forces members stationed at bases in Japan, Europe,

Cuba, the Caribbean, and Bermuda. Doing those tours was gratifying. Most of the young servicemen had not experienced live entertainment by name artists from the US for two or three years.

We left the Roxy and were asked to produce a few shows for the soft launch of the House of Blues in Hollywood. We were running on fumes and surviving but weren't getting closer to achieving the bigger picture I had envisioned. Around the same time, I had a catch-up meeting with my business manager, Bruce Kolbrenner. He asked if I knew how much money I had put into R & B Live since its inception, and I wasn't sure. He said more than you probably realize, and cited a number in the low six digits. All I could muster was "Wow!" That revelation tipped the scales, and I realized I just couldn't justify continuing it.

The End

I rank R & B Live as one of my top career highlights but also my most disappointing failure. I passionately believed in the concept, and it was successful enough to earn a few minutes of fame—despite my pecuniary losses. In retrospect, developing the brand from scratch was gratifying, and we did create an unforgettable music and entertainment experience that many people claimed was the best in their lives. Bill had blossomed and contributed significantly to the growth of the brand. It would not have been as successful without his passion and energy. He later parlayed the skill set he had learned into opening his own thriving event production company, Hammond Entertainment, which celebrated its twenty-fifth anniversary in 2021. It has been gratifying to witness his professional growth as well as share a close and lasting friendship. He's like a brother to me.

My failure to leverage a moderate level of success and fame has always tempered the exhilarating ovations the shows once evoked—and kept me from taking bows for something I loved doing. But I've found comfort and peace in just accepting the fact that it was fun while it lasted.

TALE FOUR: STARTING RIGHT TO FINISH STRONGER

As a parent, I've always encouraged my children to choose their own paths in life. Don't try to please anyone, including me, by doing what you think is expected of you. My mantra is to stay true to yourself, work hard, concentrate, and focus on chasing your dreams. I've suggested the same approach to developing artists I've managed who were searching for an authentic artistic identity. One of the biggest challenges young artists face is starting off on the right foot, having clarity about their artistry, defining their artistic vision, and knowing how to package and sell their brand.

My middle daughter, Jillian, and her creative partner, Lucas Goodman, surprised me when they shared "Treat Me Like Fire," a song they were cowriting and producing for a potential digital release. They had spent months developing it, but Jillian refused to let me hear it. She said, "Dad, it's not ready for your ears yet." When I finally listened to it, I thought it needed a few structural changes, but it stood out as unique—both Jillian's voice and the musical vibe of the track. They let me listen to a few more iterations, and each time the song improved. Their artist brand name was Lion Babe. They had been collaborating and dating for a year or so.

They shared the video, and it was full of raw energy—edgy, creative, and well-crafted on what I knew was a shoestring budget. She had a massive amount of hair—the most I had ever seen on her head. I admired and respected their entrepreneurial spirit and desire to forge a daring and authentic brand concept.

On December 1, 2012, they uploaded the song on SoundCloud and released the video on YouTube the following week. Shortly after the release, *World Star Hip Hop Music Blog* wrote about the song and video, which spurred considerable viral traction. Incredibly, they were an overnight success with their debut single and video—a rare feat for an indie self-released debut. Within a few weeks I got flooded by calls from industry friends, managers, record label execs, and lawyers who had realized that Jillian was my daughter. They wanted to know if I managed Lion Babe or if they were seeking representation. Jillian and Lucas were being inundated with calls as well. I said I wasn't involved but I'd pass on their inquiry.

Jillian grew up with Vanessa being a recording artist and entertainer and had a music manager as a father. Lucas's parents, Daang and Ray Goodman, had established Trash & Vaudeville in the '70s as one of New York's most popular and seminal rock 'n' roll boutiques, and it has remained as a favorite staple for rock and hip-hop stars. They're also avid music lovers. But Jillian and Lucas were total novices about the music industry and how to capitalize on their sudden momentum—they had never been artists.

Several heavy hitters were pursuing them, including managers Ben Mawson (Lana Del Rey), Troy Carter (Lady Gaga, John Legend), David Massey (Island/Mercury), Amanda Ghost (Outsiders/Polydor UK, Island Mercury), Scooter Braun (Taylor Swift, Justin Bieber), Rocket Management (Elton John's company), Andrew Keller (Columbia Records), and attorney Michael Guido (Kanye West and several of my former clients, including Andraé Crouch).

They were overwhelmed and treading water, but taking care of expedient responses in this formulative stage is crucial. Finally, I told them it was time for them to make some decisions before the momentum subsided. I offered to manage them on a temporary basis to help them set up their artist brand. They needed a master course and insight about how to navigate the complexity, treachery, pollution, and egotistical land mines that one must endure to be successful in the music industry—and survive.

Imparting such wisdom to aspiring artists and other people's children is much easier than imparting it to your own—which I would soon find out. I never contemplated managing any of my children. I had a nightmare lurking in the back of my mind, where I wake up one day and Jillian says, "Dad, you're fired!" That had already happened with her mom and didn't sit well with me—but I didn't plan to be around that long. Since I had managed their mother, I felt that met my family quota. But as with her mom, I was motivated by love and wanted to get them sailing in the right direction.

Setting Up the Lion Babe Brand

My initial priority was to help them build a competent support team. They met and retained attorney Michael Guido, who had already expressed interest in representing them. Simultaneously, I advised them to register Lion Babe, form a business partnership or LLC, set up and register a publishing company, create a collaboration agreement, sign with ASCAP or BMI (the top performing rights organizations), and set up a bank account for their LLC before any potential revenues were generated.

They needed to define their brand. Were they a duo or a band, or would Jillian be the face of their brand? Would they promote themselves as a couple, or hide it and say they were just collaborators? I recommended they take the same approach Annie Lennox and Dave Stewart did when they formed the Eurythmics: they promoted themselves as a couple and duo on their album covers, videos, advertising, and promotional materials. Jillian said they wanted to establish their brand as a duo but not promote their personal relationship out of the box, so I reminded them they'd have to mandate and enforce it once they had signed with a label. I shared a story about my clients A Taste of Honey (two females and two males), who broke up after the label decided to only feature Janice Johnson and Hazel Payne on their album cover. People presumed they were a duo. In addition, I recommended that they not leverage Vanessa being Jillian's mom, but rather create their own persona and path. People would find out soon enough. And I convinced them to create a definitive graphic brand logo initially to establish Lion Babe as their brand identity. Once Lion Babe built brand currency, their fans would start identifying with them individually.

And lastly, I wanted them to upgrade their stage presentation as soon as possible. I had seen their first live show, and I thought it was a train wreck—but it could be fixed. We developed a twenty- to thirty-minute showcase comprising four songs that was tight, dynamic, and gave them both time to shine. I impressed upon them that being a successful live attraction would ultimately sustain their financial livelihood as artists—much more than their potential streaming royalties.

Meeting Amanda Ghost

I had started following up on calls they had not returned. Amanda Ghost, who had launched Outsiders as her own boutique label distributed by Polydor/UK/Universal Music Group, seemed the most enthusiastic. Amanda was a veteran songwriter, singer, and artist who later developed into a multiple award–nominated songwriter and producer for several top artists, including Beyoncé, Shakira, John Legend, and James Blunt, and served a controversial stint as president of Epic Records (February 2009–December 2010). She had signed two developing UK artists, Laura Welsh and Joel Compass, and had secured the licensing rights to release the *Fifty Shades of Grey* original motion picture soundtrack.

In response to all the media interest, we scheduled the showcase in mid-February 2013, and Lion Babe delivered an impressive show. There was a good turnout from industry execs, and the club was packed with their fans as well. Amanda couldn't attend, but she sent an A & R rep from the label. Within a few days after the show, she expressed interested in signing them and promised to submit a formal offer.

The UK manager Ben Mawson was vigorously pursuing them as well. He had turned Lana Del Rey into a huge commercial success and star. Without any commitment or agreement in place, he took the initiative to pitch Lion Babe and "Treat Me Like Fire" for a major Ray-Ban sunglasses television campaign in Europe. Ray-Ban wanted to use a remix of songs done especially for them to shoot a commercial in New York using Kate Moross, one of the UK's hot young photographers and video directors. They also wanted them to attend a VIP event in London in June to launch their campaign and premiere the commercial. We agreed to the deal.

Since all the serious interest was coming from London, I proposed they consider signing with a UK manager, especially if the deal with Amanda came to fruition. They could break their album in the UK and leverage the momentum to launch in the US.

We shot the commercial in New York, and it went extremely well. Kate Moross was excellent and easy to work with and shot it in black-and-white, so it had a retro vibe, and they both looked fabulous. Since Ray-Ban wanted them to attend the event at the end of June, we decided to devote some of our visit to scheduling meetings with managers and meeting the major players at Polydor/UK.

Wheels Up to London

Traveling to London with Jillian was eerie, sparking déjà-vu memories of when I relocated in London in the early 1970s. We were the exact same age, twenty-three. My adventure and experiences there changed my life and view of the world, and sentimentally I thought it might do the same for her. With assistance from Amanda's office, I confirmed management meetings with Mawson; Roger Ames, a well-respected and internationally renowned record executive (London Records, Warner Bros. Polygram) who had gone into the management business; Elton John's Rocket Management; and Sarah Stennett, founder of Turn First Artists (who had managed Iggy Azalea, Ellie Goulding, Rita Ora, and Jesse James). I had interacted with Ames while he was at Polygram and had met Elton John's longtime manager John Reid in the early '70s when Rocket Management was formed, but I was familiar with the current execs at the company.

There was little movement on the contract with Outsiders, and several deal-breaking points still needed to be ironed out. The most important one was a guaranteed US release with Universal, which Amanda intimated was secure and part of her joint venture with them. However, without a signed agreement, she was setting up writing and producing collaboration meetings for Jillian and Lucas with superstar producer Mark Ronson (who worked with Bruno Mars, Lady Gaga, and Amy Winehouse, and one with Pharrell upon our return to the States. Her lawyer, Jeremy Pierce, was also helping to get clearance on a sample that Lucas used on the single. They didn't feel comfortable releasing it without securing the clearance rights first.

Our London trip was productive on all fronts. We ironed out all the major deal points on their recording contract and secured the sample rights for "Treat Me Like Fire." Outsiders/Polydor wanted to release an EP of four songs prior to releasing an album, so Lion Babe began focusing on that. We had good meetings with the managers and agreed that Sarah Stennett's company would be the best fit. I planned to stay active until the record contract and the management contract were executed, to make their transition to Sarah as seamless as possible.

My Exit

Before I exited, they were learning how fragile the creative process can be between self-contained artists who have a strong belief in their own music vision and songs and a label executive who has a different view of the commercial appeal of those songs. I tried to emphasize that fostering a healthy relationship with any label requires compromise. And there's even more pressure on developing artists to do the lion's share of compromising, because they don't have success or fame to serve as leverage when major creative decisions are at stake. They had a strong foundation to build upon. I continually reinforced that they needed to continue to learn how use their artistry and the inherent power that comes with it as an asset—and not make it a liability.

Sarah aligned them with LeRoy Benros (based in New York), who became their day-to-day global manager and has been responsible for guiding their career ascension and success since 2014. They released their debut album, *Begin*, in February 2015, then a string of singles and videos, headlined national and international concert tours, and secured a list of sponsorships (H & M, the Gap, Pantene, Apple Music Japan, Tidal, and Spotify). They released a second album, *Cosmic Wind*, in March 2019, and a third album, *Rainbow Child*, in August 2021. In February 2022, they released one of their most popular singles, "Harder" featuring Busta Rhymes.

I've immensely enjoyed their rise to stardom while sitting on sidelines as a loving father and loyal and supportive fan. On December 28, 2021, Jillian and Lucas also made me a granddad with the birth of their son, Sunny Rise. The short time we shared as business partners will always be special. They have a twenty-four-hour access pass for any kind of consultation they need. They pick my brain and keep me abreast of what they're up to. But the real joy for me is just watching my children carve out their own paths in life and achieve their own happiness and success.

TALE FIVE: A FINAL HURRAH!

In 1977, during my freshman year at Rogers & Cowan, my boss, Paul Bloch, signed St. Louis Cardinal All-Star outfielder Lou Brock, who was in the twilight of his stellar nineteen-year career as a superstar in major league baseball. He was on the cusp of breaking the all-time record of 892 stolen bases set by baseball legend Ty Cobb, which Cobb had held for forty-nine years (1928–77). The record had been one of the most durable in baseball history, on par with Babe Ruth's long-standing career record of 714 home runs. Baseball pundits considered it unbreakable. Playing against the San Diego Padres on August 29, 1977, at San Diego Stadium, Brock finally broke the record. He was also within reach of joining the elite club with three thousand career hits, a feat only fourteen players had achieved. Lou had also committed to retiring and planned to make his exit at the end of the 1979 season.

I was assigned as the executive on the account from our Beverly Hills office, and I worked with Joe Dera, who was based in our New York office. I had played baseball in Little League, American Legion, high school, college, and later in the softball leagues. I was an avid fan of the sport and Lou, so I was grateful to be able to represent him. He was charismatic; bright; culturally, socially, and politically in tune with the times; had a great sense of humor; and was a likable and fun person to be around. We clicked immediately.

Six years after I worked with Lou, he was elected to the Hall of Fame in 1985 in his first year of eligibility, becoming just the twentieth player elected in his first year on the ballot. Over his career, he totaled 3,023 hits, 1,610 runs, 900 RBI, and 938 steals—a stolen base mark that stood until it was broken in 1991 by Rickey Henderson. He had a phenomenal nineteen-year professional career that started in 1961 with the Chicago Cubs when he was twenty-two years old. In his rookie season of 1962, Brock became one of four players to hit a home run into the center-field bleachers at the old Polo Grounds in New York City since its 1923 reconstruction. During the 1964 season he was traded to the St. Louis Cardinals, where he played left field for the rest of his career. Four months to the day after Brock's trade, the Cardinals won the 1964 World Series in seven games over the favored New York Yankees. Lou hit .348 and stole thirty-three bases during the Cardinals' final drive to win the world championship.

Brock was an All-Star for six seasons and a National League stolen base leader for eight seasons. In 1966, Brock ended Maury Wills's six-year reign as the National League's stolen base champion with seventy-four steals. In the 1967 World Series, Brock batted a .414 average, scored eight runs, and set a World Series record with seven stolen bases as the Cardinals defeated the Boston Red Sox in seven games. In the 1968 World Series against the Detroit Tigers, Brock once again stole seven bases and was the leading hitter in the series, posting a .464 batting average with six runs and five runs batted in, but the Cardinals lost the series after being up 3–1 games. In August 1973, he broke a record set by Ty Cobb when he stole his fiftieth base of the season, marking the ninth time he had stolen fifty or more bases in a season. On September 10, 1974, Lou broke Wills's single-season stolen bases mark of 104 and ended the season with a new major league single-season record of 118 stolen bases.

When I started representing Lou, he was closing in on Ty Cobb's record and I was strategizing with the Cardinals' head of PR on how we'd handle the postgame press conference. Lou notified the team's management that he wanted them to clear all media requests with me. He also got me clearance to come into the Cardinals' press box and their club house, which were both firsts, since no other Black players had their own publicists. St. Louis was a racially repressive and divided city, so walking into the Cardinals' press box wearing sunglasses and a huge Afro drew gazes of wonderment from the room full of white journalists, who looked like they had seen a ghost. Once it became apparent that Lou would break the record, he started being bombarded by inflammatory and threatening racial hate mail from whites who revered Cobb and couldn't stomach a "nigger" breaking his record—which was the word that was proliferated in the letters.

The Cardinals were making a West Coast road trip when the feat seemed imminent. They were playing the San Francisco Giants, the Los Angeles Dodgers, and the San Diego Padres. I planned to attend all the series. By the time they met the Dodgers for a weekend series, he only needed to steal two bases to break the record, which would have been optimum for media coverage. But he stole only one base and sat out the next game.

On Monday, August 29, 1977, the Cardinals were opening a series with the San Diego Padres with an evening game at San Diego Stadium. I planned to catch a flight after work for a 7:30 p.m. start time. It's only about a thirty-minute flight. While driving to the airport, I got stuck in traffic and missed my flight. After grabbing the next available flight, I heard Lou steal his 892nd base to tie the record in the cab on my way to the stadium. I couldn't believe it. I had been trailing him for two weeks, then I miss one inning, and he ties the record.

Immediately upon my arrival in the stadium parking lot, I sprinted into the stadium and heard my name being publicly announced over the stadium's intercom system, "Ramon Hervey please come to press box immediately." That was a first. By the time I found the press area, Lou had stolen his 893rd base and made history, eclipsing Cobb's record to become the all-time MLB stolen base leader. The Cardinals' press rep had set up the room nicely. The after-game presser would be about thirty minutes, and we expected a packed crowd—not only because of the historical significance of Lou breaking the record, but I'd also been asked to comment about Lou chasing the record in a *Los Angeles Times* magazine story.

I had mentioned that I was pulling for him to break the record in LA because it was a national media hub, and the story would probably get more coverage there than in San Diego. So there was extra media turnout, intent on proving that the San Diego media market wasn't going to play second fiddle to L.A. I was just being honest and didn't mean to disrespect the city or the media, but I was happy that they took it that way and delivered major coverage for Lou in San Diego and nationally. The highlight of the evening was getting a chance to retrieve the second base from the game for his two steals.

Next on the list to secure his legacy and become a first-time electee to the baseball Hall of Fame was to get his three-thousandth hit. Going into the 1978 season, he needed 221. But '78 was a down season, and he had announced plans to retire at the end of the '79 season. His longtime agent Richie Bry was trying to renegotiate his salary for his last year, which was at $222,000—and that's after nineteen years. Meanwhile, I was also representing Dave "the Cobra" Parker, who in 1978 became the first professional athlete to be paid a million-dollar annual salary (in a five-year deal) as a rookie. That's how far baseball had come in eighteen years.

During the 1979 season, I was coordinating press with the Cardinals, who were getting requests from all the National League teams that Lou would be playing against for the last time. Many of the teams wanted to pay tribute to him, either with on-field gift presentations or video salutes, and they wanted him to attend the postgame media press conferences. I had to clear all requests with Lou, and while he was amenable to most teams honoring him, he had unhealed scars from others. I was also pitching mainstream media, TV, and radio for him as well. Lou was a hustling entrepreneur and had his fingers in a lot of things. He had invented a rainbow-colored sun hat called the Brockabella, which folded and was made of the same weather-proof material as an umbrella. It was attached to an adjustable headband you wore on your head. I attended numerous meetings with him, which he scheduled on his off days and game days.

His final season got off to blistering start, and in May he hit .433 and was named the National League Player of the Month. Mainstream media was responding to Lou, and he was getting coverage in print and on TV, including the *Tonight Show Starring Johnny Carson*. I had my sights on getting Lou to the White House so he could meet President Carter. I had never met a US president or visited the White House, but I researched and was able to find a contact who worked in the Carter administration, Scott Burnett, who was a special assistant to the president.

Scott knew who Lou was, and I proposed having Lou meet the president. Lou would gift him with memorabilia items from his stolen base record and his three-thousandth hit. Scott was enthusiastic and got President Carter's blessing, and the process was set in motion.

Lou was forty when he was chasing the record. By August he was hitting .326 and had one hundred hits. He was just two shy of three thousand when the Cardinals played the Chicago Cubs on August 13, 1979. Brock got hits in the first and fourth innings to become the fourteenth player in MLB history to reach the elite three-thousand-hit mark, ironically against the team that traded him in 1964.

Now that Lou had broken the record, I was able to finalize the Lou's visit to the White House with Scott. Lou was excited, and I was very pleased the meeting was happening. Lou wanted to give the president his spikes and a bat to commemorate his two history-making records. The date was set for September 24.

Shortly after it was confirmed, I received a cold call from Senator Thomas Eagleton, the Democratic senator from Missouri. He was requesting for his office to take the lead and present Lou to the president on behalf of the state of Missouri. I told him that we had been working directly with the White House and were tying up few loose ends, but I would run his request by Lou.

I called Lou and shared Eagleton's request, and he said he had no desire to be involved with him. Lou explained that Eagleton was a big Stan Musial fan, had fervently supported all of Musial's business endeavors, and had never given Lou a minute of his time. They were not friendly, and he didn't like the idea of him using this opportunity to exploit and pretend they were. I told him I'd take care of it.

I called Senator Eagleton and explained that we were too far down the line, and I felt it was too late to make any readjustments for the visit. Before I could finish and thank him for the offer, he went ballistic. He started screaming and yelling, calling Lou an egotistical, selfish, ungrateful, spoiled athlete. He emphasized that he was a US senator, and that he couldn't believe Brock had the nerve to reject, etc. etc. It felt like the n-word was on his tongue and he was a breath away from letting it out. I had let him speak without interruption, but I felt he had well exceeded his venting quota. I jumped in and retorted that his incendiary remarks were not appreciated and that we were finished. He finally shut up and hung up the phone.

At noon on Monday, September 24, we met President Carter in the Oval Office of the White House. Lou brought his wife, Virgie; his son, Lou Brock Jr.; and Bob Conway, the mayor of St. Louis. President Carter exuded the same down-to-earth and unpretentious natural southern charm he projected whenever he spoke. He took time to chat with everyone personally and posed for pictures. It was memorable for all of us. While in DC we also visited Senator Ted Kennedy, who was a lifelong fan of baseball and of Lou as well.

Lou ended the season with a .304 batting average and was named the National League Comeback Player of the Year, becoming the first player to receive that honor in their final MLB season. I had a clubhouse pass for the final game of his career in St. Louis on September 30, and he received thunderous applause and appreciation for the enormous impact he had on the Cardinals' organization and the city of St. Louis for two decades as one of the greatest players of all time.

12

TENETS OF FAME

There is no proven formula for acquiring fame. Each person's journey is different. I follow an old school precept and a more traditional tenet that fame should be viewed as a reward. It's an honor bestowed on exceptionally talented individuals who are passionate about their art form or profession and have struggled and prepared themselves for years to forge a legitimate and successful career.

Whenever I mentor burgeoning young musical artists and talent, I stress that the best path to success is to hone their craft and create quality content, songs, videos, live performances, and brand imaging materials. Music is one of the most difficult art forms to monetize and commercially exploit, and the caliber of an artist's brand presentation and product is the key to get in the game.

One of my favorite adages was coined by my friend and mentor, the esteemed record company industry legend, Bob Krasnow. Bob's sarcasm at times could sting like a fresh wound. He had a keen eye for talent but also believed as a skillful music executive that he couldn't deliver miracles. His assessment of talent could be blunt and unforgiving. Often he would say, "You can't turn horseshit into ice cream."

To reach stardom or superstardom today, I also emphasize the importance of being aware of all the tools and prevailing media and distribution platforms that can influence the development of their brand. And to take the initiative to learn and understand the technical language and key words, such as brand platform, messengering, elevator pitch, clicks, views, viral campaigns, posts, algorithms, analytics, demographics, usernames, passwords, memes, characters, and hashtags, that can impact their ability to be successful.

I've always preferred longevity over flash-in-the-pan success and believed that legitimate talent should be the driving force of the entertainment industry. I've never chased the quick buck and was willing to hedge my bet on building and developing brand integrity and artistry over gimmicks. Mining legitimate fame that can be monetized and sustainable can't be achieved overnight. It requires sweat equity and unflinching self-confidence.

I've dedicated years to honing and refining my own talents and methodology as a publicist and manager. Along my path I've shaped my philosophical view of fame and success based on what I learned from firsthand interactions with the famous artists I've represented. Each dealt with his or her level of fame differently.

I've created a baker's dozen of tenets that embody my approach to fame, which I think can be inspirational, helpful reminders for artists and other people who aspire to success and fame or may be grappling with it psychologically or philosophically. Fame has its inherent threshold, pressure, and stress points that can be disruptive. Failure to identify and navigate through those stressful times can cause things to spiral in an unfavorable direction. Comedian Chris Rock and Will Smith's epic crisis earlier this year are prime examples of the fragility of fame.

Like everybody else, there are days when famous people need to remind themselves who they are—and not how they're perceived. These rules are applicable during various iterations of fame or in dealing with a major crisis. They can serve as a gentle reminder to get recentered, as a brief mental pep talk, or as a shot in the arm.

Tenets of Fame

1. Fame is not a destination—it's an accolade.
2. Don't obsess about fame. Obsess about being your best.
3. Be authentic—don't let fame define you.
4. Avoid self-assessing—the public dictates fame.
5. Fame begets fame. The more you get, the harder it is to manage it.
6. Fueling a path of self-destruction can derail fame.
7. Success and fame don't come with a warranty.
8. You can chase fame, achieve it, and lose it.
9. Fame is currency. Infamy is a liability.
10. Fame doesn't entitle you to be an asshole—a famous asshole is the worst kind to be.
11. Dream beyond the glass ceiling.
12. Attaining fame requires the media's endorsement.
13. Face a crisis with honesty. The first lie triggers more lies.

ACKNOWLEDGMENTS

This book would not have been possible without the help, guidance, support, love, and encouragement of scores of people who have touched me throughout my journey. There are a handful of professional mentors who deserve acknowledgement, although a few have passed away: Peter Walsh, from Starlite Artists in London, gave me my first professional gig in the UK music business; Bob Jones, legendary PR veteran at Motown, my first music gig in the US at Motown; Paul Bloch; Henry Rogers and Warren, Rogers & Cowan; Shep Gordon, my first job in management; and Bob Gibson, my partner in my first PR company. I'm forever grateful and owe a debt of gratitude to all the artists that I've represented, managers, and label executives who believed in me, trusted, and supported me throughout my career, and all my employees who helped me sustain my businesses over the years. All my close friends and associates who incessantly kept advocating, coercing, and bugging me, "You have such remarkable stories, you really need to write a book." Thank you, here it is.

Special thanks to my loving sister Wini Hervey, the late Nicole Meoli, and Christine Farrier (for the 6:30 a.m. prompts to write one hour every day for three weeks, which became the genesis for my initial book treatment), who read and gave me valuable critical assessment of the early iterations of my book proposal. My lifeline, co-conspirator, editing muse, and literary agent, Marie Brown, who believed in me, secured my book deal, nurtured, pushed, and challenged me to give more throughout the writing process; Patrik Bass, executive editor at Amistad, who took a leap of faith, championed me at HarperCollins, and encouraged me to use all the senses; Judith Curr, president and publisher at HarperOne Group, for her endorsement, blessings, and welcoming me to the HarperCollins family of authors; and the entire Amistad/HarperCollins team.

My family, whose love means everything to me; my mother, for giving me life, her unrelenting love, encouragement, prayers, and candle lighting; my sisters Christie and Wini; my nieces and nephews, Stacy, Esa, Jamie, Otto, and George. And of course my loving and adorable children, Melanie, Jillian, and Devin.

ABOUT THE AUTHOR

Over the past four decades, Ramon Hervey II has earned global recognition as a highly regarded entertainment manager, brand consultant, and public relations specialist. His imprint Hervey & Company is a multifaceted boutique firm that has represented a diverse roster of celebrated recording artists, actors, and companies. The partial list includes Richard Pryor, Bette Midler, Little Richard, Lenny Kravitz, the Jacksons (with Michael Jackson), the Commodores (with Lionel Richie), Paul McCartney, Herb Alpert, Vanessa Williams, Kenny "Babyface" Edmonds, Peter Frampton, Andraé Crouch, Nick Nolte, James Caan, Daphne Rubin Vega, and the Soul Train Music Awards. He has served as an executive producer for films, television, and live events, including the Peabody Award–winning PBS documentary *Chisholm '72: Unbought & Unbossed*; the NBA's 50th Anniversary album, *NBA at 50*; and the NAACP Award–winning film *Free Angela and All Political Prisoners* (as music supervisor). In addition, he cofounded R & B Live, a live club concept in Los Angeles (1991–1996) that featured top contemporary music artists including Stevie Wonder; Prince; Natalie Cole; Chaka Khan; Earth, Wind & Fire; Al Jarreau; Lisa Stansfield; Brian McKnight; Heavy D; BeBe and CeCe Winans; and Mick Hucknall; among others.